高职高专商务英语、应用英语
浙江省高校重点教材

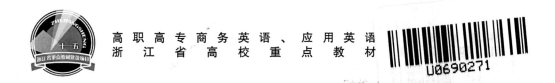

# 外贸函电实训教程

主　编　王星远　孟建国

副主编　邱　月　朱杨琼　李　佳　徐国盛　程　煜　刘有成
　　　　朱雪桢　陆金英　孟　望　孟祥瑞

主　审　沈银珍

Practices of

Business English

Correspondence

ZHEJIANG UNIVERSITY PRESS
浙江大学出版社

**图书在版编目(CIP)数据**

外贸函电实训教程 / 王星远，孟建国主编. —杭州：
浙江大学出版社，2013.6（2025.8 重印）
ISBN 978-7-308-12185-9

I. ①外… II. ①王… ②孟… III. 对外贸易—英
语—电报信函—写作—教材 IV. ①H315

中国版本图书馆 CIP 数据核字(2013)第 201774 号

高职高专商务英语、应用英语专业规划教材

外贸函电实训教程

王星远　孟建国　主编

---

丛书策划　张　琛
责任编辑　张　琛
封面设计　墨华文化
出版发行　浙江大学出版社
　　　　　（杭州市天目山路 148 号　邮政编码 310007）
　　　　　（网址：http://www.zjupress.com）
排　　版　杭州金旭广告有限公司
印　　刷　浙江新华数码印务有限公司
开　　本　787mm×1092mm　1/16
印　　张　14.5
字　　数　425 千
版 印 次　2013 年 6 月第 1 版　2025 年 8 月第 5 次印刷
书　　号　ISBN 978-7-308-12185-9
定　　价　38.00 元

---

版权所有　侵权必究　　印装差错　负责调换
浙江大学出版社市场运营中心联系方式：0571-88925591；http://zjdxcbs.tmall.com

# PREFACE 前 言

现代经济的实际发展表明：国际贸易是经济发展的重要部分和强大动力。改革开放以来，外贸业务迅猛增长，这对中国经济乃至世界经济贡献巨大，外贸人才的需求也随之越来越大。本书借鉴国内外外贸英语函电实训教材结构与体系，紧密结合我国外贸业务的实际，通过大量案例、实例，系统介绍了外贸业务活动中各种商务英语的格式与结构、写作特点、专业术语、常用专业词汇、相关句型和常见表达方式等，使学生通过相关实训，能举一反三，学以致用，从而提高外贸英语水平，熟练掌握外贸业务中常用的英语基本术语、表达技巧与技能，完成外贸英语函电所能涉及的相关工作。

本书倡导"工学结合、任务驱动、项目导向"的要求，一是在编写的每个实训项目、每个部分都明确工作任务，将外贸英语函电的工作任务定位为外贸英语函电表达，并将此任务分解到整个工作单元和工作过程中；二是将外贸英语函电表达这一工作过程融入学习过程，工作场地融入教学场地，工作情景表现在教学情景中；三是职业资格融入考核标准，每个实训项目都通过案例分析，启发引导学生思考和研习所学的内容。教材的编写融英语语言与外贸实务为一体，融函电与商务为一体，融思考与动手为一体，融案例分析与解决问题为一体，融课文与习题为一体，凸显了显性能力与隐性能力培养的结合。

本书在编写中突出了"应用为主，够用为宜，贴近实际"的原则，有助于培养学生尽快掌握技能，成为应用型、复合型、外向型的外贸人才。本书按照外贸实务发展过程排列，共分 14 个实训项目。

本书由教育部职业院校外语教学指导委员会商务英语分委会委员、硕士生导师、嘉兴职业技术学院孟建国教授和浙江工贸职业技术学院王星远老师担任主编。孟建国教授负责本书大纲的编写、总体的框架设计、部分实训项目编写及其全书包括实训教材教案的统稿，修订，王星远老师参加了部分实训项目的编写。副主编为邱月、朱杨琼、李佳、徐国盛、程煜、刘有成、朱雪桢、陆金英、孟望、孟祥瑞。本书由浙江嘉兴职业技术学院、浙江工贸职业技术学院、浙江经贸职业技术学院、三峡大学、平顶山工业职业技术学院、浙江良友进出口公司、浙江信汇进出口公司、浙江腾腾电气有限公司等多家院校、单位和公司的同仁合作完成，具体编写情况如下：

王星远、孟建国编写了实训项目 1、5；王星远、邱月编写了实训项目 2、3、4；朱杨琼、孟建国编写了实训项目 6、7、8、9；徐国盛、孟建国编写了实训项目 10、11；程煜、孟望编写了实训项目 12；刘有成、孟祥瑞编写了实训项目 13；朱雪桢、陆金英编写了实训项目 14。

王星远、孟建国对本书进行了校订，李佳制作了本书配套的 PPT，孟建国对每课内容、词汇表和词汇总表等进行了校勘。教育部高校英语专业教学指导分委员会委员、浙江大学博士生导师、浙江省外文学会会长、杭州师范大学外国语学院院长殷企平教授，嘉兴职业技术学院院长、博士生导师单胜道教授，教育部职业院校外语类专业教学指导委员会委员、浙江省高职高专院校大学英语研究会会长、浙江经贸职业学院党委委员、国际贸易与文化交流分院院长沈银珍教授，湖北兴山县陈晓玲副县长，浙江良友进出口公司副总王力东先生，复旦大学硕士生导师康志峰教授，上海金融学院硕士生导师魏耀川教授，在编写过程中都提出了许多宝贵意见。本书最终付梓出版以飨读者，也离不开浙江大学出版社张琛、张远方的编辑、校对，以及排版等工作人员的辛勤工作。在此一并感谢。

本书有以下主要特点：

1. 针对性。高等职业教育要求学生在了解基础知识的同时，重点掌握商务业务的实际操作能力。本书的编写针对学生的实际和社会岗位需求，结合高职院校"工学结合、任务驱动、项目导向"的要求，通过项目导入和案例分析，让学生了解自己的弱项，强调学生实际操作能力的培养，让学生能学会、能用上、能够用。通过对本书的学习与实训，使学生熟练掌握外贸中的基本知识以及日常业务用语，操作外贸一般性业务，能够起草规范的对外贸易业务交往中的信函、电报、电传和外事函件，能够翻译规范的外贸业务函件。通过对本书的学习与训练，学生能够达到一般外贸岗位的业务能力要求。

2. 实用性。本书有针对性地选取了大量实用的国际商务函电样本，通过对样本案例的分析和课程学习与实训，学生能熟悉翻译和写作外贸业务中各类书信、电传、电邮，掌握外贸业务中英语术语、常用业务词汇和短语以及有关业务缩略语、惯用句型和表达方法，同时熟悉合同及各类外贸单证，通过大量的技能训练把基础英语技能和外贸英语知识有机地结合起来，使学生具备撰写国际商务英语书信的能力。各实训项目主题突出，内容实用，配有针对性极强的练习，并有相关实训教材配套，以帮助巩固和深化所学内容。

3. 时代性。通过对本书案例的分析和课程学习与实训，熟悉翻译和写作外贸业务中各类书信，掌握外贸业务中英语术语，使学生具备撰写国际商务英语书信的能力。采用双语教学的形式讲授该门课程，是适应教育面向现代化、面向世界、面向未来的发展要求的，可以提高学生应用英语的水平，尤其可以提高学生的专业英语水平。

4. 系统性、连贯性、真实性。本书按外贸业务的流程分为 14 个实训项目，内容包括安排外事、商务活动、邀请、介绍、致谢、建立商务关系、政策、询价、报盘、还盘、订货、发票、支付、折扣、寄售、开立与延展信用证、装运、催货、索赔、理赔、换货、代理、包销、技术贸易、合资等。由于本书的编写人员在编写前期进行了大量的实际调查和资料搜集，在编写时注重内容体系和项目模块的安排，从而确保了本书内容的系统性、连贯性和紧贴外贸实际情况的真实性。

本书可供各高职高专院校作为教材使用，也可供从事相关专业的在职人员作为参考书或初学者作为模版教材使用。

本书系浙江省高校重点教材建设项目《外贸英语函电》（ZJG200931，主持人：孟建国）项目成果；又系教育部高等学校高职高专英语类专业教学改革课题"高职外贸英语函电教材建设与教学的有效性研究"（GZGZ7611-478，主持人：王星远）的研究成果之一。

由于编写经验和水平有限，教材中难免还有不足乃至错误，敬请体谅并不吝赐教。

编　者

2013 年仲夏

# CONTENTS 目 录

# 目  录

# 实训项目 1

## Layout of Business Letter Writing
## 商务书信写作格式

知识目标：了解商务信函的构成，掌握商务信函的撰写原则。

能力目标：能够了解 7C 原则，撰写商务信函、信封等。

## 工作任务

### 工作任务 1

上海金幕有限公司将于 6 月 9 日举行新厂的开工典礼，邀请美国博格贸易公司的采购部经理格林女士参加。请你以上海金幕有限公司业务员的身份，写一封邀请函。

## 工作任务 2

请按照要求完成信封的编写：

发信人：Mr. Zhang Yongjun, Forever Bicycle Company, Xuhui Road, Shanghai, China

收信人：Mr. M. Johnson, Sales Manager, United Bicycle Company, 456 Eastern Avenue, Pittsburgh, Pennsylvania, USA

## 操作示范

### 操作示范 1

Dear Mr.Wang,
Thank you very much for having given me this opportunity to take ..........

**Invitation to Opening Ceremony of New Company**

Dear Ms. Green,

Our new company will be commencing production on June 9 and we would like to invite you to be present at the celebration to mark the occasion.

This is an important milestone for this organization, and is the result of continued demand for our products, both at home and overseas. We are inviting all those individuals and trust that you will pay us the compliments of accepting.

Please confirm that you will be able to attend by advising us of your time. We can arrange for you to be met. All arrangements for your stay overnight (on June 9) will, of course, be made by us at our expense.

Yours faithfully,

×××

## 操作示范 2

Zhang Yongjun

Forever Bicycle Company　　　　　　　　　　　　　　stamp

Xuhui Road

Shanghai

China

Mr. M. Johnson, Sales Manager

United Bicycle Company

456 Eastern Avenue

Pittsburgh

Pennsylvania, USA

## 知识链接

1. 商务信函的作用是什么？

Generally speaking, the roles of business letters are: (1) get or convey information; (2) make or accept offers; (3) deal with all kinds of problems on business negotiations. In addition, some letters just remind receivers of the existence of the writers.

2. 商务信函的撰写很难掌握吗？

In fact, writing business letters is not different from other kinds of writing. And a good command of English is one of the important bases of writing wonderful business letters.

3. 在撰写商务信函时要注意些什么呢？（写作技巧）

A. Make sure that what you have written has no grammatical mistake.

B. Make sure that what you have written won't be misunderstood.

## 一问一答

## Asks

1. In your opinion, what kind of principles shall we need to abide by?

2. In your opinion, what does "to keep clear" mean?

3. Do you think a concise letter is a short one?

4. In your opinion, is it necessary to paragraph a letter? Why or why not?

5. Before writing a business letter, in your opinion, what should we do first?

# Answers

1. The 7Cs are (1) consideration, (2) correctness, (3) completeness, (4) concreteness, (5) conciseness, (6) clarity, (7) courtesy.

2. "To keep clear" means to avoid ambiguity. It is essential to make sure that your letter is so clear that it cannot be misunderstood. An ambiguous letter will cause trouble to both sides, and further exchange of letters for explanation will become inevitable, thus it is a waste of time. And in business, time is valuable.

3. No, a concise letter is not necessarily a short one. In a concise letter, we use simple words and straightforward expressions.

4. Yes, it is. By paragraphing carefully a letter can be made clearer, easier to read and more attractive to look at.

5. Before writing a business letter we should first of all consider and know what we want or have to say, and then say it in plain and simple words.

## 疑难解析

1. commence：begin 开始

    *e.g.* The performance will commence in a minute.

    演出马上就要开始。

2. be present：出席

    *e.g.* You are sincerely requested to be present at the party.

    敬请您光临晚会。

    It was right that I should be present.

    我自然应当到场。

3. milestone：an important event in the history or development of something or someone 里程碑，划时代事件

    *e.g.* The company passed the £8 million milestone this year.

    今年公司越过了 800 万英镑这个里程碑式的数字。

    Starting school is a milestone for both children and parents.

    对孩子和家长而言，开始上学是一件大事。

4. at one's expense：由某人付款，由某人付费

    *e.g.* We would be pleased to send you a sample at our own expense.

    我们很高兴给你方寄送样品，费用由我们自己支付。

5. 邀请函：邀请函是邀请收信人参加某项活动的书信，包含三个方面：邀请对方参加活动的内容、时间和地点；与该活动有关的注意事项；期待对方接受邀请，并表示感谢。

## Invitation

Dear Prof. Johnson,

　　To celebrate the sixtieth anniversary of the founding of our company, we request the honor of your presence at reception, which is to be held at Bogeda Hotel, Urumqi on September 30 from 7 to 9 in the evening.

　　We would be glad if you could come.

Yours faithfully,

George  Meng

## The Reply to Invitation

Dear Mr. Meng,

　　Thank you very much for your invitation to join the sixtieth anniversary of the founding of your company at Bogeda Hotel, Urumqi on September 30.

　　I will be happy to be there at 6:50 p.m. to take in the reception and look forward to it with pleasure.

Yours faithfully,

Johnson

## The Notification for Sending a Document

Dear Mr. Ruperez,

　　Enclosed herewith is a list of "Sales promotion in European countries, July / December 2013" compiled by this organization. I hope you will find it informative and useful.

　　I send you my best regards and look forward to your continuous support and cooperation.

Sincerely  yours,

C.P.  Chang

Deputy Secretary General

## The Notification for Price Adjustment

Dear Sarah,

　　We enclose our new catalogue and price list. The revised prices will apply from May 1, 2013. You will see that there have been a number of changes in our product range. A number of improved models have been introduced.

　　Out range of washing machines has been completely revamped. Many popular lines, however, have been retained unchanged.

You will be aware that inflation is affecting industry as a whole. We have been affected like everyone else and some price increases have been unavoidable. We have not, however, increased our prices across the board. In many cases, there is a small price increase, but in others, none at all.

We can assure you that the quality of our consumer durables has been maintained at a high standard and that our service will continue to be first class. We look forward to receiving your orders.

Sincerely yours,

Brance

##  Notes

1. anniversary：a day which is an exact year or number of years after a particular event 周年纪念日

   anniversary celebration 周年庆典

   wedding anniversary 结婚周年纪念日

   *e.g.* It's the twentieth anniversary of our country's independence.

   今天是我国独立二十周年纪念日。

2. honor：respect and admiration 荣誉，尊敬，敬意，欢迎

   *e.g.* The queen was welcomed at the airport by a guard of honor.

   女王在机场受到仪仗队的欢迎。

3. enclosed herewith is：随函附上

   *e.g.* Enclosed herewith is our catalogue and price list for your reference.

   随函附上我们的目录和价格单供您参考。

4. comply：act in accordance with demand, rule, etc. 服从，依从，遵从

   *e.g.* He reluctantly complied with their wishes.

   他勉强地服从了他们的愿望。

   The factory was closed for failing to comply with government safety regulations.

   工厂由于未能遵守政府的安全条例而被关闭了。

5. for your reference：供您参考

   *e.g.* Samples will be forwarded to you in a week for your reference.

   样品将于一周内发给您以供您参考。

6. price list：价格单

   *e.g.* If you want to know detailed information about price, please read our price list enclosed.

   如果您想了解详细的价格信息，请阅读我们附上的价格单。

7. out range of：超出界限的，超出范围的

   *e.g.* The products you want to purchase are out of our business range.

   您要订购的商品不在我们的经营范围内。

8. revamp：修改，改进，更新

 *e.g.* We must fight the urge to revamp our diplomatic relations.

  我们必须极力修补我们的外交关系。

  It may be time to revamp an old sayings: "A chocolate bar a day keeps the doctors away."

  可能是时候修改一下谚语："一日一巧克力棒，医生远离我。"

9. retain：保留，保持，保有

 *e.g.* This village still retains its old-world character.

  这个村庄仍然保持着古香古色的特色。

  His business has been taken over by a big corporation, but he still retains some control over it.

  他的企业已经被一家大的股份有限公司收购了，但他对该企业仍旧保持一些控股权。

10. maintain：维持，保持

 *e.g.* He took the lead, and maintained it until the end of the race.

  他在赛跑中一直保持领先到终点。

## 技能操练

**I. Choose the best answer from A, B, C and D.**

1. Our latest design has won worldwide _____.

 A. popular     B. popularity     C. popularly     D. popularize

2. Art. No.8905 enjoys the fame of wide _____.

 A. selling      B. salable      C. sales       D. sell

3. We are unable to satisfy your requirements, for the goods are _____ great demand.

 A. in       B. on       C. of        D. having

4. Payment by D/P should be _____ to you.

 A. agree      B. agreed      C. agreement     D. agreeable

5. As we are _____ urgent need of Art. No.5609, please ship our order without delay.

 A. on       B. of       C. in        D. to

6. We _____ you of our prompt shipment after receipt of your order.

 A. assure      B. assurance     C. insure      D. insurance

7. We have to claim for your delay in _____ of our order.

 A. shipping     B. shipment     C. ship       D. deliver

8. Our company has wide experience _____ the textiles line.

 A. on       B. in        C. about      D. of

9. You have delayed in dispatching us the shipping _____ after shipment.

 A. advice      B. instruction     C. information     D. data

10. Please effect payment when the draft _____.

 A. expires      B. due       C. falls due     D. falls expiration

## II. Compose a dialogue in the following situation.

Jay is a businessman who works on gymnasium equipment, and it was the first meeting between Yoyo and him. In just a few minutes of the conversation, Yoyo felt that this big fellow with a straightforward appearance kept a mind of a cunning rabbit. Known that the guy was skilled in this way, he took great care in the negotiation.

## III. Write an envelope with following information.

The sender: China Import and Export Corporation (Chongqing Branch), Xilin Road, Yonghang District, Chongqing, 100023, China

The receiver: Turner Smith, the sales manager, Hamser Electronic Corporation, 8 Shenton Way, Sydney, Australia

## Read More

### How to Write Business Correspondence

The Internet has changed a lot of things within the business world, including business correspondence. Here once traditional, formal business letters were normal, quick business e-mails now rule the day. The ease and informality of the Internet often makes it seem we can write a business e-mail poorly and get away with it; yet, it's actually the contrary. Because e-mail is so accessible, people receive much more of it and disregard anything less than perfect. Your business e-mails must stand out from the junk. The following tips will help you to create concise, engaging business e-mails for any purpose.

**STYLE**

The human eye reacts differently to a computer screen than a piece of paper, so how you format your e-mail is vital. Use short, succinct sentences that get to the point immediately; remember, your goal here is to dispense important information, so give that to the reader right up front. Always include a greeting and a signature, and use as many line and paragraph breaks as possible which makes the e-mail easier to read, and resist the urge to write a book. Business e-mails are better off short; the equivalent of a page or so is sufficient.

**TONE**

For better or worse, the Internet breeds a nasty habit of informality. It's acceptable to be slightly informal with your e-mail (people tend to expect it lately), but don't write as if you're talking to your mother or best friend. You need to strike a balance between traditional formality and e-mail informality. Think about your recipient and how they'd most likely write an e-mail. What words would they use? Would slang or jargon offend your readers? Use these considerations to create a concise, customized e-mail.

## GRAMMAR

Informality, whatever its root, does not excuse grammatical errors, and these can damage your e-mail. Grammatical errors show that you didn't spend much time on your business e-mail and you probably don't care much about your message. Go through your e-mail carefully to make sure you have spelled correctly, and you have fixed all grammar and punctuation mistakes. Remove all redundancies and get rid of any clichés. Recipients, especially professional business people, will appreciate your attention to details and they will respond better to your message when no error exist in your e-mail.

## RESPONSE

Since e-mail is an immediate medium, and a highly accessible one, it's far easier than in paper letters to request a response—and far more likely that you'll get one! Before signing off with your signature, be clear about what you want the recipient to do. Need a response via phone or with certain information attached? Say so! Your recipient will have a difficult time responding if they have no idea what you want from them. But remember: be polite when requesting action. There's little worse than an overly forward or pushy ending.

# 实训项目 2

## Establishing Business Relation
## 建立业务关系

**学习目标**

知识目标：了解建立业务关系信函的组成部分，掌握相关专业术语和常用句型。

能力目标：能够撰写建立贸易关系的信函，做到内容清楚，叙述完整，礼貌得体。

**工作任务**

### 工作任务 1

2013 年 2 月 14 日，Daisy 浏览网页，想要寻找新的客户。她在阿里巴巴网站上看到了一则广告：

欲求购设计新颖，功能独特，价格合理的商务休闲鞋。

公司名称：德国博豪进出口有限公司

联系方式：电话：0049-2332-55285-29

传真：0049-2332-55285-29

E-mail: info@Boihau.cn

网址：http://www.Boihau.cn

Daisy 查阅了德国博豪进出口有限公司的网页后，认为该公司需要的商务休闲鞋属于温州奥古斯都鞋业有限公司的经营范围，因此，她按照所提供的地址向联系人 Harry 先生发了一份电子邮件。

请以 Daisy 的名义写一封建交函，表达与之建立业务关系的意愿。要求：

1. 告知获得对方信息的途径并说明来信意图；

2. 介绍自己公司的主要情况并表示如果对方需要，可以尽快寄一份最新的详细价格单供参考；

3. 表达与对方合作的诚意，并希望早日得到回复。

---

## 工作任务 2

2013 年 9 月金立贸易有限公司业务人员从报纸上看到：

> 国际商报
>
> ### 国际贸易与经济合作机会
> ### 国际市场快递
>
> **加拿大求购瓷器**　　　　　　　　**马来西亚求购**
>
> 加拿大一公司求购中国的瓷器　　　马来西亚一公司求购碳酸钙
>
> **阿尔及利亚求购**　　　　　　　　马来西亚一公司求购天然宝石
>
> 阿尔及利亚一公司求购各类服装　　马来西亚一公司求购 60cm 直径，890cm
>
> 阿尔及利亚一公司求购纺织品　　　长的钢丝绳
>
> ### 感兴趣者请与本台《回音台》联系

了解上述信息后，金立贸易公司立即与《回音台》取得联系，得知该加拿大客户系多伦多一进口批发商，具体联络方法为：

Mr. Paul Lockwood

Purchasing Division

James Brown & Sons

304-310 Jalan Street, Toronto, Canada

Tel: (01) 7709910

Fax: (01) 7701100

E-mail: plockwood@jbs.com.cnd

请根据上述背景资料，以金立贸易公司日用品部业务员的名义，给 James Brown & Sons 公司去函，表达与之建立业务关系的热切愿望，并随寄 HX 瓷器系列的商品目录。

**操作示范**

## 操作示范 1

**Wenzhou Augustus Import & Export Company**

106 Wenfeng Road Economy and Technology Area

Wenzhou, Zhejiang, China 518112

Tel: 0086-755-82130055

Fax: 0086-755-82130045

Website: http://www.augustusect.cn

E-mail: info@augustus.cn

February 14, 2013

Mr. Harry

Germany Boihau Import & Export Company

Bergedorf No. 89

Hamburg, Germany

Dear Mr. Harry,

We have learned your name and address from Internet that you are one of the largest importers of leather shoes in Germany and you are in the requirement of business style leather shoes with comfort. We are glad to write to you with the purpose of establishing business relationship with you.

Our company, established in 1990, is located in Wenzhou, the south of China with lots of experience in manufacturing leather shoes. We have enjoyed high reputation both at home and abroad among customers.

Our products, such as leather shoes, sports shoes, heighten shoes, etc., are excellent in quality and reasonable in price, which are quite popular in Russia, Japan, Australia, Middle East and European countries. You are able to visit our website to get more details about our products. We shall be appreciated to send you our latest price list if receiving your enquiries.

We are sincerely looking forward to your early reply.

Daisy

# 操作示范 2

**Jinli Trading Company, Ltd.**
106 Wenfeng Road Economy and Technology Area
Shanghai, China 200082
Tel: 0086-21-82130055
Fax: 0086-21-82130045
Website: www.jilitc.com
E-mail: info@jinli.cn

September 24, 2013

Dear Mr. Lockwood,

From the September issue of the *International Business Daily* we have learned that you are in the market for chinaware, which just falls within our business scope. We are now writing to you to establish long-term trade relations.

As a leading trading company in Shanghai and backed by more than 20 years of export experience, we have good connections with some reputable ceramics and, sufficient supplies and on-time delivery are thus guaranteed.

Enclosed please find our latest catalogue. You'll see that we can offer a wide selection of high quality dinner and tea sets, ranging from the elegant Chinese traditional styles to the popular European modern designs.

In particular, we would like to inform you that we have a new line that may be most suitable for your requirements—HX series (see catalogue). They are all made of first-class porcelain, decorated with hand-painted pattern, and packed in eye-catching gift cases. Most of articles are available from stock.

We are sure you will find a ready sale for our products in Canada as have other retailers throughout Europe and the USA.

Please let us know if we may be of further assistance, and we are looking forward to your specific inquiry.

Yours sincerely,
Huang Huiming (Mr.)
Daily Articles Division
Jinli Trading Co., Ltd.

## 知识链接

1. 为什么要建立贸易关系？

   If a firm wishes to open up a market to sell something or to buy something from firms in foreign countries, the person in charge must find out whom he is going to deal with. No customer, no business.

2. 买卖双方怎样互相认识？（通过什么途径认识）

   A. Attending the trade fairs or exhibitions

   B. Internet

   C. Through banks

   D. Chambers of commerce in foreign countries

   E. Trade Directory (a book from which you can get much information of sellers and buyers)

   F. Chinese Commercial Counselor's Office in foreign countries

   G. Business Houses of the same trade, etc.

   H. Advertisements

   I. Embassy or Consulate

   J. Other channels

3. 根据上述情况，怎样写建交函？（写作技巧）

   A. Tell them how you obtain their names and address, express your wish of establishing business relations

   B. Introduce your company and your products or business scope.

   C. Express your wishes and look forward to their reply or cooperation.

## 一问一答

### Asks

1. What is business relation?

2. Why business relation establishment is important to international trade?

3. Which department and who will involve in establishing business relation in a company?

4. What kind of information you need for prospective dealers you are going to establish business relation with?

5. What are the basic ways to obtain the information of business individuals to be dealt with?

6. Are there any other ways that you can gain supply and demand information from besides the newspaper and the net mentioned in the 2 cases? Name some.

7. What kind of role do mass media and the internet play in business world nowadays?

## Answers

1. Business relation is the commercial connections between companies and firms.

2. Business relation establishment is important to international trade because it can open up a market to sell or buy something from the other firms or maintain or expand business activities, and it is the first step in a transaction in foreign trade.

3. This is an open question. In the Public Relation Section or Market Section anyone may involve in establishing business relation through writing a letter to a new customer.

4. You'd better need some credit information such as financial conditions, business activities, honesty integrity and so on.

5. The basic ways to obtain the information of business individuals are: Advertisements in the Media; Market Survey; Trade Negotiation; Investigation to the Foreign Countries; Exhibitions and Trade Fairs; Banks; Trade Directory; Chambers of Commerce; Commercial Counsellor's Office; Trade Press.

6. Sure, Market Survey, Exhibitions and Trade Fairs.

7. The mass media and the internet are playing a very important role in business world nowadays.

### 难点解析

1. be glad to do sth.：be pleased to do sth.; sb. have (has) pleasure in doing sth. 很高兴做某事

   *e.g.* We are glad to inform you that we are willing to establish business relations with you.
   我们很高兴告知你们，我们愿意与你方建立业务关系。

2. enter into：establish; set up; build 建立

   *e.g.* We would like to enter into business relationship with you.
   我们希望跟你方建立商业关系。
   We are desirous to establish business relations with your company.
   我们非常渴望与你公司建立商业关系。

3. specialize in：be specializing in; be specialized in; be engaged in; deal in 专营

   *e.g.* We are specialized in the above business and recall that many years ago, considerable business was done with your country on such items.
   我方专营上述业务，而是在此商品上与你们国家在很多年前就有相当多的业务往来。
   We specialize in leather products for twenty years.
   我们专注于皮革制品二十年。
   We are engaged in the exportation of Chinese foodstuffs.
   我们专营中国食品出口。

4. We have learned... from...：We have obtained... form... 我们从……获得

   *e.g.* We have obtained your name and address from China Council for the Promotion of International Trade.
   我们从中国国际贸易促进会得知贵公司的名称和地址。

We have learned your company from Internet.

我们从互联网上得知你公司。

类似的表达方式有：to owe one's name and address to; to be recommended/introduced/given to sb by; on the recommendation of; through the courtesy of。

*e.g.* We owe your name and address from the Commercial Counselor's Office of American Embassy in Beijing, through whom we have learned you are importers of textiles.

我们是通过美国驻北京使馆商务参赞处得知您的名字，并了解到你方是纺织品进口商。

Your company has been recommended to us by Shanghai Chamber of Commerce.

上海商会把贵公司介绍给我们。

We find your company through the courtesy of a friend.

承蒙一个朋友的介绍，我们才知道贵公司。

5. enjoy a reputation：won a reputation; be famous of; get the honor of; be well-known by  享有很高声誉

   *e.g.* We have learned that you have enjoyed a high reputation at home and abroad.

   我们获知贵公司在国内外都享有声誉。

6. be in the market for sth.：want to buy sth.  想要购买

   *e.g.* We are in the market for different kinds of gloves which are excellent in quality and reasonable in price.

   我们想要购买物美价廉的手套。

7. price list：price sheet  价格单，价格表

   *e.g.* We have prepared relative price list to send to you as soon as possible.

   我们已经备好价格单以尽快寄给你们。

   We have enclosed price sheet for your reference.

   我们随函附上价格单供您参考。

8. be appreciated：be obliged; be appreciating  感激，感谢

   *e.g.* We shall be appreciated if you could make shipment as soon as possible.

   如果你方能够尽快安排装运，我们将会非常感激。

   We are obliged to receive your price list.

   感谢你方的价格单。

9. company：corporation; firm; incorporation  公司

   英式英语中常用 company 表示公司，company 的缩写形式是 Co.，凡是已经注册登记、具有法人资格的公司，不论规模大小，都可以用 company 来表示。

   例如：Union International Co. （粮食加工）联合国际公司

   　　　Ford Motor Company  福特汽车公司

   　　　General Electric Company  通用电器公司

   　　　N.& O. Navigation Co. 汽轮航运公司

   美式英语中常用 corporation 表示公司，corporation 的缩写形式是 Corp.。例如，Corporation Law 指公司法。incorporation 在美式英语中表示股份公司，缩写形式为 Inc.。

firm 的意思是"商号"、"公司"，是指两个或两个以上的人合办的企业，也可以指任何商务组织、从事商贸活动的公司。

It is a reliable firm.

这是一家值得信赖的商行。

firm 也可以指不从事贸易的公司，例如：

Law Firm　律师事务所

Consulting Firm　咨询公司

## 拓展提高

**The Exporter Asking for Establishing Business Relations with the Importer**

Dear Sirs,

　　We are writing to you on the recommendation of our Commercial Counselor's Office in your country and we are desirous of entering into business relationship with your company.

　　We take the liberty to introduce ourselves as one of the leading import and export companies in China and we mainly deal in silk piece goods, which we have been exporting to European countries. We are enclosing catalogues for your further guidance. If you are interested in the items listed, please inform us of the quantities required.

　　We look forward to your early reply.

**The Importer Having a Reply to the Exporter**

Dear Sirs,

　　Thank you for your letter of October 23, 2012 and we wish to extend you our warm welcome for your desire to establish business relations with us. We are pleased to inform you that the goods you engaged in are falling within the scope of our business activities.

　　We have strong business relations with famous wholesalers and companies in China and shall appreciate it if you could send us a copy of the latest price list and samples. Our specific enquiry will be forwarded without delay.

　　We hope we may soon be able to work with you to our mutual advantage.

## Notes

1. be desirous of:  be eager to; long for sth. 期望，渴望

　　*e.g.* We are now desirous of extending our business to your market and shall be much obliged if you
　　　　will introduce us to some reliable firms in your city who are interested in this line of business.
　　　　现在，我们期望扩展业务，进军你方市场，如果你们能够介绍一些你们当地对我们这
　　　　个行业感兴趣的公司，我们将不胜感激。

2. take the liberty to do sth.：take the liberty of; venture to say sth. 冒昧做某事

   *e.g.* We take the liberty of writing to you with a view of building up business relations with your corporation.

   我们冒昧地写信以期和贵公司建立贸易关系。

   When you take the liberty of calling me mean or base, or anything of that sort, you are an impudent beggar.

   要是你竟敢说我卑鄙、龌龊这一类的话，那你就是一个大胆无耻的叫花子。

3. leading：important; essential; crucial 重要的，主要的

   *e.g.* We are one of the leading manufactures in this line in China.

   我们是中国这个行业主要的生产商之一。

   Policy responses to economic crisis must come from leading nations.

   金融危机的应对政策必须来自领先国家。

4. enclose：随函附上；封入

   *e.g.* We have enclosed a set of pamphlet to you for your reference.

   我们已经随函附上一整套小册子供您参考。

   Referring to our conversation of this morning, enclose a pamphlet describing our new articles.

   依照今天上午的谈话，随函呈上本公司新产品的小册子一本。

5. for one's guidance：for one's reference; for one's information 供……参考

   *e.g.* Enclosed you will find the latest price list for your reference.

   我们随函附上价格单供您参考。

   At the back of the card is our business scope for your guidance.

   名片背后是我们公司的经营范围供您参考。

6. Thank you for your letter of…：感谢你方……的来信(一般用于回信的开头)

   类似的表达还有：We have received your letter of…; With reference to your letter of…

   *e.g.* We have received your letter of May 8, 2013 with thanks.

   我们已经收到你方 2013 年 5 月 8 日的来信，非常感谢。

   With reference to your letter of July 20, 2013, we have learned that you are one of the leading exporters in Canada.

   我们已经收到你方 2013 年 7 月 20 日的来信，从信中我们获悉贵公司是加拿大主要的出口商之一。

7. extend：give; offer 提供，给予

   *e.g.* The bank will extend you credit.

   银行将向你提供贷款。

   Those investors who cannot extend credit directly to individuals or small businesses can get exposure to these assets via securitisation.

   那些无法直接给个人和小企业提供信用贷款的投资者可以通过证券化获得这些资产。

8. inform：tell 告知，通知

   *e.g.* We are glad to inform you that we will make shipment tomorrow.

我们很高兴告知你方我们将在明天装运。

9. fall within the scope of：属于……经营范围

　　*e.g.* Your letter of Sep. 2, 2012 has been received. We are glad to inform you the goods that you
　　need fall within the scope of our business activities.

　　你方2012年9月2日来函收到。我们很高兴告诉你, 你所要的商品属我公司的经营范围。

10. We shall appreciate it if…：如果……我们将会非常感激, 类似的表达方式还有：

　　We shall be appreciated if…; We shall be obliged if…; We shall be grateful if…

　　*e.g.* We shall appreciate it if you could send us your shipping advice early.

　　如果你方能够尽早寄来装船通知, 我们将会非常感激。

11. forward：send 寄送, 发送

　　*e.g.* We will forward shipping advice on receipt of your L/C.

　　一旦收到你方信用证, 我们立刻发送装船通知。

　　Quotation will be forwarded to you if we receive your specific enquiry.

　　我们一收到你们的具体询盘, 就会寄给你们报价。

12. mutual advantage：mutual benefit 共同的利益

　　*e.g.* We trust that this business may prove to mutual advantage.

　　我们相信这一交易对双方都有利。

　　We trust this decision will be to our mutual advantage.

　　我们相信此项决定必将使我们双方获益。

**Status Enquiry**

Dear Sirs,

　　We have received a letter from Wenzhou Augustus Import & Export Company in China, expressing their desire to enter into business relations with us on condition that we allow them a standing credit of USD 2,000 to start business. As stated in their letter, their reference is Bank of China, Wenzhou.

　　For safety's sake, we would like to know the financial and credit standing of the above-mentioned company. We should be very pleased if you would assist us in this respect, and we can assure you that any information you may give us will be treated in absolute confidence.

**The Reply to Status Enquiry**

Dear Sirs,

　　We have completed our enquiries with Bank of China, Wenzhou. Wenzhou Augustus Import & Export Company, you mentioned, is a private company and founded ten years ago. It enjoys good reputation. As far as our information goes it is punctually meeting its commitments and credit in the sum you mention would seem to be safe.

　　This information is confidential and is given without any responsibility on our part.

## Notes

1. on condition that：（这里的 that 不能省略）if

   *e.g.* I will go abroad on condition that my husband goes with me.

   如果我丈夫能和我一起去，我就出国。

2. allow sb. sth.：grant sb. sth., give sb. sth. 给予某人某东西

   *e.g.* We will allow you a discount of 3% if you could order more than 1,000 pieces.

   如果你订货量超过 1000 件的话，我们会给你 3% 的折扣。

   Two jobs allow me an apartment, food and child care payment.

   做两份工作使我得以有房住、有饭吃，并能支付雇人看孩子的费用。

3. standing credit：长期贷款；credit standing：信用状况

4. reference：证明人，推荐人

   *e.g.* If reference is needed, we will provide relevant information in time.

   如需资信证明人，我们将及时提供相关信息。

   Their reference is the Bank of Switzerland.

   瑞士银行是他们的资信证明人。

5. for safety's sake：for the sake of safety 为了安全起见

   *e.g.* For safety's sake, don't drive more than 30 kilometers per hour in the city.

   为了安全起见，在市内开车时速不要超过三十公里。

6. in absolute confidence：as confidential 绝密

   *e.g.* The information you give us will be treated in absolute confidence (as confidential).

   对于你们提供的信息，我们绝对予以保密。

7. as far as… goes：as far as… concerned 据……所知，就……来说

   *e.g.* As far as I am concerned, I prefer the latter view.

   就我而言，我更喜欢第二个观点。

8. meet one's commitments：honor one's commitments, meet one's promise 履行诺言，履行义务

   *e.g.* As far as our investigation, that company could meet its commitments during the past ten years.

   据我们的调查，那家公司在过去的 10 年间都能够履行义务。

### 技能操练

**I. Choose the best answer from A, B, C and D.**

1. Your woolen goods are _____ interest to us.

   A. in      B. of      C. at      D. for

2. Should your products prove _____in quality and reasonable in price, I trust substantial order will follow.

   A. satisfy     B. satisfactory     C. satisfied     D. satisfaction

3. The goods you offered are _____ line with the business scope of our clients.

A. out of　　　　　　B. without　　　　　　C. outside　　　　　　D. not

4. We are making you our best offer for Leather Shoes _____.

　　A. as follow　　　　B. as following　　　　C. as follows　　　　D. follow

5. We shall be pleased to receive from you all necessary information _____ these goods.

　　A. regarding　　　　B. in regard　　　　C. as regard　　　　D. with regard

6. We highly appreciate _____.

　　A. your kind cooperation　　　　　　B. you cooperation

　　C. that you cooperate　　　　　　　D. it your kind cooperating

7. We _____ some brochures _____ to illustrate the products we manufactured.

　　A. enclose, to you　　B. enclose you　　C. enclose　　D. enclose, you

8. If you will send us a catalog by air, we shall _____ very much.

　　A. appreciate　　B. appreciating　　　　C. appreciation　　D. appreciate it

9. _____ our S/C No. 301，we wish to say that the goods will be shipped by Oct.10.

　　A. With reference to　B. Refer to　　　C. Referring　　D. With refer to

10. _____ your letter of March 5, we are pleased to inform you that the L/C has been received.

　　A. In reply to　　　　B. Replying for　　　　C. Replied to　　　　D. Replied for

**II. Translate the following phrases into English or vice versa.**

1. 建立业务关系 _____

2. 专营 _____

3. 供您参考 _____

4. 属于我们的经营范围 _____

5. 随函附上 _____

6. 商会 _____

7. 享有很高声誉 _____

8. 咨询 _____

9. 价格单 _____

10. 批发商 _____

11. upon receipt of _____

12. mutual advantage _____

13. Commercial Counselor's Office _____

14. Enquiry Agency _____

15. be desirous of _____

16. specific enquiry _____

17. leading _____

18. take the liberty _____

19. with reference to _____

20. forward _____

**III. Translate the following sentences from English into Chinese or vice versa.**

1. We have learned your corporation from a friend and are pleased to inform you that we specialize in both exportation of the automobile's parts and components. We are willing to enter into trade relations with you.

2. Thank you for your letter of January 9, 2013, in which you expressed your willingness to enter into business relations with us.

3. We have experience in this line for more than 20 years, so we are sure to give our customers satisfaction for our products and service.

4. We have been asked by the Sales Division of British United Motor Corporation to write to you regarding the credit status of one of your clients.

5. Your any assistance will be highly appreciated, and we earnestly look forward to your reply.

6. From your letter, we are pleased to learn that you are especially interested in shipping electronic machines tour market.

7. 我们很高兴地向您介绍我们，期望我们能在贵公司的商务拓展方面有机会进行合作。

8. 我们期望贵公司能尝试我们的服务并认识到他们将完全满足您的需求。

9. 随函附上我们的最新产品目录供你们参考。

10. 若能告知该公司在支付货款方面是否可靠和及时，我们将不胜感激。

11. 我们是享有声望的出口商，经销各类中国产品，尤其是电子高保真(Hi–Fi)音响产品。

12. 尽管目前市场不太活跃，但只要你们的价格有竞争力，我们仍可以与你们达成相当数量的交易。

**IV. Fill in the blanks with the proper words.**

1. In _____ with our company's growth, to further expand our market, we have decided to establish an office in Dalian.

2. Please be good enough to provide the necessary information _____ us.

3. If your price is competitive, we shall be glad to place a substantial order _____ you.

4. This article is of particular interest _____ us.

5. Our sales contract _____ that the seller shall ship the goods within one month after signing the contract.

6. We are gearing our production to your requirements and shall soon be _____ a position _____ offer you substantially.

7. If your price is _____ _____ the market price, we can place a large order with you.

8. Enclosed _____ _____ a copy of our price list.

9. _____ a Chamber of Commerce, We have learned that you are one of the representative importers of electric goods.

10. We take _____ _____ _____ writing to you with a view to building up business relations with your firm.

## V. Compose a dialogue in the following situation.

Mr. Henry, an official of American Locuster & Mainletr Company, encountered Ms. Wang, manager assistant of Wenzhou Huahui Shoes Company, in the Internet. Ms. Wang mentioned Guangzhou Trade Fairs and invite Mr. Henry to come. Now they are meeting in Guangzhou Trade Fairs.

## VI. Write a letter with the ideas given below, express your wish to establish business relations with them.

(1) Recommended by the Bank of China

(2) You are the exporter of Wenzhou shoes with long experience in this line

(3) Ask them to tell you their trade terms and forward samples

(4) Hope early reply

## █ **Read More**

### Business Negotiation

Business negotiation plays a very important role in conducting an export or import transaction. The conclusion of a satisfactory contract results largely from the careful and meticulous business negotiation taking place between the exporter and importer. The negotiation is the dealings between the seller (or exporter) and buyer (or importer) in order to reach an agreement on the terms in respect of quality, quantity, packing, price, shipment, insurance, payment, inspection, claims and disputes, arbitration, etc. Only when the parties all agree on the various terms consulted can the business be done and the contract of sales be concluded. Business negotiation can be conducted through correspondence, telephone, cable or telex. Under normal circumstances, establishing business connections through correspondence is still widely employed.

Generally, four stages or links should be gone through the business negotiation to reach agreement of the various terms mentioned above. They are enquiry and reply, offer and counter offer, acceptance and conclusion of a contract. In practice, it is not necessary for every transaction to cover these four stages. In some cases, only offer and acceptance will serve the purpose. It is stipulated in the laws of some countries that only offer and acceptance are the two indispensable factors, lack of either will make no contract.

# 实训项目 3

## Enquiries and Replies
## 询盘及答复

**学习目标**

知识目标：了解询盘与回复信函的组成部分，掌握相关专业术语和常用句型。

能力目标：能够撰写询盘与回复的信函，做到内容清楚，叙述完整，礼貌得体。

**工作任务**

## 工作任务 1

2012 年 11 月 4 日，美国 ABC 公司回信，表示对广交会上型号为 BJ123 的镜框很感兴趣，希望思科公司报含 3%佣金的 CIF 到蒙特利尔的美元价格，同时希望思科公司告知付款方式、保险、包装、装运时间、起订量等相关的贸易条件，并希望对方邮寄样品。此次寄样要求思科公司通过 DHL 国际快递第 99648752 号账户寄送，邮寄费由进口方承担。根据以上交易情境，以 ABC 公司进口商的身份写一封询盘函。

_____

_____

_____

_____

_____

_____

_____

_____

## 工作任务 2

建立业务关系的信函发出不久，金立贸易有限公司就收到了 James Brown & Sons 公司的下列询盘：

Dear Mr. Huang,

Thank you for your e-mail and your latest catalogue.

We are much impressed by your HX series, especially HX1115, HX1128, HX2012 and HX4405. We would be appreciated if you could quote us your best prices on CIF Toronto all including 5% commission.

Meanwhile, we would like to have some samples of the above items for our customers to test before we could place an order. If the lab tests go well, and your prices are competitive, we'd certainly be able to place a substantial order.

Looking forward to hearing from you.

Yours truly,

Paul Lookwood

Purchasing Division

James Brown & Sons

请根据上述背景资料，以金立贸易有限公司业务员的名义，给加拿大 James Brown & Sons 公司去函，表示感谢，并按照来函要求进行回复。

_____

_____

_____

_____

_____

_____

### 操作示范

### 操作示范 1

A.B.C. Corporation

Yerhe District, Montreal, American

Tel: 001-626-780-7552    Website: www.abc.corp

Sike Spectacles Company

Xi'an Street, Lucheng Area

Wenzhou, Zhejiang, China

Dear Sir,

We are interested in your BJ123 range spectacle-frames, which we have talked about in the Canton Fair. And we shall be appreciated if you could make us a quotation per pair CIF Montreal, inclusive of our 3% commission. We are able be obliged if terms of payment, insurance, packing, date of shipment and minimum order quantities are informed.

It is understood that Chinese products are excellent in quality and reasonable in price. We have great confidence in your goods and hope you could forward us the samples by DHL (99648752 account) at our expense.

We are looking forward to hearing from you soon.

Jim

Manager

ABC Company

## 操作示范 2

Jinli Trading Co., Ltd.

14th Floor Kingstar Mansion, 676

Jinlin Road, Shanghai, China

Tel: 0086-21-62597480

Fax: 0086-21-62597490

March 16, 2012

Dear Mr. Lockwood,

We are pleased to make you a quotation regarding our HX series chinaware.

For 35-Piece Dinnerware and Tea Set Art No. HX1115, the price is USD 25.11 CIFC5 Toronto. For 15-Piece Tea Set Art No. HX1128, the price is USD 16.33 CIFC5 Toronto. For 20-Piece Dinnerware Set Art No. HX2012, the price is USD 20.88 CIFC5 Toronto. For 47-Piece Dinnerware Set Art No. HX4405, the price is USD 25.12 CIFC5 Toronto.

In addition, we have airmailed to you some samples. Our own laboratory reports, enclosed with this letter, showing that our HX series perform up to the FDA, and in some respects, out-perform it.

We are looking forward to your initial order.

Yours sincerely,

Huang Ming

Daily Articles Division

1. 在对外贸易中，询盘通常由谁提出？

Foreign trade enquiries are usually made by buyers.

2. 针对询盘进行回复时要注意什么？

The reply to the enquiries should be prompt, courteous and helpful.

3. 什么叫做"第一次询价"？

A "first enquiry" is an enquiry sent to a supplier whom we have not previously dealt with. Just like the above writing task.

### Asks

1. What is the aim of making business enquiries?
2. When making enquiries, what should be considered?
3. In what way can the enquiries attract more prompt attention after being sent?

### Answers

1. The aim of making enquiries is to get the information about the goods to be ordered, such as price, catalogue, delivery date and other terms.

2. In making enquiries, it is essential to consider the regions the enquiries are to be sent to, because some regions don't supply the goods you want. Furthermore, the number of suppliers to be approached in one and the same region should be limited; otherwise the suppliers will think that the goods enquired are in great demand, and consequently they will raise the price.

3. Enquiries should not be addressed to an individual, because if the particular person is away from office, the enquiries will have to wait, or the enquiries may be addressed to a wrong person, which means delay.

## 难点解析

1. Canton Fair: 广交会，又称中国进出口商品交易会(China Import & Export Fair)，创办于 1957 年春季，每年春秋两季在广州举办，迄今已有五十余年历史，是中国目前历史最长、层次最高、规模最大、商品种类最全、到会客商最多、成交效果最好的综合性国际贸易盛会。

    *e.g.* Canton Fair shall be held continuously with innovation which in turn achieves magnificence.

    广交会要继续办下去，不断创新，办得更好。

2. make a quotation：give a quotation　报价

    *e.g.* Such as item quality and quantity that you are interested, I will make a quotation first.

    如果您对产品的质量和数量感兴趣，我将给您报价。

    Listen to your valuable customer's need and then make a quotation.

    细心倾听尊贵客人的需要，然后为客人做初步报价。

3. inclusive：containing or including　包含的。inclusive of　包含一切费用在内的

    *e.g.* It's an all-inclusive price; there is nothing extra to pay.

    这是包括全部费用的价格，不要另付什么钱了。

    The rent is $80 inclusive of heating charges.

    房租为 80 美元，包含暖气费在内。

4. be obliged：be grateful　感激，感谢

    *e.g.* I'm much obliged to you if you could send us your catalogue and price list.

    如果您能寄来目录和价格单，我们将会非常感激。

    We shall be obliged if you make a specific enquiry.

    如果您能做具体询盘，我们将会非常感激。

5. commission：佣金

    *e.g.* There is a salary of $10,000, plus the opportunity to earn commission.

    工资是 1 万美元，还加上可以赚取佣金的机会。

    He gets a 10% commission on everything he sells.

    他每卖一件东西得百分之十的佣金。

6. minimum order quantities：最低起订量

    *e.g.* There are no minimum order quantities, you can get attractive pricing without placing larger volume orders.

    无需最低起订量，无需大数目订单，同样可以得到最具竞争力的价格。

    We would like to know the minimum order quantities per color and per design.

    我们想知道每种颜色，每种图案的最低订购数量。

7. be excellent in quality and reasonable in price：物美价廉

    *e.g.* We hope the products we are willing to purchase are excellent in quality and reasonable in price.

    我们希望我们将要购买的商品是物美价廉的。

8. forward：send　寄送，发送

    *e.g.* We are forwarding you a copy of our latest catalogue under separate cover.

我们另函把一册最新目录寄给你。

We will forward the goods when we receive your cheque.

当收到你们的支票时，我们就发送这批货物。

9. DHL：Dalsey, Hillblom and Lynn 敦豪速递公司（国际快递公司）。中外运–敦豪国际航空快件有限公司于 1986 年 12 月 1 日在北京正式成立。合资双方为中国对外贸易运输集团总公司和敦豪国际航空快递公司，双方各占一半股权。合资公司将敦豪作为国际快递业领导者的丰富经验和中国外运集团总公司在中国外贸运输市场的经营优势成功地结合在一起，为中国各主要城市提供航空快递服务。

10. laboratory report：化验报告，实验室报告

   *e.g.* Your laboratory report should contain answers to the questions.

   实验报告要包含对问题的答案。

11. FDA：Food and Drug Administration，（美国）食品和药物管理局的简称，是一项食品标准。食品和药物管理局（FDA）主管：食品、药品（包括兽药）、医疗器械、食品添加剂、化妆品、动物食品及药品、酒精含量低于 7% 的葡萄酒饮料以及电子产品的监督检验；产品在使用或消费过程中产生的离子、非离子辐射影响人类健康和安全项目的测试、检验和出证。根据规定，上述产品必须经过 FDA 检验证明安全后，方可在市场上销售。FDA 有权对生产厂家进行视察、有权对违法者提出起诉。

12. initial order：首次订购，首次订单

   *e.g.* Your initial order shall be appreciated very much。

   我们感谢你方的首次订购。

## 拓展提高

**Enquiry to Ask for Samples**

Dear Sir,

   Thank you for your letter of April 20, 2013 and we are pleased to enter into business relationship with you.

   As you know, we are the biggest importers in North America with an import value for more than 9 million Dollars per year.

   We are interested in your children's sport clothes. Our requests are as follows: 100% cotton, green, S, M, L size respectively. We shall be obliged if you could send us samples recently and if your products are satisfactory, we will place a large order with you.

   We look forward to your early reply.

Yours sincerely,

Jim

### The Reply to Enquiry

Dear Sir,

　　We have been in receipt of your samples with many thanks. Frankly speaking, we are quite satisfied with them. Therefore, we shall be appreciated if you would like to make us an offer on the children's sport clothes. If your price is competitive and favorable, we would like to consider placing an order for 10,000 pcs of 100% cotton children's sport clothes.

　　We are looking forward to your reply.

Yours sincerely,

Costa

## Notes

1. import value：进口值

　*e.g.* The customs authorities attributed the surging import value of crude oil, automobiles and iron ore, which climbed by 180%, 96% and 36% respectively, to the growing trade deficit.

　　海关认为贸易逆差主要表现在原油，汽车和铁矿石，分别上升了 180%、96%和 36%。

　　Sample also should pay tax, import value added tax follows custom duty.

　　样品也要交税，交进口增值税跟关税。

2. be interested in：对……感兴趣

　*e.g.* After study your catalogue enclosed, we are interested in your Lenovo personal computer.

　　在看过贵方随函附上的目录之后，我们对你方的联想牌电脑感兴趣。

3. respectively：分别地，各自地，独自地

　*e.g.* The nurses and the miners got pay rises of 5% and 7% respectively.

　　护士和矿工分别加薪 5%和 7%。

4. satisfactory：令人满意的，适合的

　*e.g.* He could not provide a satisfactory excuse for his absence.

　　他对自己缺席给不出令人满意的理由。

　　Sales are up 20% from last year, that is very satisfactory.

　　销售额比去年增涨了 20%，这真令人满意。

5. place an order：订购。place an order with sb. for sth. 向某人订购某东西

　*e.g.* If your price is competitive and reasonable, we will place an order for large quantities with you in the near future.

　　如果你方的价格是有竞争性和合理的，在不久的将来，我们将向你方定购大量的商品。

6. in receipt of：收到

　*e.g.* We are in receipt of your letter of the May 10, with your order for five printing machines, which I herewith acknowledge with best thanks.

贵公司 5 月 10 日来函及五部印刷机器的订单均已收到，在此表示感谢。

7. frankly speaking：坦白地说

*e.g.* Frankly speaking, we have very slim chances of managing our time because we have very little control over it.

坦白地说，我们很少有机会去管理时间，因为我们很少能够控制它。

Frankly speaking, I understand why Europeans are so concerned about the rapid development of a big country like China.

坦率地讲，我非常理解欧洲人对中国这样一个大国的快速发展的担忧。

8. competitive：有竞争性的

*e.g.* But we also have some competitive advantages that we should explore more.

但是我们也有一些应该进行更多探索的竞争优势。

First of all, if we want to stay competitive, we need to modernize our factory.

首先我们如果要保持竞争力的话，就需要使我们的工厂现代化。

### Enquiry about Price

Dear Sirs,

We are glad to learn from your letter of October 25, 2012 that as a manufacturer of lighters, you are desirous of entering into direct business relations with us. This is what we want to do, too. We have studied your catalogue and are interested in your MLK series of metal lighters. Please quote us your lowest price, CIF Wenzhou, inclusive of our 3% commission, stating the earliest date of shipment.

Should your price be found competitive and delivery date be acceptable, we intend to place a larger order with you.

Please reply as soon as possible.

Yours sincerely,

Heidi

### The Reply to Enquiry

Dear Sir,

Thank you for your letter of October 26, 2012 enquiring for our metal lighters. We wish to inform you that MLK series are in adequate stock at present, the price of which are $30 for silver one, $39 for gold one, FOB New York with 3% commission. We assure you that you will find it worth buying after studying our prices.

We welcome your order and are able to promise you that shipment will be made within 15 days after receipt of your L/C. Do not hesitate to contact us again if you have any further questions on this or any other matters.

We await your early decision.

Yours sincerely,

Tom

# Notes

1. manufacturer：制造商，制造公司

   *e.g.* The washing machine didn't work, so we sent it back to the manufacturer.

   这台洗衣机坏了，所以我们把它送回了制造厂家。

   The manufacturer of this excellent violin has really sweated the details.

   这把精美的小提琴的每个小地方都经过制造人的细致雕琢。

2. study：研究

   *e.g.* The government has ordered a feasibility study in connection with the proposed new airport.

   新政府下令做一项与所提议的新机场有关的可行性研究。

   She has made a study of the language of Shakespeare's plays.

   她对莎士比亚戏剧的语言做了研究。

3. date of shipment：装运时间

   *e.g.* Please inform us the specific date of shipment so as to catch our selling season.

   请告知我们具体的装运时间以便我们赶上热销季节。

4. delivery date：交货日期

   *e.g.* What I will say is the reason we postponed the delivery date.

   我要说的是延缓交货日期的理由。

   As the goods are needed urgently, we'd like an earlier delivery date.

   因急需，我们希望能提前供货。

5. be in stock：有现货的，备有现货，存货

   *e.g.* We have many patterns in stock for you to choose from.

   我们有多种现存的式样供你选择。

   The store had children's shoes in stock.

   这家商店童鞋有现货。

6. assure sb. that：assure sb. of　向某人保证

   *e.g.* I can assure you that the medicine is perfectly safe.

   我可以向你保证，这种药物绝对安全。

   He assured us of his ability to solve the problem.

   他向我们保证他有能力解决这个问题。

7. after receipt of：收到……之后

   *e.g.* We will effect shipment immediately after receipt of your shipping instruction.

   收到你方的装运通知后我们立刻安排装运。

### 技能操练

**I. Choose the best answer from A, B, C and D.**

1. While _____ an enquiry, you ought to enquire into quality, specification and price, etc.

    A. giving          B. offering          C. sending          D. making

2. We would _____ very much if you send us some samples immediately.

    A. thank you          B. appreciate it          C. appreciate          D. appreciate you

3. We are sending you the samples _____ requested.

    A. be          B. are          C. as          D. for

4. _____ your Enquiry No. 123, we are sending you a catalog and a sample book for your reference.

    A. According          B. As per          C. As          D. About

5. Our company has 30 years' experience _____ the machinery line.

    A. on          B. in          C. about          D. of

6. We _____ you of our prompt shipment after receipt of your order.

    A. assure          B. assurance          C. insure          D. insurance

7. I want to acquaint myself _____ the supply position of steel products.

    A. of          B. with          C. for          D. about

8. In case the said goods are not available _____ stock. Please keep us informed at all early date.

    A. in          B. by          C. from          D. out of

9. _____ our S/C No.301, we wish to say that the goods will be shipped by Oct.10.

    A. With reference to          B. Refer to          C. Referring          D. With refer to

10. We have made _____ that we would accept D/P terms for your future orders.

    A. clear          B. it clear          C. that clear          D. it is clear

**II. Translate the following phrases into English or vice versa.**

1. commission_____

2. substantial order _____

3. inclusive of _____

4. date of shipment _____

5. minimum order quantities _____

6. excellent in quality and reasonable in price _____

7. for our expense _____

8. initial order _____

9. import value _____

10. respectively _____

11. 最新的目录 _____

12. 收到 _____

13. 坦白地说 _____

14. 制造商，制造公司 _____

15. 有现货的 _____

16. 询盘 _____

17. 有竞争性的价格 _____

18. 供不应求 _____

19. 供过于求 _____

20. 订货 _____

**III. Translate the following sentences from English into Chinese or vice versa.**

1. 接到你方具体询价后，我们当即寄给你报价单。

_____

2. 我方正在研究你们的商品目录，并将告诉你们我方目前欲购的商品。

_____

3. 如果你能寄给我们样品和有关的说明书，我们将不胜感激。

_____

4. 现寄上我们的 143 号询价单一份，请您报 FOB 价格。

_____

5. 目前我方市场供过于求。

_____

6. 对于超过 100 件的订单我方将给予 8%的折扣。

_____

7. We regret that the goods you enquiry about are out of stock.

_____

8. We are now sending you, under separate cover, a list of main commodities available for export. If you need any item in this list, we will do our utmost to supply you the needed upon receipt of your detailed list.

_____

9. Please send us an offer for 3 tons walnut meat, second grade, for delivery in September with related trade terms and condition.

_____

10. Although we are keen to do business with you, we regret that we cannot accept your counter offer or even meet you half way.

_____

11. Moreover, we've kept the price close to the costs of production.

_____

12. We might say our products have met with warm reception everywhere.

_____

### IV. Fill in the blanks with the proper words.

1. Please note that our price remains valid _____ two weeks.

2. We accept payment _____ L/C. Shipment will be made 20 days after receipt of the covering L/C at sight.

3. I will respond _____ your counter-offer by reducing our price by five dollars.

4. We acknowledge _____ thanks receipt of your letter of May 10.

5. We are sending you our illustrated catalogue _____ separate cover together with some of the samples.

6. We are _____ a position to offer textile machinery from stock.

7. The goods will be sent _____ receipt of your remittance.

8. If your first order turns out _____ our satisfaction, large repeat orders will follow.

9. We trust that this will meet _____ your approval.

10. We look forward _____ hearing from you.

### V. Compose a dialogue in the following situation.

Mr. Clife from a company in Canada comes to a machinery plant for the prices of small hardware. Mr. Yang is meeting with him.

### VI. Write a letter with the ideas below.

Write to Ms. Dan, making a special enquiry on the following products and the quotation (CIF). The delivery is in two weeks after the date of June 12.

(1) 100% cotton cloth, color No.12, standard width 200 yards

(2) silk of 30% nylon, color No.9, standard width 400 yards

## Read More

**Enquiry**

An enquiry is made to seek a supply of products, service or information. In order to obtain the needed information, the enquirer should state simply, clearly and concisely what he wants—general information, a catalogue or price list, a sample, a quotation, etc. Enquiries should be specific and provide the necessary details to enable the receiver to answer the questions completely.

1. Types

(1) General Enquiry: asking for common data, such as catalogue, price list, sample and pictures, etc.

(2) Specific Enquiry: specifically enquiry about name of commodity, specifications, quantity, unit price, date of shipment, payment terms and packing, etc.

2. Structure

(1) If the seller is the buyer's constant supplier:

State the goods and services you are interested in.

Request for catalogue, price list, sample and terms of transaction, etc.

Expectation for paying attention to your enquiry and giving you an early reply.

(2) If the seller is your new supplier:

Express that you would like to establish business relationship with him.

Request for catalogue, price list, sample and terms of transaction, etc.

Expectation for paying attention to your enquiry and giving you an early reply.

Enquiries should be written concisely and clearly to the point. The reply to an enquiry should be prompt and courteous.

# 实训项目 4

## Offers and Counter-offers
## 报盘和还盘

**学习目标**

知识目标：了解报盘与还盘信函的组成部分，掌握相关专业术语和常用句型。

能力目标：能够撰写询盘与回复的信函，做到内容清楚，叙述完整，礼貌得体。

**工作任务**

### 工作任务 1

上海思科公司收到美国 ABC 公司回信，表示在广交会上对型号为 BJ123 的镜框很感兴趣，希望思科公司报含 3%佣金的 CIF 到蒙特利尔的美元价格，同时希望思科公司告知付款方式、保险、包装、装运时间、起订量等有关的贸易条件，并希望对方邮寄样品。此次寄样要求思科公司通过 DHL 国际快递第 99648752 号账户寄送，邮寄费由进口方承担。根据以上交易情境，以思科公司业务员的身份写一封报盘信函。

_____

_____

_____

_____

_____

_____

_____

_____

_____

## 工作任务 2

　　加拿大里那多公司收到上海嘉陵电动自行车厂的报盘，获知了 WEA，WEB，WEC 三种型号的电动车报价，并了解到付款条款和装运期。作为加拿大里那多公司的业务员，写一封还盘信函给上海嘉陵电动自行车厂，要求降低价格，以便继续订购。

_____

_____

_____

_____

_____

_____

_____

## 操作示范

## 操作示范 1

**Shanghai Sike Trading Company**

Xi'an Road, Xuhui District, Shanghai

www.shanaghaisike.cn

Tel: 0086-21-2584567

Dear Sir,

　　We are glad to receive your enquiry of November 4, 2012 and are pleased to know that you are interested in our BJ123 range spectacle-frames.

　　We would like to quote as follows based on per 20′ FCL.

| Commodity | Article No. | CIFC Montreal per piece | Cartons per 20′ FCL |
| --- | --- | --- | --- |
| spectacle-frames | BJ123A | USD 12.5 | 508cnt |
| | BJ123B | USD 11.5 | 497cnt |
| | BJ123C | USD 11 | 500cnt |
| | BJ123D | USD 10.5 | 480cnt |

　　Packing: 100 pieces in a carton

　　Shipment: to be delivered within 15 days after receipt of the relevant L/C

　　Payment: by irrevocable documentary L/C in favor of the seller

　　Insurance: for 110% invoice value covering WPA and FPA

　　In addition, we would like to inform you that our minimum order quantities are 5,000 pieces and we have sent you the sample you requested by DHL.

　　We look forward to your initial order.

### 操作示范 2

**Canadian Leanaedou Corporation**

Treael Road, Uior District, Canada

www.cleanaedou.corp.ca

Tel:001-834-5843956

Dear Sirs，

Thank you for your letter about the offer for the captioned electric bicycles. Although we appreciate the quality of your electric bicycles, their price is too high to be acceptable. Referring to the Sales Confirmation No. 32SP-098, you will find that we ordered 1,000 bicycles with same brand as per the terms and conditions stipulated in that Sales Confirmation, but the price was 10% lower than your present price. Since we placed the last order, price for raw materials has been decreased considerable. Retailing price for your electric bicycles here has also been reduced by 5%. Accepting your present price will mean great loss to us, let alone profit. We would like to place repeat orders with you if you could reduce your price at least by 1.5%. Otherwise, we have to shift to the other suppliers for our similar request.

We hope you take our suggestion into serious consideration and give us your reply as soon as possible.

Yours truly,

Saun

### 知识链接

1. 对于客户新的报盘，应该以什么形式回复呢？

   In response to an offer, counter-offer may be sent.

2. 还盘应该包含哪些内容？

   A satisfactory counter-offer should include the following:

   a. An expression of thanks for their last letter/E-mail

   b. Details of prices, discounts and terms of payment

   c. An undertaking as to date of delivery or time of shipment

   d. The period for which the quotation is valid.

We are glad to receive your enquiry of November 4th, 2012 and pleased to make an offer as follows.

## 一问一答

### Asks

1. What is a firm offer?

2. When you are making a firm offer, what should be mentioned?

3. If a firm offer has been accepted, can it be withdrawn?

4. If you were a buyer, what should you do when rejecting a quotation or offer?

5. What should be included in a letter of rejection?

### Answers

1. A firm offer is a promise to sell goods at a stated price, usually within a stated period of time. The promise may be expressed or implied. Usually a firm offer bears a validity, such as the wording "for accepting within… days".

2. In making a firm offer, mention should be made of the time of shipment and the mode of payment desired; in addition, an exact description of the goods should be given, if possible, pattern or sample should be sent.

3. Once a firm offer has been accepted, it cannot be withdrawn.

4. A buyer should explain the reason for rejection of a quotation or offer for the sake of courtesy as it takes the seller much trouble in making out a quotation or offer.

5. The letter of rejection should cover the following points:

   a. To thank the seller for his offer.

   b. To express regret at inability to accept.

   c. To make a counter-offer if, in the circumstances, it is appropriate.

   d. To suggest other opportunities to do business together.

## 难点解析

1. FCL：Full Container Load, 整箱货。由发货人负责装箱、计数、积载并加铅封的货运。整箱货的拆箱，一般由收货人办理。但也可以委托承运人在货运站拆箱。可是承运人不负责箱内的货损、货差。除非货方举证确属承运人责任事故的损害，承运人才负责赔偿。承运人对整箱货，以箱为交接单位。只要集装箱外表与收箱时相似和铅封完整，承运人就完成了承运责任。整箱货运提单上，要加上"委托人装箱、计数并加铅封"的条款。

　　与之相对的是 LCL（Less than Container Load）拼箱货。指装不满一整箱的小票货物。这种货物，通常是由承运人分别揽货并在集装箱货运站或内陆站集中，而后将两票或两票以上的货物拼装在一个集装箱内，同样要在目的地拆箱，拆箱费用仍向收货方收取。承运人对拼箱货的责任，基本上与传统杂货运输相同。

2. irrevocable documentary L/C：不可撤销的跟单信用证

　　*e.g.* It is our usual practice to make payment by irrevocable documentary L/C in foreign trade.

　　　　我们在对外贸易中的一贯做法是用不可撤销的跟单信用证支付。

3. in favor of：以……为受益人

　　*e.g.* Party A shall open a usance L/C in favor of Party B to pay by installments the entire cost of the Assembly Lines to be supplied by Party B.

　　　　甲方开出以乙方为受益人的远期信用证,分期支付乙方所供装配线的全部价款。

4. invoice value：发票金额

　　*e.g.* It goes against the stipulation of the contract to insure the goods at 130% of the invoice value.

　　　　按发票金额的 130%给货物投保是违背合同规定的。

　　　　To be effected by the sellers covering All Risks and War Risk for 1.5% of invoice value.

　　　　由卖方按发票总值 1.5%投保一切险及战争险。

5. WPA：With Particular Average 水渍险

6. FPA：Free from Particular Average 平安险

7. initial order：首次订单，第一次订购

　　*e.g.* We hope the new prices will meet your requirement and look forward to receiving your initial order soonest.

　　　　我方期望这个新的价钱将会达到贵方的要求，期待很快收到贵方的第一个订单。

8. refer to：谈到，提及，关于

　　*e.g.* Referring to your enquiry of September 8, we would like to make quotation as follows.

　　　　关于你方 9 月 8 日的询盘，我们愿意做如下报盘。

9. Sales Confirmation：销售确认书

　　*e.g.* The supplier faxed back to acknowledge the sales confirmation.

　　　　供应商传真告知已收到我方的销售确认书。

10. raw material：原材料

　　*e.g.* The tanner is said to be reluctant to quote firm price because of a rising and uncertain raw material market.

　　　　据说由于原材料市场上升且捉摸不定，制革商们不愿报出实盘。

11. shift：转移，转向

　　*e.g.* The wind shifted and blew the mist away.

　　　　风转了方向，并把雾吹散了。

　　　　He shifted impatiently in his seat during the long speech.

　　　　在听冗长的报告时，他不耐烦地在座位上挪来挪去。

12. take… into consideration：考虑

　　*e.g.* You should take the weather into consideration.

　　　　你应该把天气考虑在内。

拓展提高

## An Offer

Dear John,

　　Thank you for your letter of June 12, 2013. At your request, we are making you the following offer subject to your reply arriving there before June 30, 2011.

　　Article: 100% cotton bed sheet

　　Color: red, black, blue, yellow

　　Size: 1.5m, 1.8m

　　Price: $6.5 for 1.5m, $7.5 for 1.8m FOB Ningbo

　　Quantity: 10,000 pieces

　　Packing: 50 pieces in a carton

　　Shipment: before November 15, 2013

　　Insurance: to be covered by the buyer

　　Terms of Payment: By irrevocable documentary Letter of Credit in the seller's favor at sight. We will await with keen interest in your formal orders.

Yours sincerely,

Tina

## A Counter-offer

Dear Tina,

　　We are in receipt of your letter of June 12, 2013, offering us 10,000 pieces of 100% cotton bed sheets.

　　In reply, we regret to inform you that our end-user here finds your price too high. As the market is declining, you may be aware that some Japanese dealers are lowering their prices. It is no doubt that there is keen competition in the market.

　　We do not deny that your products are attractive, but the difference in price should, in no case, be as big as 5%. To step up the trade, we on behalf of our end-users, make counter–offers as follows:

　　10,000 pieces of 100% cotton bed sheets, $6 for 1.5m, $6.8 for 1.8m FOB Ningbo, other terms as per your letter of June 12.

　　We are looking forward to your early reply.

Yours sincerely,

Dian

## Notes

1. at your request：according to your request; in compliance with your request; in accordance with your request 根据你方要求

   *e.g.* At your request, we will send you the samples and catalogue as soon as possible.

   按照你方的要求，我们将尽快给你方寄过去样品和目录。

   At your request, we deducted it from the remittance.

   按照您的要求，我方已将费用从汇款金额中扣除。

2. be subject to：以……为准；以……为条件

   *e.g.* This offer is subject to our final confirmation.

   本报盘以我方最后确认为准。

   Although these targets would not be internationally binding, they would be subject to outside verification.

   虽然这些目标不具有国际约束力，但它们将受到外界监督。

3. FOB：Free on Board 离岸价

   *e.g.* We give you price of $1,350 FOB Chicago.

   我方给你方的价格是 1350 美元，FOB 芝加哥。

   Here are our FOB price lists. All the prices in the lists are subject to our confirmation.

   这是我们的 FOB 价格表，所有的价格需以我方最后确认为准。

4. at sight：即期。L/C at sight，即期信用证

5. regret to do sth.：遗憾做某事

   *e.g.* We regret to note that you have turned down our counter-offer.

   我们很遗憾，知道你方已拒绝了我方的还价。

   We very much regret to state that our end–user here find your price too high and out of line with the prevailing market level.

   我们很遗憾地声明：我们的消费者认为你的价格太高了，而且和普遍的市场价比，高得过分了。

6. end-user：终端客户

   *e.g.* An application to one end-user can be viewed as a service to another end-user.

   一个终端用户的应用程序可以被看作是其他终端用户的服务。

7. in no case：at any rate 无论如何都不

   *e.g.* Anybody should in no case be allowed to stay here.

   绝不许任何人在这里停留。

   In no case will they look on passively.

   他们绝不会在一边看热闹。

8. step up：使增加，使加快速度

   *e.g.* We should step up the development of infrastructure for research.

   我们应该加强科学基础设施建设。

9. on behalf of：代表

　　*e.g.* He spoke on behalf of all the members of the faculty and staff.

　　　　他代表全体教职员工讲了话。

　　　　I'm writing on behalf of my mother to express her thanks for your gift.

　　　　我代表我母亲写信，对你的礼物表示感谢。

## An Offer

Dear Sir,

　　We acknowledge receipt of your E-mail dated October 12, 2012, from which we note that you wish to have a firm offer from us for 10 metric tons of Apricot Kernels, 2012 crop, for shipment to Osaka.

　　We are making you, subject to your acceptance reaching us by January 12, 2013, Beijing time, the following offer:

　　"10 metric tons of Apricot Kernels, F.A.Q 2012 crop, at $300 per metric ton CIFC 3% Osaka, with shipment during March or April. Other terms and conditions are the same as usual, with the exception of insurance which will cover All Risks and War Risk for 110% of the total invoice value." We look forward to your early reply.

Yours sincerely,

Coasta

## A Counter-offer

Dear Coasta,

　　We are in receipt of your email dated October 12, 2012 offering us 10 metric tons of the captioned goods at $300 per metric ton on the usual terms. In reply, we regret to inform you that our buyers in Osaka find your price much too high. Information indicates that some parcel of Turkish origin have been sold there at a level about 15% lower than yours.

　　We do not deny that the quality of Chinese kernels is slightly better, but the difference in price should, in no case, be as big as 15%. In order to conclude the transaction, we would like to be on behalf of our buyer to make you the following counter-offer, subject to our reply reaching us before or on November 10, 2012.

　　"10 metric tons of Apricot Kernels, 2012 crop, at $280 per metric ton CIFC 3% Osaka, other terms as per your email dated October 12."

　　As the market is declining, we recommend your immediate acceptance.

Yours sincerely,

Tina

## Notes

1. acknowledge：承认，告知已收到

   *e.g.* I hereby acknowledge receipt of your letter of July 25.

   特此告知贵方 7 月 25 日的来函收悉。

   We gratefully acknowledge the contributions of everyone who helped us.

   我们衷心感谢每一位帮助我们的人所付出的努力。

2. firm-offer：实盘。实盘是指发盘人对接受人所提出的是一项内容完整、明确、肯定的交易条件，一旦送达受盘人之后，则对发盘人产生拘束力，发盘人在实盘规定的有效期内不得将其撤销或加以变更。表明发盘人有肯定订立合同的意图。如果受盘人在有效期内无条件地接受，就可以达成交易，成为对买卖双方都有约束力的合同。

3. metric ton：公吨

   *e.g.* I suggest around USD 450 per metric ton CIF Shanghai.

   我建议把上海到岸价定为每公吨 450 美元。

   The best price we can accept is RMB 135 per metric ton.

   我们能够接受的最好价格为每公吨 135 元。

4. F.A.Q：Fair Average Quality 良好平均品质，俗称"大路货"，是指国际贸易中农作物出口的品质，也就是良好平均品质

5. terms and conditions：条款和条件

   *e.g.* In a sweetheart deal, one company offers very attractive terms and conditions to another company or individual.

   在一笔甜心交易中，一家公司向另一公司或个人提出非常吸引人的条款和条件。

   Terms and conditions in the L/C should be in compliance with our Sales Contract.

   信用证的条款应该与销售合同中的条款一致。

6. parcel：一批货物

   *e.g.* Last parcel sent to us are in good condition.

   上一批运到我们这里的货物完好无损。

7. conclude the transaction：come to the transaction 达成交易

   *e.g.* We will conclude the transaction on the basis of equality and mutual benefit.

   我们将会在平等互利的基础上达成交易。

8. counter-offer：还盘又称还价，是受盘人对发盘内容不完全同意而提出修改或变更的表示，是对发盘条件进行添加，限制或其他更改的答复。还盘只有受盘人才可以做出，其他人做出无效。

9. CIFC：Cost, Insurance and Freight plus Commission 成本、保险、运费加佣金

   *e.g.* Would you please change them into CIFC 5% San Francisco?

   我们想要 CIFC 5%旧金山价。

   Will you quote us the price CIFC 3% Marseilles?

   请给我们报包括 3%佣金，马赛交货的到岸价好吗？

**技能操练**

**I. Choose the best answer from A, B, C and D.**

1. We are offering you firm _____ on the same terms and conditions as the previous contract.

　　A. as following　　　　B. as follow　　　　C. as is following　　D. as follows

2. The commodities you offered are _____ line with the business scope of our clients.

　　A. outside　　　　　　B. out　　　　　　　C. out of　　　　　　D. without

3. A firm offer _____ a time limit for acceptance.

　　A. may specify　　　　B. never specifies　　C. sometimes specifies D. must specify

4. We are offering you goods _____ the high quality.

　　A. of　　　　　　　　B. at　　　　　　　　C. for　　　　　　　　D. with

5. _____ we thank you for your enquiry, we regret being unable to make you an offer for the time being.

　　A. While　　　　　　B. When　　　　　　　C. As　　　　　　　　D. Since

6. Please let us _____ the firm offer before the end of this month.

　　A. had　　　　　　　B. have　　　　　　　C. having　　　　　　D. to have

7. _____ we would like to close the business with you, we find your price unacceptable.

　　A. Much　　　　　　B. However much　　　C. Much as　　　　　　Despite

8. We are not in a position to offer firm, as the goods are _____.

　　A. without stock　　　B. outside in stock　　C. no stock　　　　　D. out of stock

9. Our price is more attractive as _____ that offered by suppliers elsewhere.

　　A. compared to　　　B. compared with　　C. compare to　　　D. compare with

10. Thank you for your letter of September 1, _____ which you offered us 13,000 yards of printed shirting with the following terms and conditions.

　　A. from　　　　　　B. of　　　　　　　　C. in　　　　　　　　D. to

**II. Translate the following phrases into English or vice versa.**

1. 实盘 _____

2. 以……为准 _____

3. 最后确认 _____

4. 标题货物 _____

5. 还盘 _____

6. 报价 _____

7. 长期业务关系 _____

8. 达成交易 _____

9. 条款和条件 _____

10. 货号 _____

11. non-firm offer _____

12. be specialized in _____

13. irrevocable L/C _____

14. at your request _____

15. prevailing price _____

16. make an offer _____

17. initial order _____

18. F.A.Q _____

19. on the high side _____

20. average price _____

**III. Translate the following sentences from English into Chinese or vice versa.**

1. We shall be very glad to place our order with you if your quotation is competitive and delivery date is acceptable.

   _____

2. We hope you will quote us competitive CIF Liverpool for Children's shirt.

   _____

3. We shall appreciate it very much, if you will quote us your lowest price for Groundnuts.

   _____

4. The price you counter-offer is not in line with the prevailing market.

   _____

5. We want some samples of your products in order to acquaint ourselves with the material and workmanship before we place a large order with you.

   _____

6. We might add here that, owing to heavy demand, our offer remains valid until the end of this month and that there is little likelihood of the goods remaining unsold once this particular offer has lapsed.

   _____

7. 你方必须降价 3%，否则没有成交的可能。

   _____

8. 我们高兴地向你方作出 50 台 70 型铣床的如下报盘。

   _____

9. 兹报即期装船苦杏仁(Bitter Apricot Kernels)50 公吨实盘，每公吨 FOB 价 120 美元，以我方最后传真确认有效。

   _____

10. 我们愿意通知你方我们能供应标题项下的货物。

   _____

11. 如果能设法改进产品的质量，我们可能大量订货。

   _____

12. 不言而喻，你方会立即开立以我方为受益人的信用证。

   _____

## IV. Fill in the blanks with the proper words.

1. We shall make a reduction _____ our price if you increase the quantity to 5,000 pieces.

2. We would like to direct your attention _____ the quality of the goods which is superior _____ that of other makes.

3. We are prepared to keep the offer open _____ 30th this month.

4. Many of our clients requested us to approach you _____ offers.

5. If you could make a reduction _____ 1% _____ quotation, we have confidence _____ securing large orders for you.

6. We will withdraw the offer if we should not hear _____ you by the end of this week.

7. The above offer is subject _____ our final confirmation.

8. The earliest shipment is December; we hope that it will be acceptable _____ you.

## V. Compose a dialogue in the following situation.

Mr. Joe, the manager of embroidered table cross company, is making an offer with Miss Wang, an importer from China, about embroidered table cross.

## VI. Write a letter with the idea below.

Suppose one of your customers intends to buy 500–1,000 reams of A4 poster paper. Before he places an order, he'd like to see some samples and know something about price, earliest delivery date and terms of payment. You are asked to reply to his request.

## ▮ **Read More**

### What Makes an Offer Binding?

Do you know what constitutes a contract? Do you know that an offer can also be binding even if it was never written on paper? Do you know that a contract need not be in writing?

There are a number of terms, which you will need to understand:

1. What is an offer?

An offer is an expression made by one individual to another. It can be given to another individual, a group of individuals or to the world at large. It offers the promise of being bound as long as the specified terms are accepted. It can be oral, written or via conduct.

2. What is an acceptance?

An acceptance takes place when there is a final and unqualified expression of agreement to the terms of the offer. An acceptance must be communicated to the offeror. Unless Postal Acceptance Rule applies, acceptance must be made either through fax, telex or face to face. In the case of acceptance by post, an acceptance of offer is made once the letter is posted, even if the letter was lost in the mail.

3. What is a contract?

A contract occurs when an offer is accepted. And unless required by law, a contract need not be in writing. All contracts are agreements giving rise to obligations which are enforced or recognized at law. However, not all agreements are contracts as a valid contract must possess all the following element: offer, acceptance, intention to create legal relations, capacity and consideration.

During the course of negotiating the contract, many statements would have been made. Some would be legally binding while others are not. There are a number of factors, which could potentially legally bind a statement.

1. The closer the statement was made to the conclusion of the contract, the more likely it is to be binding.

2. If the maker of the statement has greater knowledge concerning the statement compared to the other party, it is more likely the statement is binding.

3. The greater the emphasis placed by a party to the contract, the more likely the statement is binding.

4. If an oral statement is later set down in writing, then it is more likely to have become contractually binding.

5. If the maker of the statement invited the other party to verify the truth of the statement made (e.g. "Why don't you get an independent party to verify if you don't believe me"), then the statement is more likely to be a representation and may give rise to a course of action in misrepresentation if false.

# 实训项目 5

## Sales Promotion
## 促 销

**学习目标**

　　知识目标：了解推销信函，振兴信函以及随访信函的组成部分，掌握相关专业术语和常用句型。

　　能力目标：能够撰写推销信函，振兴信函以及随访信函，做到内容清楚，叙述完整，礼貌得体。

**工作任务**

### 工作任务 1

　　李先生是中国大红花有限公司外贸部的业务经理，中国大红花公司主要经营中国传统蜂蜜。据考证，该蜂蜜营养价值非常高而且口感好，尤其适合欧美国家的客户。假如你是李先生，请写一封推销函，向欧美客户介绍你们公司的蜂蜜以及表达希望对方早日试订的愿望。

_____

_____

_____

_____

_____

_____

_____

_____

_____

_____

_____

## 工作任务 2

请以中国机器设备进出口贸易公司业务员的身份向其客户写推销函开拓新市场。要求推销函主要以介绍公司业务为主，主要目的是促使客户对公司产品感兴趣并尽快下订单。

_____

_____

_____

_____

_____

_____

## 操作示范

## 操作示范 1

**Chinese Dahonghua Import and Export Company**

Fudong Road, Lucheng District, Wenzhou, Zhejiang 325000

Tel: 0086-577-22365678

Website:dhhie.com.cn

Dear Gentlemen,

We are pleased to learn from the Chamber of Commerce that you are in the market for honey.

We wish to inform you that we are specialized in the export of the commodity. Chinese honey meets with warm reception from European customers with its special flavor.

As requested, we now enclose our quotation sheet with samples and catalogues to be sent under separate cover. We trust that the quoted price is acceptable to you, which is 15% lower than that of the similar article of Indian origin. A fair comparison in quality between our products and those of other suppliers will convince you of the reasonableness of our quotation.

We would suggest that you send us your trial order as soon as possible, as there is a brisk demand for this article.

Yours sincerely,

Mr. Li

Manager

## 操作示范 2

**China National Machinery & Equipment**
**Import & Export Corporation**
178 Guang'anmenwai Street, Beijing 100055, China
Tel: 0086-63451188　Fax: 0086-63261865

March 3, 2013

Messrs, Adler Bismarck & Co.
Hamburg
Germany

Dear Sirs,

We write to introduce ourselves as one of the largest exporters from China, and of a wide range of Machinery and Equipments.

We enclose a copy of our latest catalogue covering the details of all the items available at present, and hope some of these items will be of interest to you.

It will be a great pleasure to receive your enquiries for any of the items against which we will send you our lowest quotations.

Should, by chance, your corporation not deal with the import of the goods mentioned above, we would be most grateful if this letter could be forwarded to the correct import corporation.

We are looking forward to your favorable and prompt reply.

Yours faithfully,
Lucy

### 知识链接

写促销信函的要求：

1. More personal.

2. To represent the offer from the point of view of the buyer, not the seller.

3. Use concise and exact language to introduce their product's specification, capability, traits, and usages.

4. Through exchange information, build communication between buyers and sellers, and achieve the purpose of sales promotion.

5. The content of sales letter should be substantial, and use the vivid language and clear style to persuade/convince/prevail on customers. The language should be attractive, amiable, approachable, valid, and the information should be actual/authentic, genuine, unfeigned/real, believable, dependable, credible, reliable, trusty.

The common structure of a sales letter:

1. Appellation

2. The salutation

3. The main body: try to catch the attention of readers; arouse the interests of readers, and try to bring sympathy among readers; directly point out the product or services in this letter, through detail introduce product and service to make the readers clearly know what the purpose of this letter is; show your evidences: using recommended documents, reports on the media, identity to support the evidences are formal, reasonable and believable.

4. The ending

A. What do you want to do? Your purposes.

B. More information for the product.

C. The contact number, the contact name.

D. Repeat important points of the main body.

5. Signature and date

## Asks

1. What is sales promotion?

2. What's the purpose of sales promotion?

3. What does a good sales letter consist of?

4. How to create successful sales letters?

5. What is the best way to end the sales letters?

6. What are the advantages of a sales letter?

## Answers

1. Sales promotion is a marketing strategy within a short period of time. It is a sales channel to be designed for stimulating customers' purchase intentions. (Jobber, 2004)

2. Its purpose is to expand business, to persuade the reader (namely the buyer) to buy what the sellers are able to supply.

3. A good sales letter consists of four essential elements; it must:

a. arouse interest

b. create desire

c. carry conviction

d. induce action.

4. The following are some tips that help you create successful sales letters:

a. Talk about your customer, not yourself

b. Acquaint or reacquaint the reader with who you are

c. Use bullets

d. End with an action

e. Keep your letter brief

f. Show that you "get" their company

g. Use statistics

h. Give away ideas.

5. What result do you want from your letter? Are you looking forward to getting a face-to-face meeting? Are you answering questions raised at a previous meeting? Do you want to make your prospect better informed? Do you need to get a signed contract? You need to close your letter by requesting a specific, quantifiable action. For example, "I will call you on Tuesday, November 18 at 10 a.m. to schedule a meeting" or "Please return the enclosed contract on Friday, December 12, or call me if you have any other questions."

6. A. It can save customer's time, build long-term relationship with customers, repeat orders.

B. It can be stored long time, give more detail description on products, stress the memories.

C. It can be repeated reading; and it can make customer understand more and strengthen customers' memories.

## 难点解析

1. be in the market for sth.：  want to buy  想要购买

   *e.g.* After investigation of your area, we obtain that the customers in South Africa are in the market for cotton table cloth very much.

   经过调查，我们获知南非地区的客户非常想要购买全棉的桌布。

2. be specialized in：专门从事，专门经营

   *e.g.* We are specialized in the export of the commodity.

   我们专门从事此商品的出口业务。

   specialize：把……用于专门目的；使专门化；专营

   *e.g.* We specialize in this line. 我们专营此类商品。

   a specialized wharf: 专业码头

   a specialized foreign exchange bank: 外汇专业银行

   a specialized capital: 专用资本

3. under separate cover：另寄，另邮（不附寄在信中的邮品需单独邮寄时，用此短语）类似的短语还有 by another post, by separate post 等。

    *e.g.* We are pleased to send you our revised catalogue under separate cover.

        我们很乐意另邮寄出修改后的目录给您。

        We have forwarded to you by another post a full range of samples for the coming season。

        我们另邮寄给你方供下个旺季销售的全套货物样品。

4. convince：使相信，使说服。固定搭配 convince sb. of sth.

    *e.g.* The annual turnovers have convinced our agents that our products are superior to Japanese ones.

        年销售额使我们的代理商确信我们的产品比日本产品要好得多。

        You'll need to convince them of your enthusiasm for the job.

        你要使他们相信你殷切希望得到这份工作。

5. brisk demand：旺盛的需求；catch the brisk demand 抓住大量的市场需求

    *e.g.* There is a brisk demand for electronic toys.

        电动玩具需求旺盛。

        We shall appreciate it very much if you will effect shipment as soon as possible, thus enabling the goods to arrive here in time to catch the brisk demand.

        如果贵方能尽快将货物发出的话，我方会非常感激的，这样的话，货物就能及时运达，赶上旺销季节。

6. available：可得的，可用的

    *e.g.* We must utilize all available resources.

        我们必须利用可以得到的一切资源。

        The products you enquired are available, therefore, do not hesitate to place an order with us promptly.

        对于你们所询价的商品我们是有现货的，因此，不要犹豫，请尽快向我们订购。

7. of interest：有兴趣

    *e.g.* We have eliminated all statistical tables, which are of interest only to the specialist.

        我们删去了全部统计表格，因为只有专家才对这些表格感兴趣。

        It is a question of interest to biological science.

        这是生物学长期以来感兴趣的问题。

8. by chance：偶然地，意外地

    *e.g.* I got this book by chance at a second-hand bookshop.

        我赶巧在一家旧书店里买到了这本书。

        I heard their talking by chance.

        我偶然听到了他们的谈话。

**拓展提高**

**Sales Letter**

Dear Sirs,

　　We know that you may be presently in the market for high quality sunglasses at an affordable price. As this item falls within the scope of our business activities, we should be pleased to enter business relations with you in the near future.

　　We are specializing in the manufacture and export of sunglasses with high quality and competitive price. For any information about the products of Dolphin, please visit our website: www.wzdolphin.com.

　　If we can be of any further assistance, please feel free to contact us.

Best Regards,

Bonia

Wenzhou Dolphin Sunglasses Import & Export Co., Ltd.

Add: Yongqiang Industrial Park, Wenzhou City, Zhejiang, China

Tel: 0086-577-28238398　　Fax: 0086-577-28238397

E-mail:bonia@ wzdolphin.com

Web: www.wzdolphin.com.

**The Reviver**

Dear Sirs,

　　Looking back through our records, we find that from 2009 to 2012 you bought from us a large quantity of Haier air-conditioners including the Models GW-120-1 to GW-120-10. However, unfortunately, in 2013 we did not receive any order from you.

　　That makes us surprised. Did we do anything wrong? Didn't the products you ordered satisfy your requirements? Was there anything wrong with the quality of our products?

　　Whatever the reason, we would really want to know it. We hope you can tell us the real reason, so that we can improve the quality of our products and related service.

　　Recently our company has developed a new product: Haier TGW-121-1 of exchanging air-conditioner Models GW-120-1, which is very strong, tranquil and electricity-saving. We hope to receive your order of our new air-conditioners.

Yours faithfully,

John

### The Following-up Letter

Dear Sirs,

We have been expecting to hear from you concerning the captioned engine pamphlets of which we trust you have already received.

This engine is an ideal one suitable for use in rice-growing countries. It supplies motive power for hand tractors, small irrigation pumps and grain threshers. It is moderate in price and compares most favorably with other makes in quality

As we contemplate introducing this engine into Brazil, we shall be glad to have your comments on its sales possibilities. Further details, if required, will be gladly furnished to assist you in your sales efforts.

We look forward to the pleasure of hearing from you soon.

Yours faithfully,

Lily

## Notes

1. sales letter：推销信

   Sales letters is taken as a form of advertising. It aims at selling particular kinds or service to selected types of customers.

   The purposes of sales letters are to persuade the customers to buy your product now, to develop an interest in your product that will induce them to buy later, to keep the name of your organization in customers' mind, or to get customers to try your product or ask questions about it.

2. affordable price：实惠的价格，能承受的价格

   *e.g.* Often your local town will offer a series of fitness classes at an affordable price.
   你当地的镇上经常会以一个大家可以负担得起的价钱提供一系列健康课程。

3. assistance：帮助，援助

   *e.g.* You should never deny assistance to those who need it.
   你不应当拒绝帮助那些需要你帮助的人。

   We are going to render them economic assistance.
   我们打算向他们提供经济援助。

4. the reviver：振兴信

   The reviver is a kind of letter with the purpose of which is to keep the regular customers and to expend the business, because they are the main buyers of sales potential.

5. looking back through：回顾

   *e.g.* Looking back through these numbers, it's easy to see how true that statement really is today.
   回顾上面的数据，我们今天终于理解了这句话是多么正确。

   Looking back through it leaves me feeling happier, more positive and just better in general.

当我回头看这些事情的时候，它使我更高兴，更积极，反正比平时更喜悦。

6. tranquil：安静的，平静的

　　*e.g.* While many people claim that they thrive in high-stress environments, others work better in some place that is relaxing and tranquil.

　　　尽管很多人声称他们在高度紧张的环境下做得不错，其他人还是在放松和平静的地方工作得更好。

　　Just because the meaninglessness, my heart is so tranquil!

　　　就是因为没有意义，所以我的心才会如此平静！

7. electricity-saving：节电的，节能的

　　*e.g.* Industrial tests show that electricity-saving result of these equipments is obvious.

　　　工业性试验表明，该装置具有明显的节电效果。

8. the following-up letter：随访信

　　(1) refers to the customer's enquiry;

　　(2) refers to the offer the firm has previously made;

　　(3) expresses regret or surprise that no order has been received and discreetly enquire into the reason;

　　(4) If possible, put forward new points and arguments favorable to the promotion of sales;

　　(5) ends with the repeated hope that the customer will take advantage of the offer.

9. irrigation pumps：灌溉泵，灌溉水

　　*e.g.* For more long-term support, they have also supplied seeds, irrigation pumps for farmers and counseling and support for children.

　　　至于较长线的工作，则包括向农民提供种子、灌溉用的泵，为儿童进行心理辅导和支援。

10. grain threshers：脱粒机

　　*e.g.* In this paper, the shape of the air exit of cross-fan grain thresher was studied.

　　　本文对横流风机式谷物脱粒机排风管道的形状进行了研究。

11. contemplate：冥思苦想，深思熟虑

　　*e.g.* He contemplated the problem before making a final decision.

　　　在做出最后的决定之前，他仔细考虑了这个问题。

　　I have never contemplated living abroad.

　　　我从未考虑过去国外居住。

12. furnish：supply（what is necessary for a special purpose）提供

　　*e.g.* This shop furnishes everything that is needed for camping.

　　　这家商店提供各种野营用品。

## 技能操练

**I. Choose the best answer from A, B, C and D.**

1. They have _____ a price which we think will be acceptable _____ you.

　　A. bid; for　　　　　B. bid; to　　　　　C. bidden; by　　　　　D. bid; with

2. A sample of our new beef extract has been sent to you today _____ parcel post, and we hope
it will reach you _____ perfect condition.

    A. with; in            B. in; by            C. on; with            D. by; in

3. It is possible that you couldn't find the new patterns _____ you are looking in this
catalogue.

    A. for what           B. which            C. for which            D. that

4. This offer is made _____ the clear understanding that if they are not completely _____
your liking, you can return them to us without any obligation and _____ our own expense.

    A. at; to; at            B. in; for; for            C. in; in; for            D. on; to; at

5. We deem it _____ your advantage _____ avail yourself _____ our offer for 2,000
tons linseeds.

    A. in; to; of            B. in; as; for            C. to; to; of            D. of; as; for

6. The purpose of a promotion letter is to _____ the prospective customer's interest.

    A. attract            B. arouse            C. attend            D. alter

7. A sales confirmation should be counter-signed by _____.

    A. the seller            B. both parties            C. the bank            D. the buyer

8. _____ the growing needs of the fast developing market at your end, we are considering
_____ a representative office in your city.

    A.To meet; set up                     B. To meet; establishing

    C. Thinking; setting                D. Thinking of; to establish

9. We specialize _____ all kinds of metals and are always ready to buy in large quantities.

    A. in            B. from            C. on            D. at

10. We can _____ honey for sugar.

    A. deliver            B. prefer            C. replace            D. substitute

**II. Translate the following phrases into English or vice versa.**

1. 促销 _____
2. 畅销，销路好 _____
3. 做出选择 _____
4. 现行价格 _____
5. 达到标准 _____
6. 精湛的工艺 _____
7. 振兴信 _____
8. 合理的价格 _____
9. 优惠的条件 _____
10. 储备存货 _____
11. fall within the scope of _____
12. look back through _____

13. affordable price _____

14. the following–up letter _____

15. medium and small–sized enterprises _____

16. extend the scope of business _____

17. trial order _____

18. meet with warm reception _____

19. discount _____

20. trademark _____

## III. Translate the following sentences from English into Chinese or vice versa.

1. Kindly do your best to promote the new product in your area.

_____

2. As requested, we are sending you the samples under separate cover.

_____

3. As the type required is out of supply, we will replace it by the following type.

_____

4. You may be interested to see from the enclosed price-list that all the types available, we allow you a discount of 15% on the current prices stated.

_____

5. We are writing to inform you that we have been appointed agents for the famous Panda color TV. We can supply the newest models of fine quality from stock, and also provide spare components and excellent after-sales service.

_____

6. This is an exceptional opportunity for you to buy a stock of high-quality products at prices we cannot repeat. We hope you will take full advantage of it.

_____

7. 我们可以向贵方提供最新型的诱人、耐用且价格合理的玩具。玩具种类很多，适合不同年龄的儿童。我们相信这些玩具将受到儿童的喜爱，并对他们的智力开发大有益处。

_____

8. 我们能够供应几种不同的绿茶。

_____

9. 我们建议你方早日接受，因为我们已经没有多少库存。

_____

10. 由于你方以前大量订购，特给予优先机会，但望贵方尽快答复，如无兴趣，我方可撤盘。

_____

11. 第 101 货号商品的质量要比第 102 货号商品的质量好。

_____

12. 由于此产品需求甚殷，供应有限，我们建议你方尽快接受此报盘。

**IV. Fill in the blanks with the following words.**

perform(s), retail, feature(s), lowest, allow(s), manufacture (s), market, equipped

1. Let me describe our new product and then show you how it is better than those of any other _____.

2. Our Super ADF with its excellent memory capacity and procession ability, _____ better than other word–processor on the _____ today.

3. The Super ADF comes _____ with a highly efficient electronic printer that can print 500 words per second. Furthermore, Super ADF _____ for the use of up to six different languages.

4. With its _____ price of USD, Super ADF offers the _____ price ever in the word-processor market.

5. Thus, I hope no doubt that our new word-processor—Super ADF has all the _____ that are required of a successful product.

**V. Compose a dialogue in the following situation.**

Mr. James is a representative of a British company, and Mr. Liu is a staff member of China National Foodstuffs Import & Export Corporation. They hold a discussion on the seafood.

**VI. Write a letter with the idea below.**

Write a letter to MRT company, enclosing the proforma invoice they require for 200 KWH Meters, Model HH 23 with a sample to be dispatched separately for their reference. Ask them to compare our price with that of other manufacturers.

## Read More

### Sales Promotion

Sales promotion consists of those promotional activities other than advertising, personal selling, and publicity. As such, any promotional activities that do not fall under the other three activities of the promotion mix are considered sales promotion. The trade often uses the term indiscriminately. Businesspersons may use the term "promotion" when they actually mean "sales promotion". For purpose here, promotion is a broad term that encompasses sales promotion as well as the other three promotional activities.

The techniques of sales promotion are varied and numerous. The common ones used are coupons, sweepstakes, games, contests, price-offs, demonstrations, premiums, samples, and money refund offers. A combination of these can be used and sometimes is used in the same campaign.

Sales promotion is temporary in nature. Not being self-sustaining, its function is to supplement advertising, personal selling, and publicity. To launch Budweiser beer in Great Britain, Anheuser-Busch employed the "American" theme. Its TV commercials on July 4 and Thanksgiving day were spots filmed in California with American actors. To supplement its advertising effort, the company used a variety of sales-promotion techniques. It made posters, bunting, flags, pennants, T-shirts, and sweatshirts available to pubs and discos for promotional parties. Bud ashtrays, bar towels, coasters, football pennants, and similar items were offered for sale. Moreover, American disc jockeys were brought in to program American music nights.

# 实训项目 6

# Orders and Acknowledgements
# 订单和回执

## 学习目标

知识目标：了解订单中所涉及的交易条件，掌握规格、数量、价格、支付条件和交货期的内容及表达方式；了解合同、确认书、协议和备忘录的书面形式。

能力目标：能够书写订单及起草对外贸易合同，把握语言准确性和清晰度。

## 工作任务

### 工作任务 1

加拿大 Vancouver Textiles Corp. 欲首次订购 China National Textile Imp. & Exp. Corp. 的产品，即衬衫和毛衣。因此写信决定订购，并随信附上订单。现在你以加方的身份写一封首次订购函。订单如下：

| 商品 | 商品号 | 颜色 | 价格（美元） | 数量 | 小计 |
|------|--------|------|--------------|------|------|
| 衬衫 | 325 | 红 | 10.00 | 100 | 1,000.00 |
| | | 蓝 | 10.00 | 100 | 1,000.00 |
| | | 黄 | 10.00 | 100 | 1,000.00 |
| | | 白 | 10.00 | 200 | 2,000.00 |
| 毛衣 | 456 | 蓝 | 15.00 | 100 | 1,500.00 |
| | 543 | 绿 | 20.00 | 200 | 4,000.00 |
| | | 总计 | | 800 | 10,500.00 |

要求：

1. 感谢贵方的来函及目录。

2. 货物交付地点为加利福尼亚约克镇前进路 634 号的仓库。

3. 预期收到信用证后的 1 个月内交付货物，因此表明在收到确认后即准备信用证。

4. 表明如果初次交易成功的话，将来会有更大的订单。

5. 希望将来有一个长期和成功的合作。

6. Vancouver Textiles Corp. 地址：245 Madison Street, Vancouver, Canada。

_____

_____

_____

_____

_____

_____

_____

_____

## 工作任务 2

加拿大 Victorian Trade Co.在收到浙江嘉兴晓栋进出口公司的报价和样品后，决定订购一批山地自行车，并随附订单。

Victorian Trade Co.

6103 Dahousie Street Toronto

B4H53A, Canada

August 12, 2013

Xiaodong Imp. & Exp. Co.

Jiaxing, Zhejiang, China

Dear Sir or Madam,

Thank you for your letter of August 5 sending us your quotation and samples. We find both quality and prices satisfactory. Enclosed herewith please find our Order No. 363A.

As we are in urgent need of these goods, we hope you will make delivery at an early date.

Please send us your Sales Confirmation in duplicate as soon as possible. Thank you for your prompt attention.

Yours faithfully,

Encl. As stated

W. James   (Manager)

订单：

Victorian Trade Co.

6103 Dahousie Street Toronto

B4H53A, Canada

Order Form

No. 363A

Aug. 8, 2013

Xiaodong Imp. & Exp. Co.

Jiaxing, Zhejiang, China

| Quantity | Description of Goods | Unit Price (CIF Toronto) | Price |
|---|---|---|---|
| 10 | Racing Bike Standard yellow | $1,500 | $15,000 |
| 10 | Racing Bike Standard green | $1,500 | $15,000 |
| 100 | Mountain Bike blue/white | $1,000 | $100,000 |
| 100 | Mountain Bike pink/white | $1000 | $100,000 |

Total: $230,000

2% discount: $4,600

Grand Total:$225,400

Packing: in wooden cases

Shipment: from Jiaxing no later than October 15

Payment: by confirmed irrevocable L/C payable by sight draft

Authorized by: Xiaodong Gu (manager)

Tel: 416-288-0506    Fax: 416-061-0321

E-mail: Victorian@trading.com.ca

你认为如何处理较为妥当？根据订购单写一份回函。

_____

_____

_____

_____

_____

## 操作示范

### 操作示范 1

Vancouver Textile Corp.

245 Madison Street

Vancouver, Canada

May 19, 2013

China National Textiles Import & Export Corporation

Shanghai Branch,

Shanghai, China

Re: Order No. 52765

Dear Sirs,

　　Thank you so much for your letter of May 10, 2013 and the catalogues. Pursuant to our e-mail since that date, we have decided to place an initial order as follows:

| Item | Item No. | Color | Price（USD） | Quantity | Subtotal |
|------|----------|-------|-------------|----------|----------|
| Blouse | 325 | Red | 10.00 | 100 | 1,000.00 |
| | | Blue | 10.00 | 100 | 1,000.00 |
| | | Yellow | 10.00 | 100 | 1,000.00 |
| | | White | 10.00 | 200 | 2,000.00 |
| Sweater | 456 | Blue | 15.00 | 100 | 1,500.00 |
| | 543 | Green | 20.00 | 200 | 4,000.00 |
| | | Total | | 800 | 10,500.00 |

　　If this order is executed successfully, we will be placing larger orders in the future.

　　Please deliver the goods to our warehouse at 643 Front Drive, Newtown, CA 99989. We understand you will be shipping from stock and should expect delivery within one month after you receive our letter of credit. The letter of credit will be prepared as soon as we get your confirmation.

　　We look forward to a long and successful cooperation.

Yours sincerely,

Vancouver Textiles Corp.

John

Purchasing Manager

## 操作示范 2

Xiaodong Imp. & Exp. Co.

Jiaxing, Zhejiang, China

August 18, 2013

Victorian

Victorian Trade Co.

6103 Dahousie Street Toronto

B4H53A, Canada

Dear Mr. James,

Re: Your Order No. 363 and Our S/C No. 1475

We are pleased to inform you that we have looked your Order No. 363A for our bikes. As requested, we enclosed herewith our Sales Confirmation No. 1475 in duplicate. Please sign and return one to us for our file.

It is understood that an L/C in our favor covering the captioned goods will be established on or about Aug. 31. You may rest assured that we shall effect shipment with the least possible delay upon receipt of your credit.

We appreciate your cooperation and look forward to receiving your further orders.

Yours faithfully,

Encl. As stated

Xiao Dong (General Manager)

### 知识链接

1. 什么是订单?

Simply speaking, an order may result from an offer or an enquiry with subsequent quotations. After receiving an offer the buyer may write an order.

2. 订单的主要特点是什么?

The main characteristics of an order are: correctness and clarity.

3. 订单或订购信应包含哪些内容呢?

Name of commodity and specifications，quantity, price, packing, date and method of shipping, terms of payment.

## 一问一答

### ▌ Asks

1. What should be mentioned in a letter of confirmation?
2. Should a first order be acknowledged by letter or not? Why?
3. In a reply to a first order, what should we pay attention to?
4. How do the seller deal with rejecting orders?
5. If faulty goods are delivered, how do the buyer respond?

### ▌ Answers

1. Details of description, quantities, prices, article numbers, mode of packing, port of destination, time of shipment, and terms of payment as agreed upon.
2. First order should be acknowledged by letter, because it is the first order from a new customer. Besides, for the sake of courtesy and in order to consolidate business relations for future dealings, it is advisable to acknowledge the "first order" by letter.
3. In a reply to a first order, it is advisable for the seller to draw the buyer's attention to some other products so that business can be enlarged to the benefits of both parties.
4. Letters rejecting orders should be written carefully, because such letters always offend the buyers. Who fail to secure their supplies will lose the chance of making profits.
5. If faulty goods are delivered, the buyers can demand either a reduction in price, or replacement of the goods, or cancellation of the order. He may also be able to file a claim for the losses he sustained.

## 难点解析

1. pursuant to：according to a particular law, rule, contract, etc. 依照，遵循
   *e.g.* The doctrine of privity of contract provides that only the parties to a contract receive rights and obligations pursuant to the contract.
   合同当事人的相互关系原则规定只有合同双方的当事人才有权依照合同享有权利、承担义务。
   The ships in fault shall be liable for the damage to the ship, the goods and other property on board pursuant to the proportions prescribed in the preceding paragraph.
   互有过失的船舶，对碰撞造成的船舶以及船上货物和其他财产的损失，依照前款规定的比例负赔偿责任。
2. initial：first 开始的，最初的
   *e.g.* After the initial cheers, the noise of the crowd began to die away as the band started playing.

开始的欢呼声结束以后，乐队开始演奏，人们的喧闹声也随之逐渐消失。

We are through the initial testing period.

我们通过了最初的考试阶段。

3. execute：执行，实行，处决，完成

  *e.g.* We can execute big volume orders in 20 days.

  我们可以在 20 天内完成大批量的订单。

4. warehouse：a large building for storing large quantities of goods 仓库

  *e.g.* Bales of cotton were piled up in the warehouse.

  大捆大捆的棉花堆积在仓库里。

5. ship from stock：to supply goods available from stock 发现货

6. herewith：在此，因此

  *e.g.* Thank you for your samples of striped coatings received today. Please make shipment in accordance with our Order No. 2602 enclosed herewith.

  很感谢今天收到你们寄来的带条纹外衣料样品。请按照信内附寄的第 2602 号订单发货。

7. in duplicate：一式两份的

  *e.g.* Credit available with any bank by negotiation, against presentation of beneficiary's draft(s) at sight, drawn on us in duplicate.

  本信用证可由任何一家银行议付，议付时需提供由受益人向开证行开出的即期汇票一式两份。

8. in our favor：我方受益

  *e.g.* With so much working in our favor, we can see what is holding us back.

  有这么多有利因素，我们可以看到是什么在阻止我们。

9. upon receipt of：一收到

  *e.g.* Upon receipt of a copy of the arbitration application, the respondent shall, within the time limit prescribed by the Arbitration Rules, submit its defense to the arbitration commission.

  被申请人收到仲裁申请书副本后，应当在仲裁规则规定的期限内向仲裁委员会提交答辩书。

**拓展提高**

### Placing an Order

Dear Mr. Chou,

  From the samples you sent us in March, we have made selections and are pleased to give you the following order on usual terms for shipment to Manchester.

  Order No. BA3233

| Items No. | Quantity | Color | Unit price (USD) |
|-----------|----------|-------|------------------|
| S-4 | 150 | blue | 8.50 |
|  | 150 | red | 8.50 |
| S-5 | 250 | blue | 6.50 |
|  | 250 | red | 6.50 |
| S-6 | 150 | blue | 22.50 |
|  | 150 | red | 22.50 |
|  | 150 | green | 22.50 |
| S-7 | 150 | blue | 15.50 |
|  | 150 | red | 15.50 |
|  | 150 | green | 15.50 |

For your information, we have applied for the import license and the letter of credit for this order. Since we need the goods urgently, you are requested to effect shipment a month after receipt of our L/C. There is a good market for the said items and, if this initial order is satisfactorily executed, we are prepared to place repeat orders with you in the near future.

We are waiting for your confirmation and prompt delivery.

Yours sincerely,

Ellen Bishop

Sales Manager

### Acknowledgement of an Initial Order

Dear Ms. Bishop,

We thank you for your order No. BA3233 of April 25, and welcome you as our new clients.

We confirm supply of the goods at the prices stated in your letter, and have arranged for dispatch by the end of this month. We are quite sure that you will be completely satisfied with the goods and find them of exceptional value for money.

As you may not be aware of the wide range of goods we have available, we are enclosed a copy of our latest catalogue. We hope that our handling of your first order will lead to further business between us and mark the beginning of a good working relationship.

Yours faithfully,

Chou Hua

Sales Manager

## Notes

1. selection：选择，挑选

   *e.g.* As for the selection of business media, would you like to share some thoughts with us?

   对于商业媒体的选择方面，您能和我们分享一下您的想法吗？

2. on usual terms：按照普通条款

   *e.g.* Please bill us for the following on our usual terms.

   请按照我方通常的条件开出下列货物的帐单。

   I'm afraid we must insist on our usual payment terms.

   恐怕我们必须坚持我们一直采用的付款方式。

3. import license：进口许可证

   *e.g.* When can you arrange for a credit under the new import license?

   按照新的进口许可证规定，你方什么时候能开出一张信用证？

   It is important that you time the shipment to arrive here prior to the expiration of the import license.

   你们须安排此货物在进口许可证期满之前到达，这是非常重要的。

4. effect shipment：make/arrange shipment 装船、装运

   *e.g.* Could you possibly effect shipment more promptly?

   你们能否再提前一点交货呢？

5. said：mentioned before(above) 所说的，所提及的，以避免重复前面出现的事物或名称

6. execute：执行，履行，实施

   *e.g.* We execute that instruction, and we move to the next one.

   我们执行那个指令，我们继续下一轮。

7. acknowledgement：承认，确认，感谢

   *e.g.* I received a gracious letter of acknowledgement.

   我收到一封有礼貌的感谢信。

   This would allow you to receive an acknowledgement or receipt of delivery even if response message is empty.

   这样即使响应消息为空，也将使您能够收到一个消息的确认或者收到信息。

8. exceptional：异常的, 例外的；exceptional performance 非同一般的表现；exceptional hardship 严重困难；exceptional circumstances 特殊情况

   *e.g.* We all believe we live in an exceptional time, perhaps even a critical moment in the history of the species.

   我们都相信我们生活在一个特殊的时期，甚至也许是人类有史以来最为关键的时刻。

9. aware：知道的 (be aware of sth.; be aware that…)

   *e.g.* Yon can only humbug those who are not aware of your tricks.

   你只能欺骗还不清楚你的伎俩的那些人。

I need not press the urgency of the matter on you, as I know you are fully aware of it yourselves.

我无需向你们强调此事的急迫性，因为我知道，你们自己对此完全了解。

10. mark the beginning of a good working relationship：标志着我们之间良好的工作关系的开端

### Repeat Order

Dear Mr. Chou,

We have received the captioned shipment ex S.S. "East Wind" and are very glad to inform you that we find the goods quite satisfactory. As we believe we can sell additional quantities in this market, we wish to place with you a repeat order for 2,000 dozens of the same style and sizes. If possible, please arrange early shipment of this repeat order, as we are badly in need of the goods.

Please acknowledge this order immediately on receipt and inform definite delivery date. This order is of no avail if it is not signed by a responsible person of our firm.

Yours faithfully,

John Smith

Sales Manager

### Acknowledgement of an Order

Dear Mr. Esses,

Thank you for your order No. 223 and assure you that all the items you required are in stock.

We confirm with you the following order for the pillowcases at the prices stated in your letter of December 3.

| Quantity | Pattern No. | Catalogue No. | Prices |
|---|---|---|---|
| 50,000 pillowcases | 18 | 45 | $10.60 each |
| 15,000 pillowcases | 21 | 65 | $11.70 each |

**(All the prices are FOB Ningbo)**

We are expected to arrange the establishment of the relative Confirmed Irrevocable Letter of Credit through the bankers and shall inform us by fax as soon as it is opened.

We thank you again for the above order and hope that this will lead to an enduring cooperation between us.

Yours faithfully,

Chou Hua

Sales Manager

## Notes

1. captioned shipment：标题所指船货

2. a repeat order：重复订货

   *e.g.* We are very glad to be able to place with you a repeat order for TV sets.
   我们很高兴能跟你方重复订电视机。

   If the first shipment is satisfactory, we can place with you many repeats (repeat orders).
   如果第一次送货很满意，我们可以跟你方多次重复订货。

3. avail：益处；效用

   *e.g.* He tried and tried but all his efforts were of no avail.
   他试了又试，但一切努力都不起作用。

4. be expected to：预计，预期

   *e.g.* He is expected to get through to the finals.
   我们期待他进入决赛。

   He is expected to win the game with ease.
   预计他在比赛中会轻易获胜。

5. lead to：引起，把……带到

   *e.g.* The Government's present course will only lead to disaster.
   政府的现行方针后患无穷。

   Too much work and too little rest often lead to illness.
   过量的工作和过少的休息会引起疾病。

6. enduring：持久的

   *e.g.* People all want an enduring peace.
   人们都想要有持久的和平。

   And the benefits are enduring, rather than one-off.
   而且这种利润是持久的，而不是一次性的。

### 技能操练

**I. Choose the best answer from A, B, C and D.**

1. We confirm exchange of letters _____ the subject article.

   A. to regard          B. regarded          C. regarding          D. regard

2. We thank you for your quotation of April 24 and now _____ an order with you for the following items.

   A. place          B. to place          C. making          D. make

3. We would ask you to do everything possible _____ punctual shipment.

   A. ensuring          B. to be ensured          C. to ensure          D. while ensuring

4. We hope you give your usual best attention _____ this order.

　　A. for carrying out　　B. to the execution of　C. by filling out　　　D. in the performance of

5. We must have the goods not later than September 30 _____ our stock is running short.

　　A. when　　　　　　B. that　　　　　　　C. which　　　　　　D. as

6. We have accepted your order No. 333. Please open the relevant L/C _____ here two weeks

　　prior to the date of shipment.

　　A. which must reach　　B. when must reach　　C. it reaches　　　　D. that reaches

7. We have decided to place a trial order for the following goods _____ the terms stated in

　　your letter.

　　A. with　　　　　　B. on　　　　　　　　C. by　　　　　　　　D. at

8. As soon as we are _____ a position to accept new orders, we will contact you immediately.

　　A. at　　　　　　　B. on　　　　　　　　C. in　　　　　　　　D. under

9. The quality of the goods does not _____ us.

　　A. interest　　　　　B. interesting　　　　C. interested　　　　D. to interest

10. We hope the goods will give you every _____.

　　A. satisfying　　　　B. satisfactory　　　　C. satisfaction　　　　D. satisfied

## II. Translate the following phrases into English or vice versa.

1. 标题货物 _____

2. 合同订单 _____

3. 一式两份 _____

4. 以便我方保存 _____

5. 试订购 _____

6. 所附订单 _____

7. 小额订单 _____

8. 现货供应 _____

9. 缺货 _____

10. 使贵方满意 _____

11. with reference to your letter _____

12. for prompt supply _____

13. at the prices named _____

14. confirm acceptance of it _____

15. as shown in the enclosed Sales Contract _____

16. sign and return for our file _____

17. in stock _____

18. decline your order_____

19. inability to entertain any fresh orders

_____

20. ensure the fulfillment of the order

_____

**III. Translate the following sentences from English into Chinese or vice versa.**

1. We have accepted your order for 20000 yards of article No. 244.

_____

2. Please send us color assortment immediately and open the covering L/C according to the terms contracted.

_____

3. are delighted to We are pleased to find that your materials appear to be of fine quality.

_____

4. We send you a small order for 2,000 dozen rubble shoes.

_____

5. If this order is acceptable, please let us know by fax.

_____

6. We have received your catalogue and price list, and now we order the following goods at the prices named.

_____

7. 我方随附试订单，如贵方产品质量达到我方期望，我方不久将有大量订货。

_____

8. 产品材料必须为防水材料，我方订单以此为准。

_____

9. 我方非常重视贵方订单，我方将在有限时间尽快发货。

_____

10. 如你方对商品质量不满意，15 天之内我们愿意接受退货。

_____

11. 随信附寄销售确认书一式两份，请查收。

_____

12. 你订购的货物可随时交付。

_____

**IV. Fill in the blanks with the proper words.**

1. We have the _____ of sending you an order for 1,000 dozen umbrella.

2. We shall place a large order with you provided the quantity of the goods and shipping period meet our _____.

3. Please cable your acceptance, _____ _____ _____ which we shall open an L/C in your favor.

4. Thanks for your letter of December 23 with catalogue and price _____.

5. Please inform us whether you still have products in _____.

6. Both the quality and price are _____, and we are please to confirm the letters and E-mails exchanged between us and to enclose Order No. 344.

7. We have instructed our bank to _____ an L/C for the amount of this order.

8. We confirm _____ of the goods at the prices stated in your letter, and have arranged for _____ by the end of next month.

9. We hope that our handling of your first order will _____ _____ further business between us.

10. If the first order is satisfactory executed, we are prepared to place _____ orders in the near future.

**V. Compose a dialogue in the following situation.**

Mr. Hall, a manager of German Import and Export Company, is now discussing with Mr. Liu, the boss of Wenzhou Lelian Clothing Company, about the trial order for T-shirt.

**VI. Write a letter according to the following situation.**

Write a letter to The Western Trading Co. ordering 15,000 pairs of household slippers for delivery during the next month at the price and on the terms quoted by the manufacture.

# Read More

Market Analysis in Practice

The goal of a market analysis is to determine the attractiveness of a market and to understand its evolving opportunities and threats as they relate to the strengths and weaknesses of the firm. Let's have a look at the following dimensions of a market analysis:

◆　Market Size (current and future)

◆　Market Trends

◆　Key Success Factors

Market Size

The market size of the market can be evaluated based on present sales and on potential sales if the use of the product is expanded.

Market Trends

Changes in the market are important because they often are sources of new opportunities and threats. The relevant trends are industry-dependent, but some examples include changes in price sensitivity, demand for variety, and level of emphasis on service and support. Regional trends also may be relevant.

Key Success Factors

The key success factors are those elements that are necessary in order for the firm to achieve its marketing objectives. A few examples of such factors include:

◆ Access to essential unique resources

◆ Ability to achieve economies of scale

◆ Access to distribution channels

◆ Technological progress

It is important to consider that key success factors may change over time, especially as the product progresses through its life cycle.

# 实训项目 7

## Packing and Transportation
## 包装和运输

**学习目标**

知识目标：了解国际货物运输的方式、装船指示和装船通知、装运单证以及国际贸易中货物的包装、唛头等。

能力目标：能够熟练使用有关国际货物运输和包装方面的术语、缩略语和基本英语表达方式。

**工作任务**

### 工作任务 1

你方接到客户的电话，客户对刚刚预定的玩具提出了一些包装要求。包装如下：产品内包用透明包装，以便消费者能直接看到产品；为了节省成本，外包建议使用纸箱；在外包上注明"小心轻放"。你如果是直接负责这批货物的业务员，你觉得纸箱很容易受损受潮，因此你建议客户使用木箱子。请你给客户写一封包装确认函，说明你对产品的包装意见。要点如下：

1. 同意使用开窗盒子包装，可以提高产品销售率；
2. 建议使用木箱子作为外包装，更加坚固。
3. 同意在外包上印上"小心轻放"。

China National Import & Export Co.

13 Fudong Road

Wenzhou

China

March 23, 2012

Japan International Trade Co., Ltd.

Tokyo

Japan

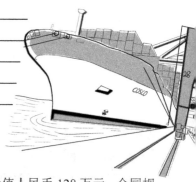

## 工作任务 2

2013 年我国某对外贸易出口公司出口到加拿大一批货物，价值人民币 128 万元。合同规定用塑料袋包装，每件要使用英、法两种文字的唛头。但我方公司实际交货时改用其他包装代替，并仍使用只有英文的唛头，国外商人为了适应当地市场的销售要求，不得不雇人重新更换包装和唛头，后来该公司的负责人十分气愤，给我方业务员写信，商讨处理此事的方法。作为此笔交易的主要负责人，你应该如何面对？

### 操作示范

### 操作示范 1

China National Import & Export Co.

13 Fudong Road

Wenzhou

China

March 23, 2013

Japan International Trade Co., Ltd.

Tokyo

Japan

Dear Sirs,

Re: Our order No. 335

Further to our telephone conversation on 23th regarding the packing of the above order for Disney toys, we would like to propose the following:

We would like to have the products packed in window packing for inner packing so that the products can be seen directly. I believe it will help to promote the sales.

I prefer wooden cases to cartons for outer packing. I fear that cartons are not strong enough for ocean transportation. They might be easily damaged through rough handling. They are more susceptible to damage by moisture.

Handle with care, the port of destination and our order No. will be stenciled on the outer packing.

Please let me know if you have any other requests.

Yours sincerely,

×××

# 操作示范 2

许多国家对于在市场上销售的商品规定了有关包装和标签的管理条例，近年来这方面的要求愈来愈严。有的内容规定十分繁杂，不仅容量或净重要标明公制或英制，还要注明配方、来源国、使用说明、保证期限等，甚至罐型、瓶型也有统一标准。进口商品必须符合这些规定，否则不准进口或禁止在市场上出售。这些管理条例一方面用来作为限制外国产品进口的手段，另一方面也是方便消费者的需要。从本案例来看卖方未严格按照合同规定的包装条件履行交货义务，应视为违反合同。根据《联合国国际货物销售合同公约》第 35 条规定："卖方交付的货物必须与合同规定的数量、质量和规格相符，并须按照合同所规定的方式装箱或包装。"我出口公司的错误有二，一是擅自更换包装材料，虽然对货物本身的质量未造成影响；二是未按合同规定使用唛头，由于加拿大部分地区原是法国殖民地，为此，销售产品除英文外常要求加注法文。加拿大当局对有些商品已在其制定的法令中加以规定。本例中买卖双方已订明用英、法两种文字唛头，更应照办。总之为了顺利出口，必须了解和适应不同国家规定的特殊要求，否则会造成索赔，退货等经济损失，并带来其他不良的影响。

## 知识链接

1. 为什么包装在国际贸易中更为重要？

To some extent, packing is a kind of art. On the one hand, packages should reach importers in perfect shape, even if they meet with nasty storm or other kinds of bad weather during the roughest journey. No exporter would expect to find their goods damaged or partly missing on arrival. On the other hand, commodities should be kept in good condition for the protection of their quality and quantity. Besides, packing is considered as a means of promotion to attract more customers so that advantages could be obtained in such a highly competitive market.

2. 装箱单的作用是什么？

Specifically speaking, it indicates the name, net weight, gross weight, the length and width of every piece of goods so as to let the consignee declare, identify and check at the customs more easily after receiving the goods.

3. 为什么海洋运输是国际贸易中通用的运输方式？

Because it is cheaper to deliver large quantities of goods over long distances.

 一问一答

## Asks

1. What do you mean by packing mark? And what are the categories of it?

2. How do you understand shipping instruction and shipping advice?

3. Is bill of lading an essential document in our trade and why?

## Answers

1. Packing mark is also called transport package shipping mark, which is composed of a few simple geometric figures, letters, numbers or words. It is generally divided into two categories: (1) shipping mark, (2) indicative mark and warning mark.

2. Shipping Instruction is a kind of document given by the buyer to the seller before the shipment for the requirement and instruction of the goods about its mode of packing, the stencil of shipping mark, mode of transportation and so on. Shipping Advice is a kind of notification given by the seller to the buyer after the shipment which contains the time of shipment, the ports of loading and destination, means of conveyance, partial shipment, transshipment, name of ship, dates of effecting shipment and arrival, number of sales contract, quantity of shipment, etc.

3. Yes. It is a receipt of the goods given to the shipper by the shipping company, an evidence of ownership of the goods and a contract for the performance of certain services upon certain conditions.

### 难点解析

1. packing：包装，打包

   *e.g.* Do you have specific request for packing?

   你们对包装有什么特别要求吗？

   The speed of the machine may be regulated to pace the packing operation.

   机器的速度可调节得同包装的速度相一致。

   compression packing 压缩包装; hanging packing 挂式包装; neutral packing 中性包装; window packing 透明包装

2. inner packing：selling packing, small packing 内包装，小包装

   *e.g.* The inner packing with a little bit of flower design is best on our market.

   内包装上带一点花卉图案，这样最适合我们的市场需要。

For this kind of inner packing product, its positive-negative error of the weight should be controlled within the regulated limits.

这种内包装产品的重量、正负误差应控制在规范标准之内。

3. promote：促销，促进

*e.g.* The meeting discussed how to promote this latest product.

这次会议讨论了如何开展这种新产品的推销工作。

The meeting discussed how to promote cooperation between the two countries.

会议讨论了如何促进两国的合作。

So what should we do to promote peace, in addition to the proposals mentioned above?

那么，除了上述提到的方案外，我们应该采取什么行动来促进和平呢？

4. wooden case：木箱，木盆

*e.g.* Our strip scissors are packed in boxes of one dozen each, 200 boxes to a wooden case.

我们的旅行剪刀是用木箱包装的，每个木箱装 200 盒，每盒一打。

The wooden case should be not only seaworthy but also strong enough to protect the goods from any damage.

木箱不仅要适合于海运，还要十分坚固，足以保护货物不受任何损失。

5. cartons：纸板箱

*e.g.* We pack the products in cartons.

我们把货物打包在纸箱里。

The cartons lined with plastic sheets are waterproof.

有塑料纸做衬里的纸盒是防水的。

We plan to use cardboard or plastic cartons for the outer packing.

我们打算利用纸板箱或塑料箱作为外包装。

6. outer packing：外包装

*e.g.* On the outer packing, please mark wording, "Handle with Care".

在外包装上请标明"小心轻放"字样。

As to the outer packing, we plan to use corrugated cardboard boxes.

至于外包装，我们计划用皱波纹纸板箱。

7. rough handling：粗暴搬运

*e.g.* I am sorry to say it's not on the way, but during loading. The tins inside the cases were broken evidently through rough handling.

很遗憾，我想这不是在途中损坏的，而是在搬运过程中损坏的，箱子里的罐子很明显是因粗野的搬运打碎的。

8. susceptible：易受影响的，易感染的

*e.g.* We are all susceptible to advertising.

9. moisture：湿度，潮湿

*e.g.* Moisture in the atmosphere condensed into dew during the night.

大气中的水分在夜间凝结成露珠。

10. be stenciled：被刻印

*e.g.* Port of destination, package number, gross and net weights, measurement and shipping mark shall be stenciled conspicuously on each package.

每件货物上应刷明到货口岸、件号、毛重及净重、尺码及唛头。

## 拓展提高

### Packing Requirement

Dear Sirs,

Thank you for your letter of Mar. 15 informing us that the subject goods could be shipped.

With regard to the packing for the above order, the goods should be packed in wooden boxes of 10 kilos net, each wooden box containing 2 cardboard cartons of 5,000 grams net. All cases are to be marked as usual. Kindly stencil our shipping marks in letter 4 inches high, and give gross and net weight on each case.

We hope that the result of packing turns out to be satisfactory for our customers. If so, you may continue using this packing in the future. As soon as the goods reach us, we shall let you know.

Yours truly,

×××

### Stating Packing Requirement

Dear Sirs,

We have received your consignment of 30 cases of machine parts you shipped to Sydney on March 23.

We regret to inform you that five were seriously damaged. In consideration of the long and friendly relationship between us, we refrain from lodging a claim this time. But we feel it necessary to stress the importance of trustworthy packing for your future deliveries to us.

As machine parts are susceptible to shock, they must be wrapped in soft-materials and firmly packed in seaworthy cases.

Please let us know whether these specifications can be met by you and whether they will lead to an increase in your prices.

We look forward to your early confirmation.

Yours faithfully,

×××

# Notes

1. the subject goods：标题项下的物品

   *e.g.* Please open an L/C covering the subject goods as soon as possible.

   请尽快开立标题项下商品的信用证。

   We intend to place an order with you for 20 metric tons of the subject goods.

   我们想向你方订购 20 公吨标题项下的货物。

2. cardboard：硬纸板

   *e.g.* Paper folds more easily than cardboard.

   纸较纸板易于折叠。

3. shipping marks：唛头

   *e.g.* Do you have any objection to the stipulations about the packing and shipping marks?

   有关包装运输唛头的条款你们有什么异议吗？

4. turn out to be：结果是，原来是

   *e.g.* However, even if the study turns out to be accurate, those without the relevant genes need

   not despair.

   然而，即便这项研究是准确的，没有相关基因特征的人们也不需要感到绝望。

5. consignment：委托，运送

   consignment invoice 寄售发票；consignment note 发货通知书；consignment order 寄售单

   *e.g.* Products of more than 100 designers, from clothes, accessories to furniture, will be sold on

   consignment in the 540-square-meter store.

   这家 540 平米的商店将以寄售的方式销售 100 多位设计师的作品，包括服装、配饰及

   家具等。

6. In consideration of：考虑到，鉴于

   *e.g.* In consideration of your extensive experience in the field，we are glad to appoint you as our

   agent.

   考虑到你们在这一业务范围的丰富经验，我们很高兴指定你们为我们的代理。

7. refrain from：克制，抑制

   *e.g.* If you can refrain from calling attention to your fears and anxieties, nobody will know about

   them.

   如果你能克制住不去注意恐惧和焦虑，那么将无人会察觉到它们。

8. lodge a claim：提出索赔

   *e.g.* We are now lodging a claim against you for the short weight of fertilizer.

   我方现向贵方索赔，赔偿我方的化肥短缺。

   This consignment is not up to the standard stipulated in the contract. We are now lodging a

   claim with you.

   这批货的质量低于合同规定的标准，现向你方提出索赔。

9. trustworthy：可靠的，可信任的

*e.g.* trustworthy products 信得过的产品

In other circumstances, you might not consider me a trustworthy source of information about myself.

在其他情况下，您可能不会认为我是有关我本人信息的可信源。

10. seaworthy：适用于航海的

*e.g.* Although early submarines were less-than-seaworthy, their progression through present times has been remarkable.

虽然早期的潜艇并不适于航海，但它们直到现在取得了卓越的进步。

---

**Urging Shipment**

Dear Sirs,

Re: Contract No. WR 234

Referring to our Order No. 234 for 220,000 yards printed shirting, we wish to call your attention to the fact that the shipment is approaching, but nothing has been received from you about the shipment under the captioned contract.

As we mentioned in our last letter, we are in urgent need of the goods and we may be compelled to seek an alternative source of supply.

Under the circumstances, it is not possible for us to extend further our L/C No. 356, which expires on March 23.

As your prompt attention to shipment is most desirable to all parties concerned, we hope you will let us have your shipping advice by fax without further delay.

Yours faithfully,

×××

---

**Proposing Partial Shipment**

Dear Sirs,

Thank you for your letter of March 23 regarding your order No. 234 for 220,000 gunny bags.

In your letter, you asked for earlier shipment of the whole order. I regret to say that we are unable to comply with your request.

When the sale was agreed, we expressly stated that shipment would be made in May.

If you wish to have earlier delivery, the best we can do is to make a partial shipment of 100,000 in April and ship the remaining in May. We hope this arrangement will meet with your approval.

We expect your prompt reply so that we can ask the manufacture to expedite delivery.

Yours faithfully,

×××

## Notes

1. be compelled to：迫不得已

 *e.g.* So he might be compelled to remain here for months, and in what a state!

  这样他也许就不得不在这里住上几个月，而且是处于如此狼狈的境况。

  Children could be compelled to work, thus effectively denying them schooling.

  孩子们可能被强迫工作，因此而严重剥夺他上学的权利。

2. alternative：两者择一的

 *e.g.* Is there a credible alternative to the nuclear deterrent?

  是否有可以取代核威慑力量的可靠办法？

  There was no alternative for them to vote in favor.

  他们别无选择，只有投票赞成。

3. expire：期满，终止

 *e.g.* However, most of these contracts expire this month.

  不过，这些合同大部分在本月到期。

4. comply with：照做，遵守

 *e.g.* If you do not comply with these rules, the transaction strategy will not work.

  如果不遵守这些法则的话，事务策略将不能正常工作。

  If we reinforce the traffic security education and more people comply with traffic regulations, I believe one day traffic accidents can be avoided.

  如果我们加强交通安全教育，更多的人遵守交通规则，我相信总有一天交通事故是可以避免的。

5. partial shipment：分批装运

 *e.g.* If I were in your position, I would allow partial shipment.

  如果我处在你的位置，就会同意分批装运。

  We propose partial shipment. We can ship whatever is ready to meet your urgent need instead of waiting for the whole lot to get ready.

  我们建议先发部分，我们可以先装运现已生产出来的货物以解你们的燃眉之急，而不是等到所有的货物都备齐才发货。

6. expedite：加快，促进

 *e.g.* This will reduce your correspondence with me and expedite your processing.

  这样将减少你我间的信件往来，加快您审理的速度。

  If the order of the rows is not important, however, you can consider sending requests in parallel, to expedite processing.

  然而，如果行顺序无关紧要的话，可以考虑以并行方式发送请求，从而加快处理速度。

**技能操练**

**I. Choose the best answer from A, B, C and D.**

1. The above clarifies our view _____ this matter.

    A. with           B. on           C. to           D. for

2. We hope this arrangement will be agreeable to you. Should this be so, please amend the covering credit to allow _____ partial shipments under advice to us.

    A. as           B. as read           C. to           D. to reading

3. We are satisfied the packing is suitable for a long sea _____.

    A. trip           B. voyage           C. assured           D. sure

4. Please be _____ that your comments on packing will be passed on to our manufacturers for their reference.

    A. sure           B. ensure           C. assured           D. confirmed

5. We are confident that our cartons for canned goods are not only _____ but also strong enough to protect the goods from any possible damage.

    A. seaworthy           B. seaworth           C. for sea           D. sea

6. We should _____ the 50 books to a carton.

    A. put           B. place           C. pack           D. install

7. Claims _____ transportation should be referred to the shipping company.

    A. concerned           B. concerning           C. concern           D. to concern

8. Almost two weeks have passed _____ we e-mailed you our offer on September 30.

    A. since           B. when           C. as           D. for

9. _____ that it is necessary to protect the goods from any conceivable losses, you should insure them against all possible risk.

    A. Consider           B. Considering           C. To consider           D. Considered

10. _____ instructions are stated accurately in the captioned contract.

    A. Packing           B. Package           C. Pack           D. To pack

**II. Translate the following phrases into English or vice versa.**

1. 包装条款 _____

2. 适用于海运 _____

3. 木箱 _____

4. 内衬坚固防水材料 _____

5. 转船 _____

6. 指定包装 _____

7. 唛头 _____

8. 发货通知书 _____

9. 舱位 _____

10. 野蛮装卸 _____

11. packing list _____

12. shipping port_____

13. seaworthy packing _____

14. inner packing _____

15. make delivery _____

16. direct sailing _____

17. in two installments _____

18. the parties concerned _____

19. outer packing _____

20. annual requirements _____

**III. Translate the following sentences from English into Chinese or vice versa.**

1. 货物用适用于海运的木箱包装。

_____

2. 所以包装将特别加固，我们希望这样能防止损坏。

_____

3. 请在外包装上刷上我公司的首字母和订单号。

_____

4. 这种产品深受客户喜欢的原因就是它是由一种防水材料做成的。

_____

5.一旦货物发运，请即告详情。

_____

6. 他们尚未告知我方他们是否可以安排货物在香港转船。

_____

7. Please fax us the marks and destination.

_____

8. We assure you that your orders will be fulfilled on schedule, neither behind nor ahead of schedule.

_____

9. Stocks there are not ample. On the contrary, they are running short.

_____

10. The shipment must arrive here before the expiration of the license.

_____

11. We advice that the goods under Contract No. 21 have been shipped per S/S Peace today.

_____

12. We have modified the sizes. Please inform your manufactures accordingly.

_____

## IV. Fill in the blanks with the proper words.

1. All of canned fruits and meat are to be _____ in cartons.

2. We will not be held responsible for any damage which results _____ rough handling.

3. Each case will be marked _____ details required by the Argentinean authorities.

4. We wish to draw your attention to the fact that the date _____ delivery is approaching.

5. We shall appreciate it if you will inform us _____ the condition of packing as soon as the consignment arrives at your end.

6. Please _____ the L/C as soon as possible to enable the goods to reach you in due course.

7. Please get the goods ready for _____ at an early date.

8. On examination, we _____ to find that certain points in your L/C are not in conformity with the contract.

9. We look forward to hearing _____ you.

10. They insisted _____ having the goods transshipped at Singapore.

## V. Compose a dialogue in the following situation.

Your customer wants you to pack toy mobile phones with wooden cases. You refuse and suggest cartons. You promise that those cartons will be lined with waterproof paper.

## VI. Write a letter with the ideas given below.

The buyer of BC Co. complained that the delayed shipment had caused their clients to refuse the ordered goods. You are writing for BC Co. to the buyer telling them that although you have tried your best to meet the shipment date, you could not finish the production and failed to make delivery on time. To be worse, the following long Spring Festival Holiday made it impossible for you to deliver the goods. But now, the goods are waiting for shipment in Keelung and you request the buyer not to decline the ordered goods.

## ▌ **Read More**

### Inner Packing and Outer Packing

With the development of the modern industry, packing is becoming a crucial aspect for manufacturers. It is proved that attractive packing promotes the goods' sales. Any kind of fast-selling merchandise has at least two characters, the first one is superior in quality and the other one is attractive in appearance.

Generally speaking, packing can be divided into inner packing and outer packing. Inner packing, also called selling packing or small packing, is beautifully designed to attract consumers. In supermarkets, the packing should be attention-getting. Outer packing known as shipping packing, is used for transportation and protecting the goods from damage. So outer packages should be easy to open and close, to store and reuse, to dispose of or recycle. In this way, cartons, wooden cases, gunny bags, drums and bales are widely adopted. Collective packages like containers and pallets are practical and suitable for long-distance transportation.

Some shipping companies or logistic express will check the outer packing of every piece of goods. Once an unsuitable packing is found, it will be repacked compactly, for example, sealed up, bundled and added extra case. Those with valuables of obvious mark (such as spare parts of GE, COMPAQ and MOTOROLA) are to be packed in neutral packing, against pilferage during delivery.

# 实训项目 8

## Terms of Payment
## 支付方式

### 学习目标

知识目标：了解国际贸易货款的各种结算方式；了解汇付在国际贸易中的应用；了解托付在国际贸易中的应用；了解托收在国际贸易中的应用；掌握信用卡在具体贸易中的应用。

能力目标：能够熟练运用各种支付方式的惯用句型和表达法。

### 工作任务

#### 工作任务 1

温州乐联贸易有限公司的业务员 Tom 和一美国客户在商讨产品支付问题。美国客户有意求购下列产品，但要求采用承兑交单方式支付，但 Tom 考虑到是老客户，他回信时婉言谢绝承兑交单方式支付，要求客户采用付款交单方式支付。

| Name of Commodity | Quantity | Unit Price | Total Value |
|---|---|---|---|
| Bed Cover No. FL 123 No. FL 123 | 500 pcs 500 pcs | USD 40 USD 60 | CIF Mexico USD 20,000 USD 30,000 USD 50,000 |

温州乐联贸易有限公司联系方式：浙江省温州市鹿城区人民路 23 号，邮编：325003，电话：0577-88345566

美国公司：The United Import Co., Ltd. 地址：45 Ashanti Road, Ohio, USA, 电话：1-626-780-75521

## 工作任务 2

2013 年 9 月公司业务人员 Miss Li 与荷兰 Tivoli 儿童用品公司经多次磋商现已建立业务关系，买卖双方同意按下列条件购进、售出下列商品。

| Name of Commodity & Specs | Quantity | Unit Price | Total Value |
|---|---|---|---|
| Plush Toys. Art. No. KB0677 New Design Brown Bear Art. No. KB7900 Toy Bear in Sweater | 1,080 pcs 1,208 pcs | USD 13.35 USD 9.30 | CIFC3 AMSTERDAM USD 14,418.00 USD 11,234.00 USD 25,652.00 |

荷兰 Tivoli 儿童用品公司的具体联络方法为：

Mr. Tivoli Smith

Purchasing Division

Tivoli Kids Products Ltd.

48 Berstofsgade, Rotterdam, the Netherlands

Tel: 0031-74123721

Fax: 0031-74123737

E-mail: tivolismith@hotmail.com

请根据上述背景资料，以上海环宇工贸有限公司的名义，给荷兰 Tivoli 儿童用品公司去函，要求支付条件为买方应通过买卖双方都接受的银行向卖方开出以卖方为受益人的不可撤销、可转让的即期付款信用证并允许分装、转船。信用证必须在装船前 30 天开到卖方，信用证有效期限延至装运日期后 21 天在中国到期。

## 操作示范

## 操作示范 1

Wenzhou Lelian Trading Co.

23 Renming Road,

Lucheng District, Wenzhou, Zhejiang Province, 325003

China

May 2, 2013

The United Import Co., Ltd.

45 Ashanti Road, Ohio, USA

Tel: 001-626-780-75521

Dear Mr. Bishop,

Re: Payment for Order No.111

We have received your letter of April 30 and noted your kind intention of pushing the sale of bed covers in your country.

Although we are appreciative of your trial order for 500 pcs of No. FL 123 and 500 pcs of No. FL 123, we regret that we are unable to consider your request for payment under D/A terms, the reason being that we generally ask for payment by Letter of Credit.

In consideration of the friendly relations between us, we are, as an exceptional case, prepared to accept payment for your trial order on a D/P basis. In other words, we will draw on you a documentary draft at sight through our bank on a collection basis.

We hope that the above payment terms will be acceptable to you and look forward to hearing from you soon.

Yours truly,

Tom

Wenzhou Lelian Trading Co., Ltd.

## 操作示范 2

**Universal Trading Co., Ltd.**

Add: Rm1201-1216 Mayling Plaza,

131 Dongfang Road, Shanghai, China

Fax: 0086-21-6336141

E-mail: puppyhappy@hotmail.com

http://www.puppyhappy.com

Sep. 29, 2013

Tivoli Kids Products Ltd.

Berstofsgade 48, Rotterdam, the Netherlands

Dear Mr. Smith,

We thank you for your letter of September 28 and shall be pleased to receive your order. Our usual terms of payment is to be made by an irrevocable transferable letter of credit in our favor through a bank acceptable to the seller, payable by draft at sight to reach us 30 days before shipment, with partial shipments and transshipment allowed and valid for negotiation in China until the 21st day after the date of shipment.

We are now awaiting the arrival of your L/C, on receipt of which we shall make the necessary arrangements for the shipment of your order. Any request for further assistance or our final confirmation will receive our immediate attention.

Yours sincerely,

Miss Li

Sales Manager

**知识链接**

1. 确认对方的来信及订购意向。

   The addresser should first confirm the addressee's soon reply and appreciate the addressee's intension of purchasing or selling the captioned goods.

2. 简明扼要地写明写信人所在公司所一贯坚持的支付方式或委婉地拒绝对方所提出的支付方式并说明理由。

   There are three mainly used terms of payment in the international trade, namely, remittance, collection and letters of credit. There are M/T, T/T and D/D in remittance. There are D/A, D/P at sight and D/P after sight in collection. There are 12 kinds of different kinds of L/C. You should state clearly which mode of terms of payment you prefer to in your letter. Try to persuade your customers to accept the terms of payment which is beneficial to you. For example, our usual terms of payment is to be made by an irrevocable transferable letter of credit in our favor through a bank acceptable to the seller, payable by draft at sight to reach us 30 days before shipment, with partial shipments and transshipment allowed and valid for negotiation in China until the 21st day after the date of shipment.

3. 本着互利互惠的原则，希望对方能考虑写信人所提出的支付方式并表达良好的愿景。

   Express your wishes for the long and mutual beneficial business relationship with your customer, wish your customer could take your difficulty into consideration and accept your usual terms of payment, wish to receive your customers' soon and favorable reply so that you could make the relevant arrangements for the shipment.

4. 根据上述情况，怎样写陈述支付方式的信函？（写作技巧）

   A. Acknowledge receipt of their letter and order, express your appreciation for their intention of purchasing or selling the captioned goods.

   B. Introduce your usual terms of payment or state the reasons that you are unable to accept their required terms of payment.

   C. Express your wishes: We hope that the above terms of payment will be acceptable to you and look forward to hearing from you soon.

**一问一答**

## Asks

1. Why is the problem of payment rather complicated in foreign trade?

2. What are the popular terms of payment for small quantity or freight of samples?

3. What is the main difference between payment by L/C and payment by collection?

4. Who should be concerned under payment by L/C and how is an L/C issued?

5. Which method is safer and better for the seller, D/P or D/A? Why?

6. Under what circumstances shall a seller agree to payment by D/A?

7. What are the advantages of T/T in advance?

## Answers

1. In foreign trade, buyers and sellers are in two different countries. Sometimes sellers have to do business with unknown buyers. If the seller delivers goods before payment has been made, he runs certain risks of non-payment of the buyer, and if the buyer makes payment in advance, he likewise runs risks of non-delivery of the goods. It becomes necessary for a third party to act as an intermediate between them to solve the problem of payment. This party is the bank, who either guarantees payment to the seller and examines the seller's shipping documents for the buyer or makes collection for the seller. That is why we say payment in foreign trade is rather complicated.

2. In addition to the traditional terms of payment like L/C, remittance and collection, other modes of payment like PayPal, Master, Moneybookers, Western Union and Money Gram are also well accepted by overseas traders, especially for the small amount like commission, the express freight of samples and so on, since they are faster and more convenient for both parties.

3. In the case of payment by L/C, the opening bank offers its own credit to finance the transaction, while in the case of collection, the bank will only do the service of collection and remittance and will not be liable for non-payment of the importer.

4. The parties mainly concerned under payment by L/C are applicant (buyer), issuing bank, advising bank and beneficiary (seller). The buyer (applicant) applies to open the L/C to the seller (beneficiary) through a bank who can open the L/C at their counter. The opening bank will inform the bank at seller's counter (the advising bank) that the L/C has been opened. The seller will check all the terms and conditions listed in the L/C. If all terms and conditions are acceptable, seller will arrange the shipment within the time specified in the L/C. After the goods are loaded onto the ship without any damage, the captain will issue the clean on board bill of lading to the seller. The seller will submit the clean on board bill of lading and other relevant documents to the bank at their counter (the advising bank) to gather the payment. The bank at seller's counter (the advising bank) will send the clean on board bill of lading and relevant documents to the buyer's bank (the opening bank). The opening bank will inform the buyer that all documents are received. The buyer will go to the bank to make the payment to get the clean on board bill of lading and relevant documents. With all of these documents, the buyer can clear the Import Customs and pick up the goods as soon as the goods arrive on the port of destination. L/C is used for the larger quantity order shipped by sea. The typical L/C scenario takes 14–21 days to complete.

5. D/P. D/P is safer and better for the seller, because it calls for actual payment against transfer of shipping documents, while in the case of D/A, the buyer can get hold of the shipping documents

against his acceptance, which merely is a promise to pay after certain days.

6. Payment by D/A is accepted only when the financial standing of the importer is sound or where a previous course of business has inspired the exporter to believe that the importer will be good for payment.

7. T/T means telegraphic transfer, or simply wire transfer. It's the simplest and easiest payment method to use. T/T payment in advance is usually used when the sample and small quantity shipments are transported by air. The reason why the documents like air waybill, commercial invoice and packing list will be sent to buyer along with the shipment by the same plane. As soon as the shipment arrives, the buyer can clear the customs and pick up the goods with the documents. As it's acknowledged, T/T payment in advance presents risk to the importer if the supplier is not an honest one. For sellers, T/T advance payment is required for some high-value samples and small quantity order shipped by air. T/T takes 3–4 days for sellers to receive the wire transfer made from anywhere in the world.

## 难点解析

1. intention：意图，目的

*e.g.* I advertised him of my intention.

我把我的打算告知他。

Good intention alone is not enough.

光有好的意愿还不够。

2. push the sale：推销

*e.g.* We hope you will do your best to push the sale of our products.

我们希望你们将尽最大努力销售我们的产品。

As your agents, we'll make greater efforts to push the sale of your products.

作为你们的代理，我们将会更加努力地推销你方产品。

3. appreciative：感激的

*e.g.* The best part was seeing how appreciative the people in that village were to receive the supplies and equipment.

最让人心动的是看到村民们在收到用品和设备时所表现出来的感激之情。

To his own astonishment, Mark metamorphosed into a person who was appreciative of everything and everyone around him, but no one more than his wife.

让他自己大吃一惊的是，马克就像变了个人一样。 他对周围的人和事都充满了感激，但最最感激的还是妻子。

4. D/A：Days after Acceptance 承兑交单

*e.g.* It would help me greatly if you would accept D/P or D/A instead.

如果你们能接受付款交单或承兑交单，这会对我们有很大帮助。

We've done business for years and you should have some faith in our credit. It would help me greatly, if you could accept D/A or D/P.

我们做了很多年生意了，你应该对我们的信用有信心，如果你可以接受承兑交单或者付款交单，会对我有很大的帮助。

5. in consideration of：考虑到，鉴于

e.g. In consideration of your extensive experience in the field, we are glad to appoint you as our agent.

考虑到你们在这一业务范围的丰富经验，我们很高兴指定你们为我们的代理。

The actions taken were in consideration of uncertainties associated with the economic environment and to position the company for long-term success.

所采取的行动考虑了与经济环境相关的不确定性目的是让公司处于长期成功。

6. exceptional：可例外的

e.g. There are only a handful of stores that it is exceptable to spend more than 15 minutes in. This list does not include Bed, Bath & Beyond or the local Pottery Barn.

很少有几家商店值得花费超过 15 分钟的时间，其中不包括 Bed, Bath & Beyond 商店（卖床上用品，浴卫用品和厨房用品等家具类小商品）或是当地的 Pottery Barn 商店（家具店）。

7. D/P：Document against Payment 付款交单

e.g. It would help me greatly if you would accept D/P or D/A instead.

如果你们能接受付款交单或承兑交单，这会对我们有很大帮助。

We'd like you to accept D/P for this transaction and future ones.

我们希望你们对这笔交易和今后的交易接受付款交单方式。

8. documentary draft at sight：即期跟单汇票

e.g. We'll draw on you by our documentary draft at sight on collection basis.

我们将按托收方法向你方开出即期跟单汇票。

9. on … basis：在……基础上

e.g. In 1997, the handling of known crack is carried on. On the basis of CVDA–1984 "pressure vessel defects evaluation code" safety evaluation is executed.

1997 年，对已知裂纹进行了处理，并根据 CVDA–1984 "压力容器缺陷评定规范" 进行了安全评定。

10. irrevocable transferable Letter of Credit：不可撤销的可转让的信用证

e.g. Irrevocable Letter of Credit, confirmed Letter of Credit, and transferable and divisible Letter of Credit are common terms of payment in international trade.

不可撤销的信用证、保兑信用证、可转让分割信用证是国际贸易中常见的支付方式。

11. valid：有效的

e.g. This train ticket is valid for three days.

这张火车票 3 日内有效。

They taught me that the only valid competition is with oneself.

他们教给我，唯一有效的竞争是和自己的竞争。

12. in our favor：我方受益

*e.g.* Fortunately, we have two things working in our favor this time.

幸运的是，这次还有两个对我们有利的因素。

You could wire transfer the payment into our bank account or open a Letter of Credit in our favor.

你可以汇款到我们的银行账户，或是开一个以我方受益的信用证。

## 拓展提高

### Payment by L/C

Dear Sirs,

We thank you for your order No.223 for 2,000 dozen shirts but regret being unable to accept your terms of payment mentioned herein.

In our last letter we sent you a copy of our specimen contract in which are contained the general sales terms and conditions. If you have gone through the specimen contract you will see that our usual terms of payment are by confirmed, irrevocable Letter of Credit in our favor, available by draft at sight, reaching us one month ahead of shipment, remaining valid for negotiation in China till the 30th day after prescribed time of shipment, and allowing transshipment and partial shipments.

We hope therefore that you will not hesitate to come to agreement with us on payment terms so as to get the first transaction concluded.

We look forward to receiving your favorable response at an early date.

Yours faithfully,

×××

### Proposing to Pay by 30 days' L/C

Dear Sirs,

Thank you for your letter of October 23.

We are pleased to receive your order, and wish to say we have adequate stocks of Emery Powder in our warehouse, and that delivery date can be met.

Payment by irrevocable Letter of Credit is convenient for us, and we shall draw a 30 d/s bill on your bank.

We are now awaiting the arrival of your L/C, on receipt of which we shall make the necessary arrangements for the shipment of your order. Any request for further assistance of information will receive our immediate attention.

Yours faithfully,

×××

## Notes

1. regret：感到后悔，遗憾

   regret to do sth. 遗憾没去做某事

   regret doing sth. 后悔做了某事

   *e.g.* I regret that I cannot come.

   我来不了，很抱歉。

   I regret to tell you that Mr. White has departed from the world for ever.

   我遗憾地告诉您怀特先生与世长辞了。

   Much to my regret, I am unable to accept your kind invitation.

   不能接受您的盛情邀请，我深为抱歉。

2. herein：于此；在这方面

   *e.g.* And herein I give my advice: for this is expedient for you, who have begun before, not only to do, but also to be forwarded a year ago.

   我在这事上把我的意见告诉你们，是于你们有益的。因为你们下手办这事，而且起此心意，已经有一年了。

3. specimen：样品，样本；标本

   *e.g.* Watch him closely. He is a fine specimen of the type you want to know.

   仔细地观察他。他是你想了解的那类人的一个很好的标本。

   I found that there were these rings in every specimen except for the smallest.

   我发现年轮在几乎所有的标本中都存在，除两具最小的以外。

4. prescribed：规定的

   *e.g.* The supervisor prescribed the steps in which orders must be filled out.

   主管规定了完成订货的步骤。

5. come to agreement：达成协定

   come to an agreement 达成协议；达成一致；取得一致意见；商定

   come to agreement with 与……达成一致

   *e.g.* After a long discussion we've come to an agreement on barter trade.

   经过长时间的讨论，我们已在易货贸易方面达成了协议。

   Webster appealed to both sides to forgive each other. He urged them to come to an agreement.

   韦伯斯特请求南北双方都相互原谅，他敦促南北双方能够达成协议。

6. stock：囤积，办货

   stock market 股票市场；证券市场；股票交易

   in stock 有存货；现有

   stock exchange 证券交易所

   stock price 股票价格；股票行市；交易所卖价

   stock raising 畜牧业

7. propose：propose 的基本意思是"提议、建议"，多指在讨论或争辩中提出明确的意见或建议,强调要求对方予以考虑或同意。引申可表示"打算,计划(做某事)"。可用作及物动词，也可用作不及物动词。用作及物动词时，可接名词、代词、动名词、动词不定式或从句作宾语。后接从句时，从句要用虚拟语气。

propose 与介词 to 连用，意为"求婚"，常指男子向女子求婚。

propose 与 for 连用，表示"提(名)，推荐"。

*e.g.* What do you propose we do?

你建议我们做什么?

We propose an early start tomorrow.

我们打算明天早早出发。

### Requesting Easier Payment Terms

Dear Sirs,

Re: 2,000 dozens of shirts

Our purchases of shirts from you have normally been paid by confirmed, irrevocable Letter of Credit in the past several deals.

This arrangement has cost us a great deal of money. From the moment we open the credit until our buyers pay us normally ties up funds for about 3 months. This is currently a particular serious problem for us in view of the difficult economic climate and the prevailing high interest rates.

If you could offer us easier payment items, it would probably lead to an increase in business between us. We propose either cash against documents on arrival of goods, or drawing on us at 3 months' sight.

We shall highly appreciate your kindness in consideration of the above request and giving us a favorable reply.

Yours faithfully,

×××

### Request for Payment by D/A

Dear Sirs,

Re: 200 sets of color TV

We have received your letter of July 23 ordering for 200 sets of NK-2300 Color TV. Thank you for your interest in our products.

Although we are appreciative of your pushing the sale of our TV set at your end, we regret being unable to consider your request for payment by 30 days D/A. As you know, our usual practice is to ask for sight L/C.

However, in order to facilitate developing the sale of TV sets in your market, we would like to suggest payment by D/P as a special accommodation.

We sincerely hope that the above payment term will be acceptable to you and trust you will appreciate our cooperation.

Yours sincerely,

×××

## Notes

1. ties up funds：积压资金

*e.g.* International oil price remains high level, stockpiling of some commodities increases and hence ties up funds.

国际石油价格高位运行，国内有的商品库存增加和部分资金占压。

tie up：积压，包扎，绑好

*e.g.* You need the loan for years, but investors don't want to tie up their money for years.

这笔款你需要贷若干年,可是投资者不希望他们的钱被占用好几年。

There are no basketball or tennis courts, although some people bring rackets and balls and tie up a string between trees.

这里没有篮球场或者网球场，然而有人带来了球拍和球，并且在树干之间拉起了绳子。

2. in view of：鉴于，考虑到

*e.g.* Accordingly and in view of the importance of this issue, further discussion is needed.

有鉴于此，并考虑到此问题的重要性，各方有必要进行深入讨论。

In view of the seriousness of this problem, effective measures should be taken before things get worse.

考虑到问题的严重性，在事态进一步恶化之前，必须采取有效的措施。

3. prevailing：流行的；一般的，最普通的；占优势的；盛行很广的

*e.g.* She wears a fashionable hair style prevailing in the city.

她的发型是这个城市流行的款式。

We have a prevailing view in our society—not only in the policy world, but in many spheres—that we are divided creatures.

在我们的社会里有一种流行的观点——不但存在于政策领域，而且存在与许多其它领域——那就是我们是被分割的生物。

4. interest rates：利息、利率

*e.g.* So, if interest rates go down, the value goes up; if interest rates go up, the value of your investment goes down.

因此如果利率下降，它的价值就上涨；如果利率上扬，这份投资的价值就会走低。

Not if you realize that interest rates are going up in most of the world—except maybe in Europe and Japan—quite dramatically over the last 12 months.

但是如果你明白过去 12 个月里，世界大部分国家的利息都在涨——除了欧洲和日本——而且涨得相当显著，就不觉得(矛盾了)。

5. cash against documents：付现交单；凭单证付现金

 *e.g.* We regret we can't accept "Cash against Documents" on arrival of goods at destination.

  很抱歉，我们不能同意"货抵目的地付款交单"方式付款。

  If pricing for terms of 90 days from BL (Backed by LC) available please advise both that and cash against documents with deposit.

  假如从"根本法"（立法会撑持）90 天的订价来说，请奉告对两国当局及现金与存款的文件。

6. push the sale of：推销

 *e.g.* It's difficult for us to push the sale of your digital cameras nowadays.

  现在我们很难把您的数码相机销售出去。

  We have decided to make a further concession of 2% in the hope that this will help you push the sale of our products.

  我方决定再作 2% 的让步，希望这将有助于你方推销我们的产品。

7. at your end：在贵方所在地

 *e.g.* But that might not be the case at your end.

  但这或许跟你的情况完全扯不上边。

  All the bags are beautifully designed to come in line with the local market preference at your end.

  所有袋子都设计得很精美，符合你们当地市场的口味。

  However, if you want to have it covered for your imports at your end, you may arrange the insurance as you like.

  但是如果你方想要为你们的进口货物投保这种险的话，你们可以自行安排。

8. facilitate：促进，帮助

 *e.g.* Modern inventions facilitate housework.

  许多现代发明便利了家务劳动。

  All of these agencies and people either complement or facilitate our work, or express the health needs of populations.

  所有这些机构和人士要么补充或便利我们的工作，要么表达人民的卫生需求。

9. accommodation：(纠纷的)解决；妥协；互让

 *e.g.* Neither accommodation nor recognition would be sustainable options in the face of the zombie threat.

  在僵尸的威胁面前，既不和解也不认同是或可维持的选择。

技能操练

**I. Choose the best answer from A, B, C and D.**

1. As we must observe our usual practice, that is, payment _____ L/C.

   A. by               B. is by            C. will by          D. will be

2. In order to encourage your effort in promoting our products in your end, we shall consider _____ payment by D/P at 30 days.

   A. accepting        B. to accept        C. accept           D. acceptance

3. Considering the amount involved in this lot of goods is rather small, we agree to draw _____ you by documentary sight draft.

   A. with             B. to               C. in               D. on

4. As we must _____ to our customary practice, we sincerely hope that you will not think us unaccommodating.

   A. adhere           B. according        C. accept           D. accommodate

5. In _____ with your request, we exceptionally accept D/A payment terms, but this should not be regarded as a precedent.

   A. facilitate       B. regret           C. payment          D. compliance

6. We regret _____ unable to accept your terms of payment as mentioned in your last mail.

   A. to be            B. being            C. to               D. for being

7. The Letter of Credit does not _____ the sales confirmation.

   A. adhere to        B. agree with       C. agree to         D. according to

8. Please _____ the goods should be shipped as soon as the covering L/C reaches you.

   A. see to it that   B. see              C. see to           D. see that

9. We are sorry to inform that the listed terms of payment do not correspond to customary business _____.

   A. terms            B. payment          C. practice         D. experience

10. Since both the contracts are less than USD 110,000 in value, we would like you to _____ the terms of payment to D/A.

   A. modify           B. transfer         C. agree            D. lead to

**II. Translate the following phrases into English or vice versa.**

1. 预付货款 _____

2. 交货付现 _____

3. 凭此信用证 _____

4. 全套装运单据 _____

5. 有足够库存 _____

6. 开一张一式两份的即期汇票 _____

7. 可以如期交货 _____

8. 立即办理 _____

9. 产地证明书 _____

10. 发票金额全数加 10% _____

11. draw on Hua Feng _____

12. commercial acceptance draft _____

13. Cash Against Documents on Arrival of Goods at Destination _____

_____

14. contract value _____

15. irrevocable L/C _____

16. mail transfer _____

17. credit standing _____

18. cash against documents _____

19. pay in installments _____

20. consular invoice _____

## III. Translate the following sentences from English into Chinese or vice versa.

1. The buyer suggested D/A as the terms of payment, but the seller was unwilling to make any exception.

_____

2. We can't agree to draw at 30 days D/A.

_____

3. So it's better for us to adopt D/P or D/A.

_____

4. I suppose D/P or D/A should be adopted as the mode of payment this time.

_____

5. It would help me greatly if you would accept D/A or D/P.

_____

6. Could you make an exception and accept D/A or D/P?

_____

7. 我们坚持用信用证方式付款。

_____

8. 我们向法国出口一般使用即期信用证付款。

_____

9. 你必须意识到不可撤销信用证为出口商提供了银行担保。

_____

10. 我们要求用不可撤销的、允许分批装运、金额为全部货款、并以我方为抬头人的信用证，
凭即期汇票支付。

_____

11. 百分之五十用信用证，其余的用付款交单，您看怎么样？

_____

12. 请立即电传通知我方信用证号码。

_____

**IV. Fill in the blanks with the proper words.**

1. Will you please increase the credit _____ $1,000?

2. The credit is short _____ to the amount of RMB100.

3. Many banks in Europe are _____ _____ _____ to open L/C and effect payment in RMB.

4. When can you arrange for a credit _____ the new import license?

5. The validity of the L/C will be _____ to 30th August.

6. Please _____ L/C No. 205 as follows.

7. Your refusal to amend the L/C is _____ to cancellation of the order.

8. You ought to pay us the bank _____ once payment is wrongly refused.

9. We'll not pay until shipping _____ for the goods have reached us.

10. We're worrying that a decline in prices might _____ _____ refusal of payment.

**V. Compose a dialogue in the following situation.**

Your partner, a businessman from America, is negotiating with you about a certain business. Everything has been settled except the problem of payment. He insists on paying by installments. As this order is big enough, you finally agree to 50% by down payment and the balance by L/C.

**VI. Write a letter with the ideas given below.**

ABC Corp. asked you to supply them with goods to the value of 5,000 pieces shirts. They suggest the payment, 50% by L/C at 30 days' sight, the balance 50% by D/P at sight. Write a letter explaining that they shall pay 100% of the sales proceeds in advance by T/T.

## Read More

### PayPal

When you make a payment through PayPal that is funded by Instant Transfer or eCheck, and when you initiate an "Add Funds" transaction, you are requesting an electronic transfer from your bank account. Upon such a request, PayPal will make electronic transfers via the Automated Clearing House system from your US or Canadian bank account in the amount you specify. You agree that such requests, which constitutes your authorization for such transfers. PayPal will never make transfers from your bank account without your authorization.

PayPal provides you with protection against unauthorized withdrawals from your bank account under the terms of the Electronic Fund Transfer Rights and Error Resolution Policy. You may be charged a service fee for any ACH transactions that result in a returned ACH item, but not limited to those caused by insufficient funds in your bank account, closure of your bank account, or if the bank account number or other information you provided is incorrect. Currently, returns to non-US bank accounts are charged a returned ACH fee based on their location and returns to US bank accounts are not charged. PayPal reserves the right to resubmit for collection any ACH debit authorized by you that is returned for insufficient or uncollected funds.

PayPal allows you to send money to anyone with e-mail. PayPal is free for consumers and works seamlessly with your existing credit card and checking account. You can settle debts, borrow cash, divide bills or split expenses with friends all over the world.

## 实训项目 9

# Establishment, Amendment and Extension of the L/C
# 开立、修改及延展信用证

### 学习目标

知识目标：熟练掌握信用证支付环节中的各种贸易术语，掌握信用证开立、修改和延期的表达方式及相关信函的写作方法。

能力目标：能够撰写催开信用证、修改信用证和信用证延期等信函，做到内容清楚，叙述完整，礼貌得体。

### 工作任务

## 工作任务 1

Wenzhou Jiada Import & Export Co. 已把 J&D 向其订购的 5000 件衬衫准备好且眼看交货期临近，但却未收到相关信用证。故去函催对方开信用证，并要求对方要按合同的条款开出信用证。

请根据上述情况，以我方业务员 James 的名义向 J&D 公司去函，催促其开立信用证。J&D 公司的地址：

12 Aston Road, Birmingham, UK

Wenzhou Jiada Import & Export Co.公司的联系方式：

17 Fudong Road, Lucheng District, Wenzhou City, Zhejiang Province, China

Tel: 0086-577-88345564 Fax: 0086-577-88345565

Email: yully87@hotmail.com

http:// www. Jiada.com.cn

## 工作任务 2

J&D 在收到 Wenzhou Jiada Import & Export Co.的信后，立即回函告知该订单的信用证已开出并提醒对方按时交货。

请根据上述情况，以买方的身份向对方复函。

## 操作示范

## 操作示范 1

**Wenzhou Jiada Import & Export Co.**

17 Fudong Road, Lucheng District,

Wenzhou City, 325000, China

Tel: 0086-577-88345564　Fax: 0086-577-88345565

Email: yully87@hotmail.com　http:// www. Jiada.com.cn

September 12，2013

12 Aston Road,

Birmingham, UK

Dear Sirs，

　　As regards 5,000 pieces of shirts under the subject S/C, we wish to call your attention to the fact that we have got the goods ready for some time and the delivery date is drawing near, but up to the present moment we have not received the covering L/C.

　　Therefore, we should ask you to take immediate action to have the L/C established so that we may carry out the order within the assured time.

　　Meanwhile, in order to avoid amendments, please make sure that the L/C stipulations should be in exact accordance with the terms of the contract in question.

　　We look forward to receiving your response at an early date.

Yours faithfully,

James (manager)

The Sales Department

## 操作示范 2

J&D

12 Aston Road, Birmingham, UK

Tel: 0044-0196854675 Fax: 0044-0196987890

September 13, 2013

Wenzhou Jiada Import & Export Co.

17 FuDong Road, Lucheng District,

Wenzhou City, 325000, China

Dear James，

Re：L/C for Our S/C No.102

Thank you for your letter but we wish to invite your attention to our Order No.6241 for 5,000 pieces of shirts, and we did send you an irrevocable L/C 7 days ago which expires on November 5.

As the delivery date is approaching and our end-users are badly in need of the goods，we shall be thankful very much if you will effect shipment ASAP.

We would like to point out that any late shipment of our order will undoubtedly place us in no small difficulty and we will get heavy losses.

Thank you for your kind cooperation.

Yours truly，

Simon (Mr.)

The Purchase Department

## 知识链接

1. 为何要催证?

The seller must receive the L/C before the goods are shipped. For not effecting the shipping and for prompt shipment，the seller urge the buyer to establish the L/C is quite necessary.

2. 开证始于何方? 开证行和代理行分别属于何方?

The process of issuing an L/C starts with the buyer.

The buyer's bank is the opening bank and the seller's bank is the correspondent bank (the noticing bank).

3. 一般应该何时开证? 为什么?

It is a usual practice in export trade that the L/C is to be established and to reach the seller one month prior to the date of shipment so as to give the seller enough time to make preparations for shipment.

4. 根据上述情况，怎样写催证函？一般应该给予什么样的建议？

In writing a letter of this kind, we should do it clearly, concisely and politely. In such a letter, further suggestion is given in order to avoid amendments to the L/C, and the seller often asks the buyer to open the L/C in exact accordance with the restrictions of the contract.

## Asks

1. How many parties are involved in the Letter of Credit?

2. Why is it the usual practice that the Letter of Credit is to be opened and to reach the seller 30 days ahead of shipment?

3. What should the seller do if any discrepancies or some unforeseen special clauses are found in the L/C?

4. Under what condition is an extension of the L/C necessary?

5. What should the seller take care of when writing letters concerning L/C amendment and extension?

6. When to open the L/C is appropriate? Why?

## Answers

1. There are 6 parties involved in the Letter of Credit.

   (1) Applicant (importer/buyer): it is usually up to the importer to choose a commercial bank that is willing to open a Letter of Credit on his behalf. In international business, the applicant is often referred to as the buyer, opener or consignee.

   (2) Issuing/Opening Bank: it is the bank that issues the Letter of Credit on behalf of the applicant. It takes full responsibility for payment if the exporter presents the correct documents.

   (3) Advising Bank/Notifying Bank: it is the bank that advises the beneficiary of the arrival of the Letter of Credit.

   (4) Beneficiary: it is the party in whose favor the Letter of Credit is issued.

   (5) Negotiating Bank: it refers to the bank that is willing to buy the full set of shipping documents presented by the exporter.

   (6) Paying Bank: it refers to the bank that pays the amount of money to the exporter as stipulated in the Letter of Credit.

2. It is the usual practice that the Letter of Credit is to be opened and to reach the seller 30 days ahead of shipment so as to give the seller enough time to make preparation for shipment, such as making the goods ready and booking shipping space. For prompt shipment, it is advisable that the Letter of Credit is issued in good time.

3. It is essential for the seller to amend the L/C because a minor difference between the clauses of the L/C and the terms stipulated in the sales contract or sales confirmation. If not discovered or duly amended, it may cause the seller much inconvenience because the negotiating bank will refuse to make the payment.

4. There are times when the seller fails to get the goods ready for the shipment in time or the buyer requests that the shipment be postponed for one reason or another. Under such circumstances, the seller will have to ask for extension of the expiry date as well as the date of shipment of the L/C.

5. Message urging establishment of Letter of Credit must be written with tact. Their aim is to persuade the buyer to cooperate more closely and in fact to fulfill his obligations; otherwise they will give offence to the buyer and bring about unhappy consequences.

6. It is a usual practice in export trade that the L/C is to be established and to reach the seller one month prior to the date of shipment so as to give the seller enough time to make preparations for shipment.

## 难点解析

1. drawing near: come near, come up 走近, 临近

   *e.g.* The Beijing Olympic Games is drawing near.
   北京奥运会日益临近了。

2. take immediate action: 立即采取行动

3. carry out: 施行, 履行

   *e.g.* He will carry out his plan.
   他要执行他的计划。

   He does not have the funds to carry out his design.
   他没有资金来施行他的设计。

4. amendments: 修正, 改正

   *e.g.* The amendment is an appendage of that contract.
   这个修改案是那个合同的附件。

   The amendment will become effective next year.
   修正案将于明年生效。

5. stipulation: 规定, 条款

   *e.g.* Your remarks break the stipulation of the contract.
   你们的意见是违反合同规定的。

   There's no stipulation as to the amount you can invest.
   没有关于投资额的规定。

6. in accordance with: according to 与……一致, 依照

   *e.g.* What you do should be in exact accordance with what you said.
   你应该言行一致。

7. irrevocable：impossible to retract or revoke 不能取消的

　　*e.g.* This is an irrevocable decision.

　　　　这是不能撤回的决定。

8. expire：to come to an end; terminate 期满，届满；终止；呼气

　　*e.g.* My membership in the club has expired.

　　　　我的俱乐部会员资格已期满。

9. ASAP：As Soon As Possible, 尽快

　　*e.g.* Jack said he would pay you ASAP.

　　　　杰克说他会尽快还你钱的。

**拓展提高**

**Discussion the Issuance of L/C**

Dear Sirs,

　　We confirm supply of 200 tons of steel at the price stated in your order No. 345. Our Sales Contract No. RT-2301 in two original was sent to you by fax. Please sign and return one copy of them for our file.

　　It is understood that a Letter of Credit in our favor covering the said goods should be opened immediately. We wish to point out that stipulations in the relative L/C must strictly adhere to the terms stated in your contract so as to avoid subsequent amendments. You may rest assured that we will make shipment without delay upon receipt of your L/C.

　　We look forward to receiving your response at an early date.

Yours faithfully,

××× 

**L/C Extension**

Dear Sirs,

　　Thank you for L/C No. 3425 covering our S/C No. 345 of 3,000 sets of knitting machines.

　　We are sorry that owing to the foggy weather in our city, we are unable to get the goods ready before the end of this month. Therefore, it is impossible to ship the goods this month, and we would like to ask you to do your best to extend the L/C covering the Knitting machines.

　　It is expected that the consignment will be ready for shipment in the early part of May and we are arranging to ship it on S.S Blue Star sailing from Ningbo on or about May 10.

　　We are looking forward to receiving your fax extension of the above L/C, thus enabling us to effect shipment of the goods in question. We thank you for your cooperation.

Yours faithfully,

×××

## Note

1. in two original：一式两份

   *e.g.* This contract is made out in two original copies, one copy to be held by each party in witness thereof.

   本合同一式两份,买卖双方各执一份为证。

   This contract is made out in two original, each copy written in Chinese and English languages, both text being valid.

   本合同正文一式两份，分别以中文和英文书写，两种文本具有同等效力。

2. for our file：供我方存档

   *e.g.* Please sign and return one copy for our file.

   请将本确认书的一份签署后寄还本公司以备存档。

   Please sign and return one for our file.

   请签退一份以供存档。

3. adhere to：坚持，依附

   *e.g.* We should adhere to our opinions.

   我们应当坚持我们的意见。

   She adhered to what she had said at the meeting.

   她坚持她在会议上说过的话。

4. subsequent：随后的，后来的

   *e.g.* Subsequent events proved me wrong.

   后来发生的事证明我错了。

   He confessed to other crimes subsequent to the bank robbery.

   他供认抢劫银行案后，又坦白了其他罪行。

5. owing to：由于，因为

   *e.g.* Owing to a strange mental aberration he forgot his own name.

   由于一种莫名的精神错乱，他把自己的名字忘了。

6. extend：扩展，延展

   *e.g.* Our playing fields extend as far as those trees.

   我们的操场延伸到那些树前。

   Theoretically, a line can extend into infinity.

   从理论上来说一条线可以无限地延伸。

7. consignment：寄售物，托付货物

   *e.g.* The consignment covering our order No.12 arrived last week.

我方第 12 号订单项下货物已于上周运到。

The goods have been sent to Chicago on consignment.

货物已运到芝加哥，托人代销。

8. in question：正在考虑的

*e.g.* On the Christmas day in question, we could not go to Grandmother's house, as we do every
　　year.

在我们所谈到的那个圣诞节，我们未能像每年一样到祖母家去。

The latest report seems to call in question our previous conclusion.

这份最近的报告似乎对我们以前的结论提出异议。

---

**Amending the L/C**

Dear Sirs,

　　We have received your L/C No. 34564 issued by the Bank of America for the
amount of USD 3,000. On perusal, we find that transshipment and partial shipment are
not allowed.

　　As direct steamers to your country are few and far between, we often have to ship
via Hong Kong. It would be to mutual benefit to use partial shipment because we could
ship immediately whatever we have on hand instead of waiting for the whole lot to be
completed. Therefore, we are asking you to amend the L/C to read "partial shipments
and transshipment allowed".

　　It would be grateful if this amendment is faxed without delay, as our goods have
been packed and ready for shipment for quite some time.

Yours faithfully,

××× 

---

**Decline to Amend the L/C**

Dear Sirs,

　　We are in receipt of your letter of April 30 requesting us to amend the relevant L/C
to allow partial shipment instead of shipping all the 300 sets of knitting machine in one
lot. Unfortunately we are unable to comply with your wishes.

　　When we signed the Sales Confirmation it was expressly stated that shipment would
be effected in one lot. As we are in urgent need of the whole goods, it is not agreeable to
get only partial goods. We are willing to do whatever we can to cooperate with you to
expedite the whole shipment.

　　We would be grateful if the matter will be dealt with promptly.

Yours faithfully,

××× 

---

## **Notes**

1. issue：发表，发行

    *e.g.* Xinhua News Agency is authorized to issue the following statement.

    新华社授权发表如下声明。

    They issued an update on the snow forecast.

    他们发布了最新的降雪预报。

2. on perusal：经审阅

    *e.g.* On perusal, we find that transhipment and partial shipment are not allowed.

    在详阅后，我们发现不允许转船和分批装运。

    On perusal of your L/C, we find some clauses are not in conformity with the contract terms.

    经审阅你方信用证，我们发现一些条款与合同条款不符。

3. transshipment：转运

    *e.g.* We require that transshipment be allowed.

    我们要求允许转运。

    Please note that partial shipments and transshipment are not permitted.

    请注意，我们不允许部分装运或转运。

4. few and far between：稀少的，稀疏的

    *e.g.* Hold on to good friends; they are few and far between.

    知己难逢，应好好珍惜。

    Such a snow fall is few and far between in our province.

    这样大的雪在我们省是少有的。

5. mutual benefit：互利互惠

    *e.g.* If need be, we can work together for our mutual benefit.

    如果需要的话，双方可以协力工作，互惠互利。

    Our company will keep the client as the God, keep mutual benefit as the base, and set up a refulgent future together.

    公司将以顾客至上为宗旨，在共同发展互惠互利的基础上，与新老顾客共创辉煌的未来。

6. lot：批，套

    *e.g.* He bought two lots of 1,000 shares in the company during August and September.

    他在 8 月和 9 月买进了两批这家公司的股票，每次 1000 股。

    We've just sacked one lot of builders.

    我们刚炒掉一批建筑工人。

7. comply with：服从，照办

    *e.g.* They have to comply with social and environmental standards.

    他们必须遵守社会和环境标准。

We need all people to comply with the law.

我们要求所有的人遵从法律。

8. promptly：迅速地，准时地

　　*e.g.* He draw his hand back promptly from the hot stove.

　　　　他迅速地把手从热火炉上缩了回去。

　　　　The girl's life was saved because the doctors acted so promptly.

　　　　由于医生们行动迅速，那个女孩子得救了。

## 技能操练

**I. Choose the best answer from A, B, C and D.**

1. As requested, we have immediately arranged _____ our bankers to extend the expiry date of our L/C for two weeks _____ May 10.

　　A. with… up to　　　　B. with… on　　　　C. for… until　　　　D. for…to

2. As arranged, we would ask you to open an irrevocable credit in _____ favor and shall hand over shipping documents _____ acceptance of our draft.

　　A. your…against　　　B. your… for　　　C. our…against　　　D. our…for

3. We inform you that we have opened an irrevocable credit _____ the London Bank in your favor.

　　A. at　　　　　　　　B. in　　　　　　　　C. by　　　　　　　　D. with

4. We advised the bank to amend the clause _____ "partial shipment are permitted".

　　A. to reading　　　　B. to read　　　　C. to be read　　　　D. to be reading

5. We enclose our cheque for $ 2,000 _____ your invoice No. 345.

　　A. in payment of　　B. by payment at　　C. to payment on　　D. for payment in

6. The relative L/C should be issued through a third bank in Austria _____ the seller.

　　A. available by　　　B. available to　　　C. acceptable by　　　D. acceptable to

7. According to the stipulations in our S/C No. 1234, you should send us your L/C one month _____ the date of shipment.

　　A. preceding　　　　B. precede　　　　C. to precede　　　　D. preceded

8. Upon examination, we have found a _____ in quantity. Please amend the quantity to read "500 M/T( 3% more or less)".

　　A. difference　　　　B. wrong　　　　C. discrepancy　　　　D. problem

9. After the contract _____, we shall open an irrevocable L/C in your favor with the Bank of China, New York Branch.

　　A. will be signed　　B. signs　　　　C. sign　　　　D. is signed

10. _____ the terms of payment as stipulated in the contract, please establish an irrevocable Letter of Credit in our favor.

　　A. In fact　　　　B. As a matter of fact　　C. In contrast with　　D. In accordance with

**II. Translate the following phrases into English or vice versa.**

1. 即期信用证 _____

2. 开立信用证 _____

3. 以你方为受益人 _____

4. 佣金 _____

5. 议付行 _____

6. 受益人 _____

7. 分批装运 _____

8. 空白背书 _____

9. 保险单 _____

10. 海运提单 _____

11. European Main Ports _____

12. transshipment _____

13. discrepancy _____

14. amendment _____

15. stipulation _____

16. for an amount of _____

17. in accordance with _____

18. expiration _____

19. mutual benefit _____

20. in advance _____

**III. Translate the following sentences from English into Chinese or vice versa.**

1. We have received your L/C No. 555, but find it contains the following discrepancies.

_____

2. We are pleased to inform you that L/C No. 666 issued by the Chartered Bank of Liverpool for our S/C No. 111 has just received. However, on examining the clauses, we regretfully find that certain points are not in conformity with the terms stipulated in the contract.

_____

3. We thank you for your L/C No. 999, but on checking its clauses we find with regret that your L/C calls for shipment in October 2003, whereas our contract stipulates for November shipment.

_____

4. Commission should be 3%, not 5%.

_____

5. Shipment is to be made during June/July instead of "on or before June 30".

_____

6. Goods should be insured for 110% of the invoice value, not 150%.

_____

7. 请将你方第 789 号信用证作如下修改。

_____

8. 将单价从 0.78 美元增加到 0.87 美元，总金额增至 1234500 美元。

_____

9. 请将信用证改为允许转船。

_____

10. 请将第 898 号信用证改为："该信用证将于 2012 年 12 月 31 日在中国到期"。

_____

11. 请将你方第 518 号信用证的装运期和有效期分别延至 2012 年 10 月底和 11 月 15 日，并
安排信用证的修改通知书于 2012 年 9 月 30 日到达我方。

_____

12. 请对信用证速作修改。

_____


## IV. Fill in the blanks with the proper words.

1. We are glad to learn that you forwarded the Letter of Credit on May 5 _____ the Band of America in San Francisco.

2. We are glad to learn that you _____ a credit with the National Bank, _____ _____ _____ Messers, Smith & Co., for the amount of $100,000 _____ the said order available till December 31.

3. We have drawn on you at 60 days' sight a draft for $90,000, _____ the credit No. 450 of June 6, in favor of the Tokyo Bank.

4. The expiry date of the credit being May 31, we request that you will arrange with your banker to _____ it up to June 10, amending the said credit.

5. Please advise the beneficiaries that we shall amend the credit No. 1200 to read 10 boxes of the articles _____ _____ 5 boxes, otherwise unchanged.

6. We shall be glad if you look _____ the urgent matter and let us have a reply without delay.

7. As the season is drawing near, our buyers are _____ urgent need of the goods.

8. _____ spite of our numerous reminders, you haven't opened the Letter of Credit so far.

9. We want to make it clear that the L/C should be opened _____ time, otherwise, it will cause us a great deal of difficulties.

10. The shipment _____ your credit No. 456 has been ready for quite some time, but up to the present we haven't received any news of L/C.


## V. Compose a dialogue in the following situation.

James White, the Manager of N&M Garment Company, has just received L/C from his client but he found some terms to be amended. So he is talking with Bill, the manager of Wenzhou T&T Clothing Company. The amendment should be as follows:

(1) Piece length in 30 yards instead of 40 yards.

(2) Partial shipments and transshipment allowed.

(3) Extend the shipment date to January 15, 2012.

## VI. Write a letter with the ideas given below.

You are asked to write a letter to ABC Corp. asking for L/C amendment. The letter should cover the following points.

(1) The quantity is not sufficient in the L/C, please increase the amount by 500 pieces.

(2) Commission is 3%, not 5%.

(3) Delete insurance because this is on C.F.R basis.

(4) Transshipment should be allowed.

# Read More

Sample of L/C

Issue of a Documentary Credit

BKCHCNBJA08E SESSION: 000 ISN: 000000

BANK OF CHINA

LIAONING

NO. 5 ZHONGSHAN SQUARE

ZHONGSHAN DISTRICT

DALIAN

CHINA——开证行

Destination Bank : KOEXKRSEXXX MESSAGE TYPE: 700

KOREA EXCHANGE BANK

SEOUL

178.2 KA, ULCHI RO, CHUNG-KO——通知行

Type of Documentary Credit 40A IRREVOCABLE——信用证性质为不可撤销

Letter of Credit Number 20 LC84E0081/99——信用证号码，一般做单时都要求注此号

Date of Issue 31G 990916——开证日期

Date and Place of Expiry 31D 991015 KOREA——失效时间地点

Applicant Bank 51D BANK OF CHINA LIAONING BRANCH——开证行

Applicant 50 DALIAN WEIDA TRADING CO., LTD. ——开证申请人

Beneficiary 59 SANGYONG CORPORATION

CPO BOX 110

SEOUL

KOREA——受益人

Currency Code, Amount 32B USD 1,146,725.04——信用证总额

Available with…by… 41D ANY BANK BY NEGOTIATION——呈兑方式任何银行议付

Drafts at 42C 45 DAYS AFTER SIGHT——见证 45 天内付款

Drawee 42D BANK OF CHINA LIAONING BRANCH——付款行

Partial Shipments 43P NOT ALLOWED——分装不允许

Transshipment 43T NOT ALLOWED——转船不允许

Shipping on Board/Dispatch/Packing in Charge at/ from

44A RUSSIAN SEA——起运港

Transportation to 44B DALIAN PORT, P.R.CHINA——目的港

Latest Date of Shipment 44C 990913——最迟装运期

Description of Goods or Services: 45A——货物描述

FROZEN YELLOWFIN SOLE WHOLE ROUND (WITH WHITE BELLY) USD770/MT CFR DALIAN QUANTITY: 200MT

ALASKA PLAICE (WITH YELLOW BELLY) USD600/MT CFR DALIAN QUANTITY: 300MT

Documents Required: 46A——议付单据

1. SIGNED COMMERCIAL INVOICE IN 5 COPIES.

   ——签字的商业发票五份

2. FULL SET OF CLEAN ON BOARD OCEAN BILLS OF LADING MADE OUT TO ORDER AND BLANK ENDORSED, MARKED "FREIGHT PREPAID" NOTIFYING LIAONING OCEAN FISHING CO., LTD. TEL86)411-3680288

   ——一整套清洁已装船提单，抬头为 TO ORDER 的空白背书，且注明运费已付，通知人为 LIAONING OCEAN FISHING CO., LTD. 电话 86-411-3680288

3. PACKING LIST/WEIGHT MEMO IN 4 COPIES INDICATING QUANTITY/GROSS AND NET WEIGHTS OF EACH PACKAGE AND PACKING CONDITIONS AS CALLED FOR BY THE L/C.

   ——装箱单/重量单四份，显示每个包装产品的数量/毛净重和信用证要求的包装情况

4. CERTIFICATE OF QUALITY IN 3 COPIES ISSUED BY PUBLIC RECOGNIZED SURVEYOR.

   ——由 PUBLIC RECOGNIZED SURVEYOR 签发的质量证明三份

5. BENEFICIARY'S CERTIFIED COPY OF FAX DISPATCHED TO THE ACCOUNTEE WITH 3 DAYS AFTER SHIPMENT ADVISING NAME OF VESSEL, DATE, QUANTITY, WEIGHT, VALUE OF SHIPMENT, L/C NUMBER AND CONTRACT NUMBER.

   ——受益人证明的传真件，在船开后三天内已将船名航次，日期，货物的数量，重量价值，信用证号和合同号通知付款人。

6. CERTIFICATE OF ORIGIN IN 3 COPIES ISSUED BY AUTHORIZED INSTITUTION.

   ——当局签发的原产地证明三份

7. CERTIFICATE OF HEALTH IN 3 COPIES ISSUED BY AUTHORIZED INSTITUTION.

——当局签发的健康/检疫证明三份

ADDITIONAL INSTRUCTIONS: 47A——附加指示

1. CHARTER PARTY B/L AND THIRD PARTY DOCUMENTS ARE ACCEPTABLE.

——租船提单和第三方单据可以接受

2. SHIPMENT PRIOR TO L/C ISSUING DATE IS ACCEPTABLE.

——装船期早于信用证的签发日期是可以接受的

3. BOTH QUANTITY AND AMOUNT 10 PERCENT MORE OR LESS ARE ALLOWED.

——允许数量和金额公差在 10%左右

Charges 71B ALL BANKING CHARGES OUTSIDE THE OPENNING BANK ARE FOR BENEFICIARY'S ACCOUNT.

Period for Presentation 48 DOCUMENTSMUST BE PRESENTED WITHIN 15 DAYS AFTER THE DATE OF ISSUANCE OF THE TRANSPORT DOCUMENTS BUT WITHIN THE VALIDITY OF THE CREDIT.

Confirmation Instructions 49 WITHOUT

Instructions to the Paying/Accepting/Negotiating Bank: 78

1. ALL DOCUMENTS TO BE FORWARDED IN ONE COVER, UNLESS OTHERWISE STATED ABOVE.

2. DISCREPANT DOCUMENT FEE OF USD 50.00 OR EQUAL CURRENCY WILL BE DEDUCTED FROM DRAWING IF DOCUMENTS WITH DISCREPANCIES ARE ACCEPTED.

"Advising Through" Bank 57A KOEXKRSEXXX MESSAGE TYPE: 700

KOREA EXCHANGE BANK

SEOUL

178.2 KA, ULCHI RO, CHUNG-KO

# 实训项目 10

## Insurance
## 保　险

### 学习目标

知识目标: 了解货物运输保险的险别、学会订立合同的保险条款, 掌握相关专业术语和常用句型。

能力目标: 能够掌握货物保险信函的写作步骤, 撰写保险信函, 做到内容清楚, 叙述完整, 礼貌得体。

### 工作任务

#### 工作任务 1

买方 John Green 向卖方订购 2000 件羽绒服。买方已经开出以卖方为受益人的不可撤销的即期信用证。卖方将很快收到中国银行大连支行的文件。所以, 卖方可以毫无顾虑地准备生产和装运。买方已经基于 CFR 条款协定了 S/C 价格和 L/C。因此, 保险是卖方的责任。为了方便起见, 希望卖方代表买方按发票金额 110%投保水渍险和偷窃、提货不着险。保费当然由买方负责。

请根据上述背景资料, 你作为买方经理 John Green 致信卖方, 希望卖方代为向中国人民保险公司按发票价值 110%为 2000 件羽绒服投保水渍险和偷窃、提货不着险。

#### 工作任务 2

因客户要求, 公司需要生产一批羊毛靠垫。2012 年 5 月公司业务员向澳大利亚某羊毛公司订购了 100 公吨羊毛（100 metric tons of wool）。

> Mr. Bart Price (Research Development)
>
> Purchasing Division
>
> Ail Mohammed Omar & Co.

请根据上述背景资料，以绍兴平津纺织品有限公司业务员的名义，给 Ail Mohammed Omar & Co. 公司的经理 Mr. Eng Maamoun Elwani 去函，希望该公司代为向中国人民保险公司按发票价值 110% 为 100 公吨羊毛投保平安险。

**操作示范**

### 操作示范 1

Dear Sirs,

With regard to our order of 2,000 down jackets we have issued an irrevocable L/C at sight that takes your company as the beneficiary. You will be advised by Dalian Branch of the Bank of China very soon. So you can prepare for production and shipment without any concern.

There is another issue we want to request here. As we know, the price that has been stipulated in both of the S/C and L/C is based on CFR term and hence insurance lies within our responsibilities. For the sake of convenience we wonder if you could have the goods insured, on behalf of us, against WPA and TPND for 110% of the invoice value at your end. The premium change is, of course, for our account.

Hope this request will meet with your approval.

Best regards,
John Green
Manager

### 操作示范 2

Dear Mr. Eng Maamoun Elwani,

We would like to refer you to the goods under the L/C No. 567 for 100 metric tons of wool, from which you will see that this order is placed on a CFR basis. Hope you can effect the shipment as contracted.

As now we desire to have the shipment insured at your end, we shall be pleased if you will arrange to insure the goods on our behalf against FPA for the invoice value plus 10%. The extra premium for the additional coverage will be for our account. As finishing the insurance procedure you can draw on us a sight draft for our refunding you the premium fee.

We hope that the goods can be insured as per the above request. Please inform us whether you agree with the said arrangements of insurance.

Yours sincerely,

Shaoxing County Pingjin Textile Co., Ltd.

Wang Pinfeng (Mr.)

Marketing Division

## 知识链接

1. 什么是保险？保险的目的是什么？

Insurance is an essential procedure in international trade. In international trade, goods forwarded from the place of shipment to the destination usually have to undergo long-distance transportation in addition to warehousing, loading and unloading, in the course of which they are subject to various kinds of unexpected risks and may sustain loss or damage.

In order to have themselves compensated for any conceivable losses of their goods, the importer or the exporter should cover transportation insurance with their underwriters prior to shipment.

2. 中国人民保险公司

A. The People' Insurance Company of China (PICC), established in 1949, is the sole state-owned insurance organization in China.

B. It underwrites almost all kinds of insurance.

C. The PICC has its own insurance clauses, known as the China Insurance Clauses (CIC).

D. The PICC has become the practice of our foreign trade corporations to have their imports insured with the PICC.

3. 海运的主要三种险别

A. Free from Particular Average (F. P. A.)

B. With Average (W. A.) or with Particular Average (W. P. A.)

C. All Risks

4. 常见的一般附加险

A. T.P.N.D.( Theft, Pilferage & Non-delivery)

B. Fresh Water &/or　Rain Damage Risk

C. Shortage Risk

D. Intermixture & Contamination Risks

E. Leakage Risk

F. Clash & Breakage Risks

G. Taint of Odor Risk

H. Sweating & Heating Damage

I. Hook Damage Risk

J. Rust Risk

K. Break of Packing Risk

一问一答

## Asks

1. What is insurance?

2. What is the purpose of insurance?

3. When was the People's Insurance Company of China established?

4. What are the basic risks package?

5. What are the general additional risks?

6. Whom should an insurance claim be submitted to?

7. What documents must be presented in order to substantiate an ordinary average claim?

## Answers

1. Insurance is an essential procedure in international trade. In international trade, goods forwarded from the place of shipment to the destination have usually to undergo long-distance transportation in addition to warehousing, loading and unloading, in the course of which they are subject to various kinds of unexpected risks and may sustain loss or damage.

2. In order to have themselves compensated for any conceivable losses of their goods, the importer or the exporter should cover transportation insurance with their underwriters prior to shipment.

3. In 1949

4. A. Free from Particular Average (F. P. A.)

   B. With Average (W. A.) or with Particular Average (W. P. A.)

   C. All Risks

5. A. T.P.N.D.( Theft, Pilferage & Non-delivery)

   B. Fresh Water &/or Rain Damage Risk

   C. Shortage Risk

   D. Intermixture & Contamination Risks

   E. Leakage Risk

   F. Clash & Breakage Risks

   G. Taint of Odor Risk

   H. Sweating & Heating Damage

   I. Hook Damage Risk

   J. Rust Risk

   K. Break of Packing Risk

6. To the insurance company or its agent.

7. Insurance policy or certificate, bill of lading, original invoice, survey report, master's protest and statement of claim.

**难点解析**

1. order

（1）*n.* 订单；订货　（常用于句型 "place an order with sb. for sth."）

　*e.g.* We are glad to place an order with you for 50 cases Black Tea.

　　　我们乐于向你方订购红茶 50 箱。

　　　We'll accept your order if partial shipments are allowed.

　　　如果允许分批装运，我们可接受订单。

　　　We recommend a trial order of 10 tons.

　　　建议试订 10 吨看看。

　　　If the first order is satisfactorily executed, many repeat orders will follow.

　　　如果首批订单执行得令人满意，续订将源源不断。

*n.* 订购的货物

　*e.g.* How long does it normally take you to ship an order?

　　　通常需要多少时间可以装运所订的货？

　　　The order will be completed in three shipments.

　　　全部订货可分三批运完。

　　　Please rush shipment because our buyers are in urgent need of this order.

　　　因我方买主急需此笔订货，请从速发运。

　　　We expect to ship your order No. 10 sometime next week.

　　　我们预计在下周内将你方第 10 号订单货物运出。

（2）*v.* 订购；订

　*e.g.* If you order immediately we can probably collect this quantity.

　　　如你方立即订购，我方也许能收集到此数量。

（3）常用搭配

in order　妥当；整齐无误

　*e.g.* You'll find the documents in order.

　　　你方将会发现，各项单据齐全无误。

make… to order　定做

　*e.g.* If you do desire, we should be pleased to make these products to your order.

　　　如果你方确有要求，我们乐意为你定做这些产品。

in good ( bad) order　情况良好（不好）

　*e.g.* The goods arrived in bad order.

　　　到货情况不佳。

to one's order　以……为抬头；凭……指示

　*e.g.* We enclose a check for USD 100 to your order.

　　　兹附寄 100 美元支票一纸，以你方为抬头。

　　　The bank usually requires a B/L made out to order and blank endorse.

银行往往要求空白抬头、空白背书的提单。

2. with regard to：in regard to, as to, about, with reference to  关于，至于；在……方面，就……而论

　　*e.g.* With regard to insurance, we'd like you to have our goods insured against All Risks with PICC.

　　　至于保险，我方想请贵方向中国人民保险公司投保一切险。

　　　With regard to weight, lighter fabrics are generally more critical than heavier fabrics.

　　　就重量而言，较轻的织物一般比较重的织物更苛求。

3. beneficiary：受益人，受惠者

　　*e.g.* The suburb has been the accidental beneficiary of a large restoration program.

　　　这个郊区是一项大规模重建计划的意外受益者。

4. for the sake of：为……起见

　　for the sake of good order  为手续完备起见

　　*e.g.* For good order's sake, the sellers send the Sales Contract to the buyers to be signed.

　　　为手续完备，卖方将销售合同寄买方要求签字。

5. on behalf of

　（1）代表……一方

　　*e.g.* On behalf of my colleagues, and myself, I'd like to give a warm welcome to you all.

　　　我愿意代表我的同事并以我个人的名义向大家表示热烈的欢迎。

　（2）为了……的利益；为了

　　*e.g.* Volunteers have been working hard on behalf of the poor.

　　　志愿者一直在为穷人的利益而努力工作着。

6. approval：affirm, agree 同意，批准，赞成

　　*e.g.* The plan is likely to meet with the approval of the minister.

　　　计划很可能会得到部长的批准。

　　　Give formal approval to a proposal.

　　　正式批准一项提案。

7. insurance：an agreement by contract to pay money in case of a misfortune such as damage, loss or accident  保险

　　*e.g.* We can arrange insurance on your behalf.

　　　我们可以为贵方办理保险。

　　　Insurance is to be covered (effected/ taken up) by the seller on the subject article against All Risks for 110% of the invoice value.

　　　标题商品由卖方按发票金额 110%投保一切险。

8. insurer：one that insures, especially an insurance underwriter  保险人

9. on a CFR basis：以成本加运费方式

　　*e.g.* That order was placed on CFR basis.

　　　那个订单是按成本加运费订购的。

10. effect

（1）*n.* 效果；影响；作用

　　*e.g.* The price fluctuation will have an unfavorable effect on the market.

　　　　这一价格波动将对市场产生不利影响。

（2）*v.* 完成；实现；进行；办理

　　*e.g.* Shipment will be effected immediately.

　　　　装运即告完成。

　　　　The seller is responsible to effect insurance for 110% of the invoice value.

　　　　卖方负责按发票金额 110%投保。

　　　　At present, supply can be effected only in small quantities.

　　　　目前仅能供应少量货物。

　　　　Payment is to be effected by a confirmed, irrevocable sight L/C.

　　　　货款须以保兑的、不可撤销的即期信用证支付。

　　　　Please effect amendment to the L/C at once.

　　　　请立即修改信用证。

　　　　We hope we'll be able to effect our purpose.

　　　　我们希望能够实现我们的目的。

（3）常用短语：

in effect：实际上；有效

　　*e.g.* He is in effect a qualified manager.

　　　　他实际上是个称职的经理。

　　　　The import regulation is still in effect.

　　　　进口规定仍然有效。

take effect (come into effect / go into effect)：生效

　　*e.g.* The newly-adjusted prices shall take effect from (on) October 1.

　　　　新调整的价格从 10 月 1 日起生效。

to the effect that 大意是说

　　*e.g.* Information has been received to the effect that you are inspecting the goods.

　　　　有消息说你方正在验货。

　　　　We have cabled you to the above effect.

　　　　我们已按上述意思给你去电。

11. insure

（1）cover with insurance 保险；投保

insure… with…against…for… 为某物向（保险公司）以（金额）投保……险

　　*e.g.* She insured her house against fire.

　　　　她给自己的房屋保了火险。

　　　　We have insured the shipment F.P.A. and against War Risk.

　　　　我们已为这批货投保了平安险和战争险。

We have insured at (or for) 110% of the invoice value.

我们已按发票金额 110%投保。

（2）为……保险

*e.g.* Please insure us on the following goods.

请为我们投保下列货物。

Every company insures itself against loss or damage to its property.

每个公司都为自己的财产保险。

（3）(= ensure) 保证；担保

*e.g.* Your help insured us the success of our business.

你们的帮助保证了我们业务上的成功。

Carefulness will insure you against further errors in packing.

细心一些担保你们不再出包装差错。

12. at your end：for your account 在你处，由你方付费

*e.g.* We now desire to have the consignment insured at your end.

我方欲使货物在贵方投保。

13. premium：a payment made to buy insurance 保险金、保费

*e.g.* Since the premium varies with the extent of insurance, extra premium is for the buyer's account, should additional risks be covered.

因为保险费随保险范围的不同而不同，如果买方要求投保附加险，额外的保险费应该由买方承担。

This risk is coverable at a premium of 0.25%.

该险别的保险费是 0.25%。

14. draw

（1）草拟；制定

*e.g.* The contract is being drawn up.

合同正在草拟之中。

We'll draw up the agreement in a day or two.

我们将在一两天内起草协议。

The terms were drawn from the most common practices of international trade.

这些术语是按国际贸易中最常见的惯例拟定的。

Technical committee shall draw up a report of all its sessions.

技术委员会对其每一届会议均应起草一份报告书。

（2）开出（汇票）

*e.g.* You may draw a clean draft on us for the value of this sample shipment.

你方可向我开出光票，收取这批样货价款。

The balance of USD 110 has been drawn at sight on you.

我们已开出即期汇票，向你方索取金额 110 美元。

We will draw on you for the expenses.

我们将开出汇票向你方索取费用。

We will draw D/P against your purchase.

对你方购货，我们将按付款交单方式收款。

He drew a check on his New York Bank.

他开了一张自己在纽约银行的支票。

15. as per：according to　按照，依据

*e.g.* as per the instructions specified in your letter

按照信中指示

We are prepared to quote you our lowest price for tableware as per your enquiry of October 30.

我方打算按你方 10 月 30 日询盘报餐具最低价。

Please pack these equipments as per our packing instructions.

请按我方包装要求包装这些设备。

We have extended the offer as per your request.

我们已按你方要求将报盘展期。

The order will be executed as per the terms agreed。

订单将按商定的条款执行。

16. insured：the party who stands to benefit from an insurance policy　投保人，被保险人

17. invoice value：the value of invoice　发票价值

*e.g.* The goods should be covered for 150% of invoice value against All Risks.

保险须按照发票价值的 150%投保一切险。

18. shipment

（1）装运

*e.g.* The goods are well ready for shipment.

货物已备妥待运。

Please arrange shipment of the goods booked by us with the least possible delay.

请尽快装运我们所订的货物。

（2）装运期

*e.g.* The best shipment we can make is next month.

我们所能做到的最早船期是下月。

You are requested to extend shipment 15 days.

请延长装期 15 天。

（3）装运的货

*e.g.* The shipment has arrived in good condition.

货物已到，情况良好。

We hope this initial shipment will prove entirely satisfactory to you.

希望你方对首批订货完全满意。

（4）make (effect) shipment　装运；装船

*e.g.* Shipment is to be made (effected) during May.

将于 5 月份装船。

As we're in urgent need of the goods, please make (effect) shipment as soon as possible. 由于我方急需此货，请尽快装运。

transshipment 转船

partial shipments 分批装运

**拓展提高**

## Letter One

**(Asking for Insurance Arrangement)**

THOMPSON CONSUMPTION GROUP

78 Real Avenue

Sydney, Australia

Tel: …

E-mail: Thompson_group@thompsoncg.com

Fax: …

May 13, 2013

Zhejiang International Imp.& Exp. Co., Ltd.

265 Tianmushan Road, Hangzhou, Zhejiang Province P.R.C.

Dear Miss Wang,

We wish to refer to you Order No. 1003 for 50 metric tons of Pingyang Asparagus, from which you will see that this order was placed on CFR basis.

As we now desire to have the consignment insured at your end, we shall be much pleased if you will kindly arrange to insure the goods on our behalf against All Risks at invoice value plus 10%, that is, USD 60,000.

We shall of course refund the premium to you upon receipt of your debit note.

Looking forward to your early reply.

Yours faithfully,

Francis Steve

Vice President

## Letter Two

**(A Reply to the Above)**

ZHEJIANG INTERNATIONAL IMP. & EXP. CO., LTD.

265 Tianmushan Road, Hangzhou, Zhejiang Province, P.R.C.

Tel: …

E-mail: zjiie_cl@zjiiecl.com

Fax: …

May 19, 2013

Mr. Francis Steve

Vice President

Thompson Consumption Group

78 Real Avenue

Sydney, Australia

Dear Mr. Steve,

　　We have received your letter of May 13, asking us to effect insurance on the shipment for your account.

　　We are pleased to inform you that we have covered the shipment with the PICC against All Risks. The policy is being prepared accordingly and will be forwarded to you by next Friday together with our debit note for the premium.

Yours faithfully,

Wang Lili

Manager

## Notes

1. at your end：在你处，由你方付费

2. on behalf of us：代表我方

　　*e.g.* I'd like to thank Miss Green on behalf of us for a very interesting talk.

　　　我谨代表大家感谢格林小姐作了一场非常有趣的报告。

3. refund：退还，归还

　　*e.g.* The garage refunded the customer USD 10 for their poor service.

　　　汽车修理厂因服务质量低劣而退还顾客 10 美元修理费。

4. a debit note：借记账单，还款通知

5. for sb's account：由……支付

　　*e.g.* According to the prevailing practice, the premium of the additional insured value and
　　　insured coverage should be for the buyer's account.

　　　按照目前惯例，对额外的保险金额及保险险种所收的保险费应由买方支付。

6. cover：保险业，保险

　　*e.g.* We have arranged the necessary insurance cover.

　　　我们已经安排了必要的保险。

　cover：insure 保险，投保，对……进行保险

　cover the goods against 将货物投保……险别

　cover the insurance with 向……投保

cover against  投保······险

    *e.g.* Insurance company tries to persuade them to cover themselves against fire.

       保险公司试图劝说他们保火险。

coverage：保险范围，承保险别

    *e.g.* We want broader coverage to include some extraneous risks.

       我们要较广泛的保险，包含一切附加险。

coverable：可投保的，可承保的

    *e.g.* Please let us know the premium at which breakage is coverable by the insurers on your side.

       请告知你处保险商承保破损险的保费。

7. forward：转交，转运；发送，递送

    *e.g.* The letter was forwarded from a previous address.

       这封信是从先前的地址转来的。

    The goods will be forwarded to your house.

       这批货将发送到你家。

8. accordingly：按照；相应地

    *e.g.* I have told you the rules, so you must act accordingly.

       我已经把规则告诉你了，所以你一定要照着做。

    The world is changing rapidly; our plans must change accordingly.

       世界正发生迅速的变化，我们的计划必须相应地改变。

## Letter Three

### Asking for Insurance Arrangement

April 3, 2013

Dear Mr. Smith,

<u>Re: Order No. 550</u>

    With regard to our order of 500 porcelains, we have issued an irrevocable L/C at sight that takes your company as the beneficiary.

    You will be advised by Shanghai Branch of the Bank of China very soon. So you can prepare for production and shipment without any concern.

    There is an issue we want to request here. As we know, the price that has been stipulated in both of the S/C and L/C is based on CFR term, and hence insurance lies within our responsibilities. For the sake of convenience we wonder whether you could have the goods insured, on behalf of us, against All Risks, Breakage, and War Risk for 110% of the invoice value at your end. The premium charge is for our account.

    Hope this request will be met with your approval.

                         Yours faithfully,

                         Wang Dong

## Letter Four

(A Reply to the Above)

Dear Mr. Wang,

<u>Sub: Order No. 550</u>

　　This is to acknowledge the receipt of your letter informing the opening of L/C and requesting us to cover insurance for the captioned goods on your behalf.

　　We are willing to accept your request. Before completing the shipment we will insure the consignment with the local branch of the PICC as per the risks coverage and insured value you mentions. Then we will send you the insurance policy together with a debit note for the premium fee.

　　We hope we could serve your company to your satisfaction.

Yours faithfully,

John Smith

## Notes

1. insurance：保险

   常见的保险术语有：

   insurance agent　保险代理人

   insurance amount　保额

   insurance certificate　保险凭证

   insurance claim　保险索赔

   insurance company　保险公司

   insurance cover　保险

   insurance policy　保（险）单

   insurance endorsement　保险批单

   insurance premium　保（险）费

   insurance coverage　保险范围

   常见的保险类型有：

   air transportation insurance　航空运输保险

   marine insurance　海运险

   ocean marine cargo insurance　海洋运输货物保险

   overland transportation insurance　陆运保险

   parcel post insurance　邮包保险

   常见的表示投保、洽办保险动词短语有：

   arrange insurance

cover insurance

effect insurance

provide insurance

take out insurance

2. insure：为……保险，给……保险

常用的相关短语：

insured amount 保（险）额

insured cargo 投保的货物

the insured 被保险人

the insurer 承保人

3. insurance lies within our responsibilities：保险由我方负责办理

= We (The buyer) should have the goods insured.

4. All Risks：一切险（综合险）

5. Breakage：破损险

6. captioned goods：标题中提到的货物

*e.g.* We believe there is a promising market for the captioned goods in our area.

相信标题项下的货物在我地的销售前景不错。

7. premium：保费，较高价格

*e.g.* During Christmas, walnuts are selling at a premium.

圣诞节期间，核桃正按高价出售。

If you want us to insure against any special risk, an extra premium will have to be charged.

要是贵方有要求的话，我们可以为你们投保任何附加险，但额外的保费必须由你方承担。

常用的短语有：

premium fee 保险费

premium rebate 保险费回扣

premium rate 保险费率

8. serve your company to your satisfaction：为贵公司提供令你们满意的服务

*e.g.* We can process the supply material to your satisfaction.

我们可以进行来料加工并保证让您满意。

## 技能操练

**I. Choose the best answer from A, B, C and D.**

1. We are pleased to confirm _____ the above goods against All Risks for $2,000.

A. having insured      B. having arranged      C. having ensured      D. having assured

2. Insurance is to be _____ by the buyer is a transaction is concluded on FOB basis or CFR basis.

A. covered　　　　B. done　　　　C. taken　　　　D. made

3. We hope no difficulty will _____ in connection with the insurance claim and than you in advance for your trouble on our behalf.

　A. raise　　　　B. arouse　　　　C. arise　　　　D. rise

4. Please take note that the above-mentioned goods should be _____ shipment on May 31 and 150% of invoice value against All Risks should be _____ for.

　A. effecting, covered　B. effected, covered　C. effecting, covering　D. effected, covering

5. We had the case opened and the contents examined by a local insurance _____ in the presence of the shipped company's agents.

　A. survivor　　　　B. servant　　　　C. server　　　　D. surveyor

6. Furthermore, we wish to point out that for such articles as window glass, porcelains, etc. _____ additional Risk of Breakage has been insured, the cover is subject to a franchise of 5%.

　A as if　　　　B. even if　　　　C. if　　　　D. even

7. For your information, we have _____ an open policy with the Lloyd Insurance Company, London.

　A.turned out　　　　B. worked out　　　　C. figured out　　　　D. taken out

8. We will refund the premium _____ you _____ receipt of your debit note.

　A to, upon　　　　B. with, upon　　　　C. to, at　　　　D. with, at

9. We confirm that we hold the consignment covered as _____ today.

　A of　　　　B. per　　　　C. to　　　　D. from

10. We have opened insurance you ordered for USD 9,000 _____ the shipment by S.S/East Sun.

　A in　　　　B. by　　　　C. of　　　　D. on

## II. Translate the following terms into Chinese.

1.W. P. A _____ .

2. insurance premium _____

3. insurance applicant _____

4. insurance amount _____

5. insurance policy _____

6. warehouse to warehouse clause _____

7. TPND _____

8. PICC _____

9. invoice value _____

10. the insured _____

## III. Translate the following sentences from English into Chinese or vice versa.

1. The rate quoted by us is moderate. Of course, premium varies with the range of insurance.

2. Please quote us your lowest F. P. A. rate for USD 5,000,000 on TV sets from Hong Kong to Qingdao.

_____

3. We have insured your order No. 1202 for the invoice value plus 20% up to the port of destination.

_____

4. As our usual practice, insurance covers basic risks only, at 110% of the invoice value. If coverage against other risks is required, such as Breakage, Leakage, TPND, Hook and Contamination Damages, the extra premium involved would be for the buyer's account.

_____

5. We have covered insurance on these goods for 10% above the invoice value against All Risks.

_____

6. F. P. A. doesn't cover partial loss of the nature of particular average.

_____

7. W. P. A. coverage is too narrow for a shipment of this nature, please extend the coverage to include TPND.

_____

8. We ask you to insure our goods for USD 20,000 against W. P. A. with the PICC.

_____

9. 对于按 CIF 成交的货物，由我方按发票金额的 110%投保一切险。

_____

10. 这批塑料玩具我们将按仓至仓条款向中国人民保险公司投保一切险。

_____

11. 只要在保险责任范围内，保险公司就应赔偿。

_____

12. 我们应按发票金额的 110%投保水渍险。

_____

13. 保险事宜交由你方安排，但我们希望为这批货物投保一切险。

_____

14. 保险索赔应尽早提交保险公司或其代理人，以便使保险公司或其代理人有足够的时间向相关过失方索赔。

_____

15. 请注意保险只包括平安险和战争险。如果要求附加险，额外保险费由买方支付。

_____

**IV. Fill in the blanks with the proper words in the following passage (the initial letter of each missing word has been given).**

A contract of insurance, which is generally made in the form of an insurance p___1___, is one between a party who agrees to accept the risk—the i___2___, and a party seeking protection from the risk—the i___3___. I n return for payment of a p___4___ the insurer agrees to pay the insured a stated sum or a proportion of it should the event insured against happen.

There are a great many i___5___ companies in the world. Lloyd's is a famous organization incorporated in London in 1871. The People's Insurance Company of China (PICC), established in 1949, is the sole stated-o___6___ insurance organization in China. It underwrites almost all kinds of insurance and has a___7___ in practically all main parts and regions over the world. Since the establishment of the PICC, it had become the practice of our foreign trade corporation to have their imports insured with the PICC. Insurance on China's exports may also be c___8___ here if the foreign buyers consider it advisable to do so. But never should the buyers be forced to accept terms if they intend doing business on CFR basis with insurance at their discretion.

For CIF transaction, we usually e___9___ insurance for 110% of the invoice value against risks as per Ocean Marine Cargo Clauses of the PICC, that is to say, 110% is for CIF invoice value and 10% is to cover a reasonable profit and some expenses. Sometimes, buyers may request insurance to cover more than 110%. In such circumstances, the extra premium will be for buyer's a___10___.

**V. Write a letter for Everbright Trading Co. to People's Insurance Company of China enquiring about the insurance rate.**

100 箱丝绸女衫，价值 4000 美元，10 月 10 日左右将由宁波发运，目的港是新加坡，承载船只是威尔森号。欲投保水渍险。

## Read More

Exporters and importers face all the time uncertainties of loss of their goods. Therefore, insurance was invented to protect their economic interests against such risks and actual losses. Without adequate insurance, and protection of those goods in transit, international trade will be negatively affected.

Marine insurance is the oldest form of insurance, and undoubtedly, now there has been a "great leap forward" in the development of insurance forms, which almost have the items beyond your imagination. The Lloyd's has always been outstanding in the insurance world. Originally specializing in marine insurance, the members of Lloyd's, working in groups or syndicates, now cover any known form of insurance. The most reputable and well-established insurance body in China is People's Insurance Company of China, or PICC for short. With the rapid growth and development of the economy and international businesses, more and more insurance companies are now mushrooming in China.

It is customary to insure goods sold for export against the risks of the journey. In international trade, the transportation of goods from the seller to the buyer is generally over a long distance by air, by land or by sea and has to go through the procedures of loading, unloading and storing. During this process it is quite possible that the goods will encounter various kinds of risks and sometimes suffer losses. In order to protect the goods against possible loss in case of such risks, the buyer or seller before the transportation of the goods usually applies to an insurance company for insurance covering the goods in transit.

The premium charged for the insurance policy is calculated according to the risks involved. A policy which protects the holder against limited risks charges a low premium, and policy which protects against a large number of risks charges a high premium. The insurance value is calculated as: cost of goods + amount of freight + insurance premium + a percentage of the total sum to represent a reasonable profit on sale of the goods. For CIF transactions, we usually effect insurance for 110% of the invoice value against … (risks), that is to say 100% is for CIF invoice value and 10% is to cover a reasonable profit and some expenses. Sometimes, buyers may request insurances to cover more than 110%. In such circumstances, the extra premium will be for buyer's account.

# 实训项目 11

## Agency
## 代 理

**学习目标**

知识目标：了解建立代理关系信函的组成部分，掌握有关代理的专业术语和常用句型。

能力目标：能够撰写寻求代理、同意代理的信函，做到内容清楚，叙述完整，礼貌得体。

**工作任务**

### 工作任务 1

请根据下述背景资料，写一封信为一家印度客商申请独家代理：

首先回顾过去几年双方的合作，在帮助销售对方的家用电器的过程中得到了对方的大力支持，并对此表示感谢。其次提到两年前写信方提出过充当对方在印度的独家代理的请求。时隔两年，再次写信提出这一要求。最后建议对方起草协议条款。

### 工作任务 2

随着公司生产规模的不断扩大，永通纺织贸易有限公司打算进一步扩大出口范围。鉴于当前以美国为首的北美市场对价廉物美的纺织产品需求很旺，公司决定将出口范围扩大到美国市场。但又苦于公司对美国市场不是十分熟悉，业务网络关系尚未建立。公司又决定通过中国驻纽约的中国大使馆商务参赞处向当地发布信息，欲寻求一家经济实力雄厚，业务渠道广，商业信誉度较高的公司做独家代理业务，代理永通纺织贸易有限公司在美国销售纺织产品。史密斯贸易公司获悉此事之后，立即致信永通纺织贸易有限公司，要求与其建立独家代理商务关系，并告知其资信证明人为驻纽约的中国人民银行。具体联络方法为：

Mr. Smith Trade Corporation

10230 Street, New York (DC), USA

Tel: 001-8807210

Fax: 001-8807200

E-mail: smithtradecorporation@163.com

请根据上述背景资料，以史密斯贸易公司业务员的名义，给永通纺织贸易有限公司公司去函，表达与之建立独家商务代理业务关系的热切愿望。

## 操作示范

### 操作示范 1

Dear Sirs,

We wish to thank you for your cooperation and assistance over the past years in the sales of your household electrical appliances.

You may recall that two years ago we brought up the question of our representation as your sole agent for your household electrical appliances in India. Now we are writing to you again with the same goal, because we think we are entitled to do so for having built up a sizable volume of business in your products in the India market. Such an agreement would not only facilitate our sales promotion, but would also eliminate unnecessary discrepancies between your efforts when you are selling through different channels.

If you are agreeable to our proposal, please outline the terms on which you will be prepared to enter into an exclusive agency agreement with us.

We await your favorable reply.

Yours faithfully,

×××

### 操作示范 2

Dear Sirs,

Sub: AGENCY

We have learned from the Commercial Counselor's Office of your Embassy in New York that you are hunting for a reliable firm with good connections in the line of textile business to represent you in United States.

Having had many years of experience in handling textiles and enjoying a good reputation in textile business field, we know customers' needs very well and are confident that we can develop a good market for you in United States. We have owned special and well-equipped showrooms and experienced staff of sales representative who can push your business in our market.

We will be appreciated if you let us know whether you are interested in our proposal and what terms you would be willing to conclude in an agency agreement.

You will naturally wish to have information about us. We refer you to Bank of China in New York, and they can provide you with any information about our financial standing and business reputation etc.

We are looking forward to receiving your favorable response and feel sure that we will establish good business relations.

Yours faithfully,

Han Smith

General Manager

## 知识链接

1. 什么是商务代理，为什么要建立商务代理关系？

   Agency is a usual international practice that an agent is appointed to act as marketing behavior, such as selling or purchasing. An important reason for appointing a foreign agent is his knowledge of local conditions and of the market in which he will operate.

2. 怎样选择代理商？

   A. Their reliability should be good and their financial standing should be sound.

   B. The agent should have wide market connections and the sales organization should work effectively.

   C. The agent should have enough technical ability to handle the goods, such as after-sale services, etc.

   D. Whether the agent to be appointed are connected with the sale of other competing products.

3. 根据上述情况，怎样写建交函？（写作技巧）

   A. Tell them how you obtain their name and address, and express your wish of establishing agency business relations, namely the purpose of your letter.

   B. Introduce your company and your products / business scope，especial your financial standing and you credit.

   C. Your reference should be mentioned in your letter so that the receivers can learn your information accurately.

   D. Express your wishes: Looking forward to their favorable response or cooperation.

## Asks

1. What is agency?

2. Why agency business relation establishment is important to international trade?

3. When an agent is being selected, what qualifications should be considered?

4. What are the basic ways to obtain the information on financial standing or the credit of business individuals to be dealt with?

5. What details should be attended when you are drafting an agreement of agency?

## Answers

1. Agency is a usual international practice that an agent is appointed to act as marketing behavior, such as selling or purchasing.

2. An important reason for appointing a foreign agent is his knowledge of local conditions and of the market in which he will operate.

3. When an agent is being selected, the following qualifications should be considered:

   A. Their reliability should be good and their financial standing should be sound.

   B. The agent should have wide market connections and the sales organization should work effectively.

   C. The agent should have enough technical ability to handle the goods, such as after-sale services, etc.

   D. Whether the agent to be appointed are connected with the sale of other competing products.

4. Reference Bank, Chamber of Commerce, etc.

5. When an agency agreement is drafted, the following elements should be covered:

   A. the nature and duration of the agency,

   B. the territory to be covered,

   C. the duties of the agent and the principles,

   D. the method of purchase and sale.

### 难点解析

1. bring up：put forward 提出

   *e.g.* At the meeting next morning, they brought up many problems of agency and discussed them one by one.

   在翌日早晨的会议上，他们提出了很多关于代理的问题并逐一讨论。

2. be entitled to do：have the right or qualification to 有权力或资格去做

   *e.g.* Mr. White is entitled to see the documents about agency.

      怀特先生有权看这些关于代理的文件。

      We are entitled to act as the sole agent in our area.

      我们有资格在我们地区作独家代理。

3. build up：increase, promote 增长，增进，增强

   *e.g.* The wheat surpluses are building up, so we'd like to look for a selling agent in your area.

      小麦过剩的危机在不断增长，所以我方欲在贵地区寻求销售代理。

4. eliminate：wipe out 消除，根除

   *e.g.* They have drawn a package of plans to eliminate poverty in the underdeveloped areas.

      他们已经起草了一揽子计划来消除不发达地区的贫困。

      Different countries and areas should spare no efforts in fighting side by side to eliminate international terrorism.

      不同国家和地区应不遗余力地并肩战斗来消除国际恐怖主义。

5. discrepancy：difference, not in accordance with 差异，不符合，不一致；不一致之处

   *e.g.* The discrepancy in their climate seems not to matter.

      他们之间气候的差异似乎没有多大关系。

      The lawsuit was lost because of discrepancies in the statements of the witnesses.

      由于证人提供的证词出现多处矛盾，官司败诉了。

6. outline：summarize, draw the shape of 概述，概括；画……的轮廓

   *e.g.* I can now outline the responsibilities of a sole agent.

      现在我可以概述一下作为独家代理人的职责。

      She was outlined in the light of the lamp.

      灯光勾勒出她的身影。

7. agency：business or place of business providing a service 代理

   *e.g.* Agency business is very popular in international trade.

      代理业务在国际贸易中十分普遍。

8. establish：start having a relationship or to start discussions with someone. 建立（业务关系）

   *e.g.* We are writing to you to establish business relation with you.

      我们写信与贵方，以期望与贵方建立商务关系。

9. handle：deal with, to sell 销售

   *e.g.* We have handled this business for many years.

      在该行业，我们已经有多年的从业经验。

10. reputation：prestige 名誉，名声

   *e.g.* Our reputation is very sound in the line of textile.

      在纺织行业，我们的声誉良好。

11. confident：having a great deal of trust (esp. in oneself) 自信的

   *e.g.* We are very confident of the quality of our product.

我们对我们的产品质量很有信心。

12. representative：one that serves as a delegate or an agent for another 代表

    *e.g.* Our representative will visit your company next week.

      我们的代表将于下星期访问贵公司。

13. negotiate：arrange or settle by discussion and mutual agreement 谈判

    *e.g.* We will negotiate with you over the subject of the contract.

      我们将就合同一事与贵方进行谈判。

14. cooperation：things that you do with someone else to achieve a purpose 合作

    *e.g.* We are looking forward to our cooperation.

      我们期待着我们的合作。

15. extend：widen in scope, range or area 伸展，扩展

    *e.g.* They will extend their business to foreign market in the next month.

      他们下个月将把业务扩展到国外市场。

16. reference：something you say or write that mentions another person or thing 资信证明，资信证明人

    *e.g.* Our reference is the bank of China.

      我们的资信证明人是中国银行。

## 拓展提高

## Letter One

### Asking for Sole Agency

Dec. 1, 2012

Dear Sirs,

    This is to inform you that we are acting as agents on a sole agency commission basis. We specialize in the trade of household and decorative wares, such as porcelain wares, lacquer wares and crystals.

    We have been working with the Ceramics Department of your Dongguan Office and our cooperation has proved to be mutually pleasant and beneficial. You may refer to them for any information concerning our company.

    We are very much interested in an exclusive arrangement with your company for the promotion of sales of your products in Paris.

    We await your news with keen interest and eager attention.

Yours faithfully,

×××

## Letter Two

A Reply to the above Letter

Dec. 15, 2012

Dear Sirs,

　　We thank you for your letter dated Dec. 1, 2012.

　　As we are now only at the get-acquainted stage we deem it a little early to take into consideration the matter of sole agency. In our point of view, it would be better for both of us to try out a period of cooperation to see how things turn out. What's more, it would be necessary for you to test the market-ability of our products at your end and to continue your efforts in building a large turnover to justify the sole agency arrangement.

　　We enclose three copies of our latest pricelist covering all the products handle within the framework of your specialized lines.

　　We shall be pleased to hear from you again.

Yours faithfully,<br>×××

## Notes

1. this is to inform you that：通知你方……

   This = This letter

   这是正式场合的函电所使用的一种句型，属于旧式用语，但在商务信函中仍
   然很常见。类似的句型还有：

   This is to certify… 兹证明……

   This is to announce… 兹宣布……

   This is to acknowledge… 兹收到……

   *e.g.* This is to certify the account is correct.

   　　兹证明账目正确无误。

   　　This is to inform you that the goods you ordered have been shipped on board the vessel.兹
   通知你方订购的货物已经装船。

   　　This is to announce that, our previous pricelist will be cancelled and replaced by the new
   one which we enclose.

   　　兹宣布，我们过去的价目单作废，由随函附寄的新价目单代替。

   　　This is to acknowledge the receipt of your letter dated Jan.12.

   　　兹收到贵方 1 月 12 日函。

2. act as：担任，充当

   *e.g.* The general trading companies often act as intermediaries between banks and manufacturing
   　　and retail concerns.

综合贸易公司经常担任银行和制造商及零售商之间的中间人。

3. specialize：专门经营　specialize in… 专门经营/从事……

   *e.g.* We are a large scale corporation specializing in the import and export of chemicals.
   我们是一家大型公司，专门经营化工产品的进出口业务。

4. household wares：厨房用品，家庭用品

   *e.g.* We are in the line of a wide range of household wares, such as Wine Coolers, Bathroom Accessories and Battery Chargers.
   我们专营各种各样的家庭用品，例如葡萄酒冷却器、浴室用具和电池充电器。

5. decorative：装饰的，装潢用的

   *e.g.* We want to buy decorative items, such as handmade ornaments, decorative accessories.
   我们要采购装饰物品，如手工装饰和装饰配件。

6. lacquer：漆器

   *e.g.* Beijing carved lacquer ware is the Chinese national traditional handicraft.
   北京雕漆工艺品是中华民族的传统工艺品。

7. crystal：水晶，水晶饰品

   *e.g.* The most advanced, complex and beautiful crystals in the world were here.
   这里云集了世界上最先进、最复杂和最美丽的水晶。

8. ceramic：陶瓷（的），陶器（的）

   *e.g.* Pottery is a new ceramic art, so its meaning is not the traditional "ceramic art".
   陶艺是一门新兴的陶瓷艺术，因此其内涵已经不是传统的"陶瓷艺术"。

9. exclusive：独有的，专有的，唯一的

   exclusive agency　独家代理

   exclusive agent　独家代理人

   exclusive distribution　总经销

   exclusive economic zone　专属经济区

   exclusive sales　包销

   exclusive sales agreement　包销协议

   exclusive offer　独家发盘

   exclusive right　专卖权

   exclusive selling agency　独家经销商

   *e.g.* We will revert to the question of exclusive agency when opportunity arises.
   一旦有机会，我们当再谈谈独家代理问题。

10. at the get-acquainted stage：在初交阶段

    *e.g.* As we are at the get-acquainted stage, we have no intention of considering exclusive sales in your market for the time being.
    由于我们仅仅处于初交阶段，我们目前无意考虑你方市场的包销问题。

    acquaint：(acquaint with) 使了解，使熟悉；告知，通知

    *e.g.* You must acquaint with your new duties.

你必须熟悉你的新职责。

become (get) acquainted with　开始了解，熟悉

*e.g.* They made detailed investigations to become (get) acquainted with the needs of the rural market.

他们进行了详细的调查来了解农村市场的需求。

11. deem：认为（后面接 that 从句或复合宾语）

*e.g.* Do you deem our plan to be feasible?

你认为我们的计划可行吗？

Influence of multinational corporations on the host countries can be deemed a challenge to national sovereignty

跨国公司在东道国的影响可以认为是对国家主权的一种挑战。

12. try out：试用，试

*e.g.* Please try out this new product free for half a year.

请免费试用半年这种新产品。

We would not like to air our view on the plan until it has been tried out.

我们打算在计划试行后再发表意见。

13. test：试验；鉴定而进行测验，test for

*e.g.* We should use various methods to test for the needs of the market.

我们应该使用各种方法来测定市场需求。

We have tested the samples and found the quality satisfactory.

我们已经试验该样品，发现质量是令人满意的。

14. justify：证明……是正当的，认为……是有理的

*e.g.* We will draw on you for the shortage, which is too small to justify cabling for amendment.

我们将开汇票向你方索取缺少的金额。该金额太小，不值得发电要求修改。

The market report doesn't justify your price adjustment.

市场报告并不能证明贵方的价格调整是对的。

15. within the framework of：在……范围内

*e.g.* This line of goods falls within the framework of our business activities.

这种货物属于我们经营范围之内。

## Letter Three

### Looking for Sole Agency

Feb. 28, 2012

Dear Sirs,

　　Our company manufactures a range of carpets possessing exquisite workmanship and numerous styles, and available in full sizes. The carpets we are dealing are wool, silk and manmade silk hand-knotted carpets; wool and artificial full-cut carpets; wool and cotton hooked carpets; different machine-made carpets. The wool and pure silk carpets are elaborately made of fine spun silk, and superior natural wool. Our carpets with sophisticated designs, elegant patterns and beautiful colors will be at your selection and meet the need for the whole world.

With the steady increase in demand for our products in new markets, we are therefore hunting for a sole agent to represent us. The agent must be fully conversant with the technical side of the carpets and have a comprehensive understanding of all the features of the line.

Please contact us if you are interested in representing us in Liverpool.

Yours faithfully,

×××

## Letter Four

### Applying for Sole Agency

March 8, 2012

Dear Sirs,

We find from your letter dated Feb. 28, 2012 that you are hunting for a firm competent for promoting the sales of carpets on a large scale in Liverpool.

We have been well founded in Liverpool for over three decades and enjoy good relations with nearly all the wholesalers, chain stores and distributors either domestic or abroad. You can find it most worthwhile to appoint us as your sole agent in Northern European countries, such as Great Britain, Iceland, and Sweden, etc.

We have the necessary qualifications as your sole agent. Firstly, we'd like to point out that we have dealt in your products through other company for five years and our clients are quite satisfied with your carpets. The colors and styles are both fit for the taste of our market. Secondly, our annual sales volume was GBP 500,000 in the past. If you grant the sole agency to us, we can assure you that we will double the turnover.

If you wish to have more information about us, we refer you to our bank, the Barclays Limited, or to our customers, whose names we will be very glad to send you.

We do hope to hear from you and feel sure that we could come to an agreement.

Yours faithfully,

×××

## Notes

1. agency：代理

sole agency 独家代理

agency agreement 代理协议

sole agency agreement 独家代理协议

agency commission 代理佣金

*e.g.* The company has agencies in all parts of America.

该公司在美洲各地均有代理。

2. agent：代理人，代理商

general agent 总代理人

sole agent broker 掮客

sales agent = selling agent 销售代理人

purchasing agent = buying agent 采购代理人

manufacturer's export agent 厂家出口代理人

advertising agent 广告代理人

shipping agent = forwarding agent 运输代理人

insurance agent 保险代理人

*e.g.* The exporter may employ an agent who lives in the buyer's country to help promote the sales of his products.

出口商可以雇佣居住在买方国家的一位代理人，来帮助推销其产品。

3. exquisite：精致的，做工精良的

*e.g.* He bought an exquisite jade figurine.

他买了一尊小巧而精致的玉塑像。

4. artificial：人造的，人工的

*e.g.* We'd like to look for a sole agent for our artificial flowers in Africa.

我们打算在非洲寻求人造假花的独家代理商。

5. elaborately：精心地，精巧地

*e.g.* The plan to choose our sole agent in Thailand was made elaborately.

在泰国选择我们的独家经销商的计划是精心策划的。

6. sophisticated：精致的

*e.g.* We'd like to have a sales agent for our shirts with sophisticated pictures in South Asia.

我们想在南亚寻找一位销售代理人来销售我们生产的带有精致图案的衬衫。

7. conversant：精通的，熟悉的

*e.g.* The advertising agent is conversant with all the relevant rules.

广告代理人对全部相关规则都很熟悉。

8. comprehensive：广泛的，全面的

*e.g.* Her account of our plan hunting for a general agent in Russia was comprehensive.

她对我们要在俄罗斯寻求产品总代理人的计划的叙述很全面。

9. competent：能胜任的；有能力的

*e.g.* John turned out to be a very competent insurance agent.

约翰证明了自己是一个很称职保险代理人。

10. hunt for：look for 寻求，寻找

    *e.g.* The graduate is hunting for a new job as shipping agent.

      那个毕业生正在找一个新工作，即运输代理人。

11. promote：推销，促进

    *e.g.* The official visit of the Minister of Foreign Affairs has promoted the further cooperation of international trade between the two countries.

      外交部长的正式访问促进了两国外贸的进一步合作。

12. domestic：国内的

    *e.g.* This sort of domestic sports wears is very popular in the overseas market.

      这种国产的运动系列产品在海外市场很受欢迎。

13. distributor：销售者（特指批发商）

    *e.g.* Distributor can overall enjoy lower price, so they normally order a lot.

      总体上讲批发商可以享受较低的价格，所以他们通常订货量很大。

14. turnover：成交量，营业额，周转

    yearly（annual）turnover 年营业额

    turnover rate 周转率

    turnover tax 周转税，营业税

    *e.g.* Should you be prepared to appoint us as your agent, we would guarantee a turnover of USD 500,000.

      如你方愿意委任我方为你方代理，我们可以保证每年 50 万美元的营业额。

      We have cut down the price by 10% so as to make a quick turnover.

      我方已经降价 10%，以便加快周转。

## 技能操练

**I. Choose the best answer from A, B, C and D.**

1. We feel it would be better to consider the question of agency when business between has developed _____ our mutual satisfaction

    A. of            B. to            C. in            D. under

2. No one would be _____ the business if there was no profit.

    A. on            B. in            C. of            D. for

3. If terms prove _____, we think you would be just the firm we'd like to have to represent us.

    A. worked        B. working        C. works        D. workable

4. Do you think you are able to ascertain the prospects of _____ such products?

    A. sold          B. sell           C. to sell         D. selling

5. Miss Linda doesn't mind _____ a trial period of half a year for the agency.

    A. to undergo      B. underwent      C. undergoing      D. undergo

6. Miss Smith's reputation in this trade is _____.

    A. second to none      B. second after none      C. second on none      D. second before none

7. Anything less than 5% is not worth _____ because of such heavy expenses.

    A. the trouble      B. to trouble      C. being troubled      D. troublesome

8. All agents _____ this line are usually getting 5% commission.

    A. on      B. in      C. for      D. through

9. Our company knows that Miss White has local knowledge and good _____.

    A connotations      B. communications      C. connections      D. corruptions

10. What's the agency territory to be _____?

    A confined      B. limited      C. connected      D. covered

## II. Translate the following terms into Chinese.

1. sales agent _____

2. shipping agent _____

3. purchasing agent _____

4. insurance agent _____

5. exclusive agent _____

6. commission agent _____

7. general agent _____

8. advertising agent _____

9. exclusive distribution _____

10. exclusive offer _____

11. exclusive right _____

12. exclusive sales _____

## III. Translate the following sentences from English into Chinese or vice versa.

1. We have decided to offer you a sales agency in America subject to the following terms.

_____

2. Since you have no directly representative in our area, we'd like to offer you our service as your sole agent.

_____

3. We suggest a trial period of one year, if everything turns out satisfaction, we can renew the agreement on its expiry.

_____

4. We do not think the time is ripe from the consideration of the proposal of exclusive agent.

_____

5. The volume of business does not warrant entrusting you with exclusive agency at present.

_____

6. A 5% commission on invoice value of actual shipment will be remitted to you after receipt of payment.

_____

7. Regarding your proposal to represent us in the district you defined for sale of Chinese asparagus, we have decided to appoint you as our agent.

_____

8. The question of agency is still under consideration and we hope that you will continue your present efforts to push the sale of our product.

_____

9. 对于从你处获得的订单，我们将按销售净价的 5%支付佣金，另加 2.5%的保付代理佣金。

_____

10. 由于在此行业有广泛和丰富的经验，我们确信能以最有效的方式作为采购代理人代理你们的进口业务。

_____

11. 我们接受你们在代理协议草案里表明的条款，并且期待着与你们建立愉快而成功的工作关系。

_____

12. 很抱歉地通知你方，我公司的代理商已经由其他人接任。

_____

13. 我方愿意承担贵方罐装食品的代理，因为我们拥有一个广阔的国内市场和一套完善的销售网络。

_____

14. 考虑了贵方的建议并调查了贵方的资信后，我们决定依据下列条款委托贵方为中国地区的独家代理。

_____

15. 产品广告方面，贵方应尽最大努力，我方承担 50%的费用。

_____

## IV. Write a Letter.

1. 对贵方提出在南非推销我方人造皮包独家代理的询盘表示感谢。
2. 我方暂时不能答应贵方要求因为贵方的贸易量不够大。
3. 目前谈代理时机不合适，最好营业额再大一些时再谈。
4. 希望贵方体谅我方处境。

## Read More

    In the international trade, most of the business activities are negotiated between buyers and sellers directly. But when the company doesn't have a branch office or representative in one place, he (the principal) may authorize another person or firm (agent) to act as his or her behalf. Usually the seller authorizes some foreign firms to sell certain goods to the customers in a particular area during a particular period of time. There are a few reasons. The first is that it is more economical to appoint an agent than send a member of its own stuff to a foreign country. The second is that a native of any country is familiar with the market and the buyer. His knowledge of local conditions and sales channels and connections are playing a key role in promoting the sales. He knows better what goods are popular in his area and what prices the market can bear. With the peculiar advantage, it is much easier and more efficient to establish new business, maintain and develop the potential markets. Then an agent arises.

When we choose a firm or a person to be our agent, we should make sure whether he has sufficient means to develop the trade and whether the firm or person has reliable connections in that area. Once the relationship is set up, an agreement of agency is needed to bind the principal and the agent to act in strict accordance with the provisions of the agreement.

The agent is obliged to sell the goods actively and render market report. He will get a commission from the principal according to the turnover or a percentage of the price of the goods in return, maybe a fee.

There are mainly two types of agents: general agent and sole agent. Both of them have the right to sell a certain goods in a certain area under some kind of agreement or contract. But besides these, the general agent can do some non-commercial business and activities, and the principal charge for the responsibility.

## 实训项目 12

# Complaints and Adjustments
## 申诉和索赔

**工作任务**

## 工作任务 1

　　绍兴县派迅纺织品有限公司是一家专门从事纺织面料出口的外贸公司，2013 年 4 月向有着长期业务往来的马来西亚 Meng Siang Trading & Services Sdn. Bhd 公司出口了 40000 码的数码印花针织布。某天，绍兴县派迅纺织品有限公司总经理 BILL 接到 Meng Siang Trading & Services Sdn. Bhd 公司的 Parkash 先生因这批货的颜色不够明亮、手感过硬的投诉后即着手调查此事。现请你代表绍兴县派迅纺织品有限公司给 Meng Siang Trading & Services Sdn. Bhd 公司写一封邮件致歉，同时告知对方已寄去了替代产品，并答应 Parkash 先生提出的 2000 美金索赔。

> Meng Siang Trading & Services Sdn. Bhd
> (Reg No.648154-K) Jetty Awal Idaman,
> Sg Rabuan Gurab, Pulau Indah,
> 42000 Port Kelang,
> Selangor D.E. Malaysia. R.O.C. : 648154-K
> E-mail: parkash@yeah.net
> Phone: 0060-03-31015184

## 工作任务 2

作为宁波益佳玩具有限公司的采购员，2008 年 4 月你从越南某公司采购 3 万个牛仔草帽，准备出口到美国供一客户节日狂欢销售。收到货物后发现帽子的数量不对，其中的 16 箱各少了 20 顶帽子，现给对方发一封邮件投诉上述事实，要求对方立即纠正，补发缺少的数量。

越南公司的联系方式是：

Mr. Hu Weihua

11/15 Nguyen Oanh St., Ward 10, Go Vap Dist., HCMC

E-mail: deanson@yeah.net

Phone: 0084-8-9896453

## 操作示范

## 操作示范 1

Shaoxing County Passion Textile Co., Ltd.

Keqiao Industrial Zone, Shaoxing, Zhejiang, China 312000

Tel: 0086-575-84811710　　Fax: 0086-575-84811711

April 20, 2013

Meng Siang Trading & Services Sdn. Bhd

(Reg No.648154-K) Jetty Awal Idaman,

Sg Rabuan Gurab, Pulau Indah,

42000 Port Kelang,

Selangor D.E. Malaysia. R.O.C. : 648154-K

E-mail: parkash@yeah.net

Phone: 0060-03-31015184

Dear Mr. Parkash,

We are sorry to learn from your letter dated April 18, 2013 complaining about the Digital Printing Knitted Fabric we sent you by S.S. "Peace". Thank you for bringing this matter to our attention.

We shall immediately make a thorough investigation which, however, will take a little time, and shall advise you of the result upon the conclusion of our enquiry.

For your information, we arranged for the replacement to be dispatched to you upon receiving your e-mail and shall do everything we can to ensure that nothing like that will happen again.

You lodged a claim against us for the loss of $2,000 you have sustained, I took this matter up with our manager, and he agreed to your proposal in view of our long-standing business relations. We trust, there is good prospect of further development. We will make payment by check for $2,000, the amount of the claim, into your account with the Bank of China, upon receipt of your agreement.

We sincerely apologize for the trouble to you and would like to assure you that all possible steps will be taken by us to avoid any recurrence of similar mistakes in our future business.

Yours sincerely,

××× 

## 操作示范 2

Dear Hu Weihua,

We have received your shipment of 30,000 pieces of cowboy straw hats ordered in April, 2008.

Upon its arrival at the destination, the shipment was found short-delivered. We find that 16 cartons are short-shipped 20 pieces respectively. The full consignment is urgently required to complete orders for our clients. We request you to dispatch the additional 320 pieces of the same quality ASAP.

As this incident is due to your mishandling, the freight should be borne by your part.

Look forward to your soonest reply.

Best regards,

Frank

### 知识链接

1. How many types of complaints and claims in summary?

   The genuine complaints and claims  真诚的申诉与索赔

   The false complaints and claims  虚假的申诉与索赔

2. If the two parties can not reach a settlement amicably, what will they do?

   In international business, when no amicable settlement can be reached between the buyer and the seller, the disputes may be referred to a tribunal of their own choice. This method of settling disputes is called arbitration.

   Arbitration is a means of settling disputes between the two parties through the medium of a third party, whose decision on the dispute is final and binding. Generally speaking, the parties concerned should pay attention to concerning arbitration while signing a business contract.

3. How to lodge a claim successfully?

Correct negotiation strategies will guarantee successful claims.

Correct evidence is most important in claims. The buyer should lodge a claim after a thorough and careful investigation into the matter, and try to discuss the reasonable settlement with the seller. Try to discuss the problems from the points of the other side.

**一问一答**

1. 什么情况下写投诉和索赔信函?

   When the importer finds the wrong goods delivered, the quality below the requirements as specified in the sales contract, the discrepancy between delivered goods and samples, the arrived goods in damaged conditions, and so on, he will be unhappy and disappointed and make complaints.

2. 买家在发现货物有问题时应该怎么做?

   The buyer should look into the matter. If the loss is not serious, and does not influence the sale, the buyer may just write a complaint to arouse the seller's attention to avoid the matter happening again. If the loss is serious, the buyer may find the necessity of lodging a claim against the seller.

3. 投诉/索赔内容的信函应该包含哪些方面?

   (a) In the beginning of the letter, the buyer should present the problem suffered in detail. The presentation should include: the date of the order, the date of the delivery, name and quantity of goods, the contract number or any other information that help the reader easily check the order.

   (b) Mention the inconvenience and ask for an explanation.

   (c) Present the evidence such as the survey report issued by the local authorities.

   (d) Suggest how to deal with the matter

4. 解决投诉/索赔内容的信函包含哪些方面?

   (a) Apologize for the inconvenience caused to the buyer as soon as receiving the complaints or claims.

   (b) Decide whether the complaint is justified. If so, the seller should admit it readily and explain the reasons of the problems on the ground of investigation. There is no need for the seller to go into a long story of how the mistake was made.

   (c) Present the adjustment methods in detail and promise no mistakes happening again.

   (d) Hope to cooperate with the buyer again in the future.

5. 如果拒绝索赔，卖主回复时应该注意哪些方面?

   If the complaints and claims made by the buyer are not justified, the seller should point out politely and in an agreeable manner. It would be a wrong policy to reject the buyer's request without thinking. The kind of letter should begin with your regret for the trouble caused and present sufficient evidence and reasons to support your rejection. In the end of the letter, the seller should tell the buyer that you are ready to give help for the early settlement of the problem.

## 难点解析

1. complain：抱怨，诉苦；申诉，控诉，抗议

   *e.g.* I'm phoning to complain about the product.

   我打电话投诉产品问题。

   The American couple complained about the high cost of visiting Europe.

   这对美国夫妇抱怨到欧洲旅行的花销太高。

2. attention：注意，注意力

   receive one's immediate attention  得到迅速办理

   *e.g.* You can rely on us to your order immediate attention.

   请相信，我们对贵公司的订货将予以迅速办理。

3. for your information：仅供你方参考；顺便告之

   *e.g.* For your information, we are going to place another 5,000 yards of the captioned goods.

   顺便告之，我们打算再订 5000 码标题项下的货物。

4. arrange for：安排

   replacement  替换货

5. claim：索赔

   claim for damage (poor packing)  因破损（包装不良）提出索赔

   claim a compensation of the shipment from somebody for something

   claim on / against somebody  向……提出索赔

   lodge a claim against somebody for short-weight on something  因货物短重而向……提出索赔

   accept a claim  接受索赔

   settle a claim  解决索赔

   entertain a claim  受理索赔

   admit a claim  同意索赔

   dismiss a claim  驳回索赔

   reject a claim  拒绝索赔

   relinquish a claim  撤回索赔

   waive a claim  放弃索赔

   withdraw a claim  撤回索赔

   claim on account of damage  因损坏而索赔

   claim for damage  由于损坏而索赔

   claim for financial loss  要求经济损失的诉权

   claim for inferior quality  因质量低劣而索赔

   claim for payment  要求付款的诉权

   claim for proceeds  要求赔偿货款

claim for short delivery　因短装而索赔

*e.g.* 因短重买方对这批货物提出 3000 美金的索赔。

Buyers have lodged a claim on this shipment for USD 3,000 for short weight.

你方为我订单提供的货物质量与双方同意的规格不符。因此，我们须向你方提出索赔，金额为 4500 美元。

The quality of your shipment for our order is not in conformity with the agreed specifications. We must therefore lodge a claim against you for the amount of $4,500.

由于你方未能按时交货，我方将向你方提出由此而遭受的全部损失的索赔。

We shall lodge a claim for all the losses incurred as a consequence of your failure to ship our order in time.

6. take up sth. with sb.：向某人提出某事

7. recurrence：再发生

*e.g.* 这样的疏忽倘若再发生，可能有损双方的友好贸易关系。

A recurrence of such an oversight could impair our amicable relations.

## 拓展提高

## Letter One

Dear Sirs，

Our Order No. 291

We duly received the documents and took delivery of the goods on arrival of S/S "Prince" at Rotterdam. We are much obliged to you for the prompt execution of this order.

We regret to inform you that everything appears to be correct and in good condition except in case No. 51. Unfortunately when we opened this case we found it contained completely different articles. We can only presume that the contents of this case were for another order.

As we are badly in need of the goods we ordered to complete deliveries to our new customers, we must ask you to substitute them with right goods immediately. We attach a list of the contents of Case No. 51. Please check this with our Order and the copy of your Invoice.

In the meantime we are holding the above case at your disposal.

Please treat the matter as urgent. We trust you will find no difficulty in settling this matter and bring the case to a satisfactory close soon.

Yours faithfully,

×××

## Letter Two

Dear Sirs，

Your Order No. 291 per S/S "Prince"

Thank you for your e-mail of May 20 and we are glad to know that the consignment was delivered promptly，but much to our regret, Case No. 8 did not contain the goods you ordered.

On going into the matter we found that the mistake was indeed made due to a confusion of numbers when the goods were packed，and now we have arranged for the right goods to be dispatched to you. The relative documents will be sent to you as soon as they are ready. We shall be grateful if you will keep Case No. 5 and contact the local agents of World Transport Ltd., our forwarding agent，whom we have instructed accordingly.

We have already sent a fax to inform you of this, and now enclose a copy of the fax.

Please accept our apologies for the trouble caused to you by the mistake.

Yours faithfully,

×××

## Notes

1. take delivery：提货

2. execution of the order：执行订单

3. appear：似乎

   *e.g.* You appear to have misunderstood our intention.

   你方似乎误解了我们的意图。

   There appears to have been a mistake.

   其中似乎有误。

4. appear to be correct：似乎正确

5. presume：猜想；认为；推测

   *e.g.* We presume you can make us attractive prices.

   我们认为你方能给我们一个具有吸引力的价格。

6. substitute：代替；以……代替

   substitution 代替

   *e.g.* If you cannot go yourself，please find someone to substitute for you.

   如果你不能去，请找人代替你。

   We cannot agree to the proposed substitution because the substitute suggested does not suit the purpose.

我们不同意提议的代替办法，因为它不能解决根本问题。

7. at one's disposal：由某人使用(支配，处理等)

　　*e.g.* We will try our every means at our disposal to turn out the goods in a month.
　　　　我们将竭尽全力在一个月内完成这批货物的生产。
　　　　We are holding the goods wrongly delivered at your disposal.
　　　　我们将保留错发的货物由你方处理。
　　　　The whole parcel is quite useless to us and we hold the goods at your disposal pending your reply. Meanwhile, we are warehousing them at your expense.
　　　　整批货物都已无用处，你方回复前，我方将代为保存该货，等候处理。现在已仓贮，费用由你方负担。

8. treat the matter as urgent：把此事视为紧急事件

9. bring the case to a satisfactory close：给此事一个满意的结局

10. go into the matter：调查；研究

11. confusion of numbers：号码混乱；号码混淆

　　*e.g.* In order to clear up the confusion that existed in the international trade, the International Chamber of Commerce drew up a set of standard terms and definitions in l933 and revised them in l980.
　　　　为了避免国际贸易中的混乱局面，国际商会于 1933 年起草了一系列标准价格术语和定义，并在 1980 年作过一次修改。

12. dispatch：发运；发送；

　　*e.g.* We are pleased to inform you that your order has been duly dispatched.
　　　　我们欣然通知你方所订货物已按时发运。
　　　　The samples you required have been dispatched by air.
　　　　你方索要的样品已空运。

## Letter Three

Dear Sirs，

S.S. "Blue Sky"—Rice

　　We refer to S/C No. 872 in connection with the chemical fertilizer shipped per S.S. "Blue Sky". After inspection of the goods discharged at Dalian, we found that 8 bags were broken, and there was a shortweight of l,357 M/T.

　　We have just received the survey report from the Dalian CIQ evidencing the broken bags being due to improper packing, for which the suppliers are definitely responsible.

　　On the strength of the Dalian CIQ's survey report, therefore we are now lodging claims with you as follows:

| Claim for | Claim Number |
| --- | --- |
| Short—weight | USD 780.00 |

| Plus survey charges | USD 120.00 |
| Total Amount of claim | USD 900.00 |

In order to support our claims，we are sending you herewith one copy of Inspection Certificate together with our Statement of Claims which amount to USD 900.00.

Please give our claim your most favorable consideration and let us have your settlement at an early date.

Yours faithfully,

Enclosures: As stated.

## Letter Four

Dear Sirs，

S/C No.872—Chemical fertilizer

We are in receipt of your letter of March 22，with enclosures，claiming for shortweight and inferior quality of the consignment of chemical fertilizer shipped per S.S. "Blue Sky". We wish to express our deepest regret over the unfortunate incident. You must have had much difficulty in meeting the orders of your clients.

After carefully looking into the matter at the warehouse，we have found that 5 bags of our chemical fertilizer had not been properly packed in 5-ply strong paper gabs as stipulated in the contract, thus resulting in the breakage during in transit. This was due entirely to the negligence on the part of the warehouse managers, for which we, exporters, tender our apologies.

But we weighed at the time of loading and the quality was up to standard. We really cannot account for the reason of your complaint for shortweight. But since the goods were examined by Dalian CIQ，we have no choice but accept your claims as tendered.

We therefore enclose our check No.872 for USD 900 in full and final settlement of your claim.

Please accept our sincere apologies for the delay in delivery and the trouble which may have been caused to both the consignees and yourselves.

We assure you of our best services at all times.

## Notes

1. per prep.：由……装运走(从出口商的角度上看是"运走")

ex prep.：由……装运来(从进口商的角度上看是"运来")

*e.g.* We have shipped the 100 tons of wool per S.S "Rose".

我们通过"玫瑰号"装运走了 100 吨羊毛。

We have received the shipment of l00 tons of wool ex S.S "Rose".

我们收到了"玫瑰号"装运来的 100 吨羊毛。

2. discharge：卸货；履行

　　discharge cargo from a ship　从船上卸下货物

　　discharge a ship of the cargo　把货卸下船

　　discharge sb. from an obligation　免除某人的义务

　　discharge one's duty　履行职责

　　discharge oneself of one's duty　履行职责

　　discharge one's debt　清偿债务

　　discharge receipt　卸货收据

　　port of discharge　卸货港

　　e.g. They discharged the cargo at New York.

　　　　他们在纽约港卸货。

　　　　The chimney discharges smoke.

　　　　烟雾从烟囱排除。

　　　　The boss discharged him because of habitual absenteeism.

　　　　因为他习惯性旷工，老板解雇了他。

　　　　The judge found him not guilty and discharged him.

　　　　法官裁决他无罪而释放了他。

4. short-weight *n.* 短重

　　short delivery *n.* 短交；缺交

　　short shipment *n.* 短装；装载不足

　　short-calculated *adj.* 少算的

　　short-delivered *adj.* 短交；缺交

　　short-established *adj.* 少开

　　short-invoiced *adj.* 发票少开

　　short-landed *adj.* 短卸

　　short-opened *adj.* 少开

　　short-paid *adj.* 少付

　　short-shipped *adj.* 短装

　　e.g. We have to lodge a claim against you for a short-weight of 5 tons.

　　　　由于短重五吨，我们必须向你们提出索赔。

　　　　After taking delivery of the goods，we find a short delivery of 130 lbs in weight.

　　　　我方提货后发现货物短交 130 磅。

　　　　Our commission on this order is short-calculated.

　　　　本次订货的佣金少算了。

　　　　The short-delivered goods you alleged might have occurred during transit，and that is a matter over which we cannot exercise control.

你方提出的货物短交问题，可能发生在运输途中，而这是我方无法控制的。

Your L/C is short-opened to the amount of $125.

你方信用证少开了 125 美元。

The shipment is short-invoiced by $315.

此批货物的发票少开了 315 美元。

Since the loss is not negligible，we request that you make up the short-landed goods promptly.

由于这笔损失非同小可，我们要求你方立即补偿短卸的货物。

We found your L/C short-opened.

我们发现你方信用证金额少开了。

Enclosed is our Credit Note No.818 for the short-paid amount of $315.

随函附上我方第 818 号贷方通知，是我方少付的 315 美元。

The short-shipped goods will be forwarded together with your next order.

短装的货物将与你方下一批订货一道发运。

5. CIQ：中国出入境检验检疫局，英文全称：State Administration for China Entry-Exit Inspection and Quarantine

Inspection Certificate：检验证明

Survey Report  检验报告

Survey Report on Examination of Damage or Shortage  检验残损证明书

Survey Report on Inspection of Tank Hold  船舱鉴定证明书

Survey Report on Quality  品质鉴定证明书

Survey Report of Weight  重量鉴定证明书

6. statement of Claim：索赔清单

7. settlement：解决；清偿

settle：解决；清偿

settlement by amicable arrangement 以友好的办法解决

settlement by arbitration 以仲裁方式解决

settlement of balance 结清余额

settlement of loss 偿付损失

settlement of claim 理赔；解决索赔

settlement of exchange 结汇

*e.g.* The question has been settled.

这个问题已经解决了。

Please settle this long outstanding account without further delay.

请清偿这笔长期未清的账目，勿再拖延。

We enclose a check in settlement of all commissions owing.

我们附上支票一张清偿所欠全部佣金。

8. on the strength of：依靠，依据

9. tender：提供

e.g. They required us to tender the necessary documents in support of your claim.

他们要求我们提供必要的证件以支持你方的索赔。

## 技能操练

**I. Choose the best answer from A, B, C and D.**

1. They made a _____ on us for the damage.

    A. communication    B. discount    C. reference    D. claim

2. We very much regret that we fail to complete the work _____ the agreed contract time.

    A. within    B. at    C. in    D. for

3. Your claim for the damage is to be _____ with the insurance company.

    A. met    B. filed    C. satisfied    D. compensated

4. The goods _____ shipped already if your L/C had arrived in time.

    A. would be    B. must have been    C. had been    D. would have been

5. Our end-users _____ the inferior quality against us.

    A. complain about    B. complains about    C. complaining    D. complaint

6. As it _____ only a small quantity, we hope you will have no difficulty in settling this matter.

    A. has involved    B. involved    C. involves    D. may have involved

7. We have lodged a claim _____ ABC Co. _____ the quality of the goods shipped _____ S.S. Peace.

    A. against; on; by    B. with; for; under    C. on; against; as per    D. to; for; per

8. Please return the wrongly delivered goods to us for _____.

    A. replacement    B. replace    C. correction    D. service

9. _____ this reason, we cannot accept your request for a replacement.

    A. For    B. As to    C. As for    D. By

10. _____ your request, please let us know your specific inquires.

    A. Should these new products suit    B. Had these new products suited

    C. If these new products would suit    D. If these new products were to suit

**II. Translate the following phrases into English or vice versa.**

1. arrive in … condition _____

2. make a complaint _____

3. ask replacement _____

4. make an inspection _____

5. take measure _____

6. lodge a claim _____

7. up to standard _____

8. account for _____

9. public surveyor _____

10. faulty goods _____

11. 收货单，大副收据 _____

12. 短交 _____

13. 无论如何 _____

14. 求助于 _____

15. 把……归因于 _____

16. 立即，不失时机 _____

17. 任由你方处理 _____

18. 迅速处理 _____

19. 由于……的缘故 _____

20. 接受索赔 _____

**III. Translate the following sentences from English into Chinese or vice versa.**

1. We regret to inform you that the goods forwarded to us are in unsatisfactory state.

_____

2. We regret to inform you that the goods are not in accordance with your samples.

_____

3. Unless the goods ordered are delivered before the end of this month, we shall refuse them, as they will be of no use for this seasonal trade.

_____

4. Upon examination we find the whole of the contents stained. A great deal of them are damaged by wetting from sea water.

_____

5. Although the quality of these goods is not up to that of our usual lines, we are prepared to accept them if you will reduce the price, say, by …

_____

6. Upon unpacking the consignment, we find that the goods are much inferior in quality to our sample and also slightly different in shade.

_____

7. We shall be glad to have your explanation of this discrepancy in the quality, and also to know what you propose to do in the matter.

_____

8. On checking the goods received we found that several items on your invoice had not been included; we enclose a list of the missing articles.

_____

9 Much to our regret, we have found that there were only 6,952 cases against the 7,000 cases

shipped by you.

_____

10. 检查时，我们发现所有的箱子短缺 5–12 千克。

_____

11. 对本件商品，贵公司是考虑退货，还是以 8 折由我公司脱手，惠请指示。

_____

12. 我们的装运单据可以证明货物在送交承运人时是完好的，所以货物肯定是在运输途中受
损了。

_____

13. 我们提供同样的材料已有一段时间了，至今未受到投诉。

_____

14. 收到你方关于收到的材料不符合预期质量的投诉，我们深感抱歉。

_____

15. 这种产品与样品之间的偏差是在正常的允许范围之内，因此，索赔不予受理。

_____

16. 我们想给你百分分之……的折让以赔偿你方……来信中所提到的短重。

_____

17. 如果损失全加在我们头上是不公正的，因为责任应由双方共同承担。我们准备各让一半，
只付 50%的损失费。

_____

18. 我们相信我们做的安排会使你方满意，期望收到你方更多的订单。

_____

## IV. Fill in the blanks with the proper words.

1. We are lodging a claim _____ the shipment _____ S.S. "Dongfeng" _____ improper
packing.

2. We wish to express our deepest regret _____ the unfortunately incident.

3. _____ examination we found that the goods do not agree _____ the original _____
_____.

4. We hope this unfortunate incident will not affect the friendly relations _____ us.

5. We regret _____ hear that several bags of the last _____ were broken _____ in transit.

6. Please take the necessary steps _____ delay.

7. _____ the time of loading, the goods _____ in good condition.

8. We're filing a claim _____ our insurance company.

9. _____ reinsertion _____ the port _____ destination, the quality of the goods
shipped _____ S.S. "Peace" _____ contract No. 789 was found not _____ the
contract stipulations.

10. We have already raised a claim _____ the insurance company _____ $900 _____

_____ damage in transit..

## V. Compose a dialogue in the following situation.

Mr. Frank from Tivoli Products PLC in Canada is lodging a claim with Ms. Cathy from Shanghai Huaxin Trading Co., Ltd. for the poor quality.

## VI. Write a claim letter according to the following particulars.

1. 由"和平"轮装运来的首批货物，两日前抵达我港。

2. 经检验，质量太差，不适合我方市场的要求。

3. 请速告我方如何处理这批货物。我们是将货物退回给你们，还是替你们保存？

## Read More

In international trade, after concluding a deal through negotiations and signing the sales contract, the buyers and the sellers assume the obligation to perform the contract. However, breach of contract by one party occurs quite often and causes losses to the other party with the result that various trade disputes are brought about, which subsequently leads to claims and arbitration.

In international trade, claim refers to a request for compensation for losses or damages. In the course of executing a contract, if one party breaks the contract and thus bring about economic losses to another party, the suffering party may ask the defaulting party for compensation according to the contract stipulation. Handling the suffering party's claim is called settlement of claim. Therefore, claim and its settlement are two aspects of an issue.

Owing to different causes of loss and differing scope of responsibility, claims may be filed against different parties. If the sellers breach the contract, incurring losses, the sellers will bear the responsibility and the buyers should lodge a claim against the sellers in accordance with the contract stipulation. If you buyers break the contract, the buyers will be responsible for the losses sustained and the sellers should tender a claim against the buyers for actual losses. If the losses or damages take place in transit, the responsibility lies with the insurance company or the shipping company, against whom claims should be filed. It should be noted that claims must be lodged within the period of validity stipulated in the contract. If overdue, claims will be made in vain.

As regards claims and settlement, all parties concerned should bear amicable, practical and realistic attitude. The case in question should be investigated in depth to ascertain the causes of the losses or damages, and the responsibilities. The amount of losses or damages and the method of compensation should be fixed on the basis of the findings. If necessary and possible, adequate documents or certificates issued by the relevant commodity inspection organizations may be provided. In a word, claims should be carefully and tactfully handled so that arbitration and litigation are not resorted to.

Claim clauses in a sales contract usually include discrepancy and claim clause, and penalty clause.

1. Discrepancy and Claim Clause

Discrepancy and claim clause is generally stipulated to guard against differences from the sales contract stipulations in quality, quantity or packing of the goods delivered by the sellers, mainly including claim evidence, time limit and settlement. For instance, any claim by the Buyers regarding the goods shipped should be filed within 30 days after the arrival of the goods at the port of destination specified in the relevant Bill of Lading and/or transport document and supported by a survey report issued by a surveyor approved by the sellers. Claims in respect of matters within responsibility of insurance company, shipping company/other transportation will be considered or entertained by the sellers.

2. Penalty Clause

Most of the sales contracts contain on the discrepancy and claim clause, but contracts for bulk goods or machines and equipment will include not the discrepancy and claim clause but also the penalty clause. Penalty clause in the sales contract stipulations that any party who fails to perform the contract shall pay the agreed amount as penalty for compensating the other party for the losses or damages. Penalty clause is usually applied where or when the sellers fail to make timely delivery, the buyers fail to open the relevant L/C or the buyers fail to take delivery on time. The upper limit for penalty may be also included in the contract. For instance, should be the sellers fail to make delivery on time as stipulated in the contact, the buyers shall agree to postpone the delivery on the condition that the sellers agree to pay a penalty which shall be deducted by the paying bank form the payment under negotiation, or by the buyers direct at the time of payment. The rate of penalty is charged at 0.5% of the total value of the goods whose delivery has been delayed for every seven days, odd says less than seven days should be counted as seven days. But the total amount of penalty, however, shall not exceed 5% of the total value of the goods involved in the late delivery. In case the sellers fail to make delivery eight weeks later than the time of shipment stipulated in the contract, the buyers shall have the right to cancel the contract and the sellers, in spite of the cancellation, shall still pay the aforesaid penalty to the buyers without delay.

## 实训项目 13

# Electronic Correspondence
# 电子信函

学习目标

知识目标：了解常用电子信函的各种形式，掌握有关电子信函写作的基本知识，写作技巧和常用词汇和习惯表达方式。

能力目标：能够撰写常用电子信函，做到内容清楚，叙述完整，格式正确，礼貌得体。

**工作任务**

## 工作任务 1

一日，宁波荣华工艺品进出口公司业务员看到阿里巴巴网站上的一则采购信息：

Dear Sirs,

We are seeking a manufacturer to produce high quality souvenirs in wood, for retail sale to the tourist markets in the UK. Details are as follows:

The item to be produced is a replica of punt, which is a special type of river boat used in the cities of Oxford, Cambridge and other cities in the UK.

The item must be produced to scale, with an actual size of about 20cm in length.

The wood must be of good quality and finished in dark gloss varnish, with a look and feel as near to a real punt as possible.

Each Punt is to be wrapped in a small plastic bag, and packaged in a simple cardboard box.

Drawings and a detailed specification will be available at the next stage of our procurement process.

If you feel you are able to produce this item, please reply with the brief summary of your company's experience of producing similar items, prices according to different quantities, and other information relevant.

　　We look forward to hearing from you.

Mehmet

Director

Visus Ltd.

Tel: 0049-40-69668379

Fax: 0049-40-69668381

Mehmetsureyya1957@yahoo.de

　　根据上述信息，给 Mehmet 先生发一封邮件，详细介绍自己公司的信息和产品信息，表达与之建立业务关系的愿望。并随附公司报价单。

_____
_____
_____
_____
_____
_____
_____
_____
_____
_____

## 工作任务 2

经过与 Mehmet 几轮还盘之后，双方确认以下交易细节：

货名：平底船的复制品

货号：BL-011

数量：2000 件

单价：1 美元

交货：销售合同签订之后 1 个月

付款方式：见票即付之不可撤销信用证

发一份传真给 Mr. Mehmet 确认以上细节。

_____
_____
_____
_____

_____

_____

_____

_____

_____

_____

_____

**操作示范**

## 操作示范 1

From: Davidwang1977@163.com

To: Mehmetsureyya1957@yahoo.de

Subject: quotation for a replica of punt

Attachment: quotation sheet

Dear Mr. Mehmet,

I write to introduce ourselves as one of the leading exporters in China, specializing in exports such as wooden decorations, handicrafts, textiles, bags, suitcases, headwear, footwear, traveling articles, stationery and mattresses.

Enclosed please find our quotation as per your instructions. I hope it will be of interest to you.

As for our production capacity, I can refer you to John&Smith Company, with whom we have dealt for more than 8 years. We are confident that with our experience in this line for more than 16 years, we can give our customers complete satisfaction.

We look forward to receiving your further enquiry.

Yours sincerely,

Ningbo Ronghua Arts & Crafts Imp. & Exp. Corp.

David

Tel: 0086-57487178977

Fax: 0086-5748717897

E-mail: Davidwang1977@163.com

http://www.nbanc.com

## 操作示范 2

| Fax | |
|---|---|
| To: Mr. Mehmet, Director | From: David |
| Fax: 0049-40-69668381 | Fax: 0086-5748717897 |
| Date: September 10, 2012 | Tel: 0086-57487178977 |
| No. of pages (incl. this page): 1 | |
| Subject: confirmation of order | |

Dear Mr. Hehmet,

We are pleased to receive your letter of September 8 informing us that you have finally accepted our offer. Thanks.

In reply, we confirm this order with the following particulars:

Commodity: replicas of punts

Art. No.: BL-011

Quantity: 2,000 pieces

Price: $1 per piece

Delivery: within one month after signing sales contract

Payment: irrevocable Letter of Credit payable at sight

We hope this will be the beginning of our long and stable business relation between us.

Sincerely yours,

David

### 知识链接

1. 目前国际贸易往来最常用的交流方式是什么？它们有什么特点？

E-mail and fax.

E-mail has the following characteristics:

(1) It can be communicated as fast as telex and fax.

(2) It is cheaper than an international phone call, fax, and telex.

(3) The messages, pictures and sounds can be sent easily.

(4) Many e-mail addresses can be applied for free of charge, such as yahoo, hotmail, sina, ect.

(5) It provide 24-hour and 7-day service and the message can be received unattended.

Fax has the following features:

(1) It can be communicated as fast as international phone call and telex.

(2) It does not need to use abbreviations.

(3) It is cheaper than telex.

2. 发邮件时要注意哪些方面？

    (1) Write a meaningful subject line.

    (2) Use the blind copy and courtesy copy appropriately.

    (3) Use the person's name in the salutation.

    (4) Avoid writing long story.

    (5) Keep messages brief and to the point.

    (6) Use a signature that includes contact information.

    (7) Identify yourself clearly.

    (8) Proofread before sending your e-mail.

    (9) Distinguish between formal and informal situations.

    (10) Respond Promptly.

    (11) Do not use all uppercase letters.

    (12) Do not attach unnecessary files.

    (13) Use active voice instead of passive voice.

3. 电报内容为什么要简洁？撰写时有什么技巧？

Because the charge for a telegram is calculated on its type, the number of words used and the distance the telegram has to go.

There are certain techniques of simplifying telegram messages to save time and money:

    (1) Leave out pronouns of first person and pronouns in possessive case.

    (2) Leave out preposition and auxiliary verb.

    (3) Leave out article, adjective and linking verb.

    (4) Leave out conjunction.

    (5) Combine certain words if they have a definite connection with each other so that there will be fewer telegraphic words.

    (6) Use a single word instead of a phrase or a short sentence.

    (7) Change the structure of the original sentence.

##  Asks

1. Do you use e-mails in your daily life? What are the advantages of e-mails compared with traditional letters?

2. What are the differences between writing an e-mail to a friend and to a business partner?

3. Do you know how to operate the fax machine? What should we do before sending a fax?

4. What information can be inferred with this email address: wm23@marketingman.net.uk?

# **Answers**

1. Most students use e-mails in their daily life. The main advantages are as follows:

   (1) It is faster than traditional letter.

   (2) It is cheaper. There is no postal charge.

   (3) The messages, pictures and sounds can be sent easily.

   (4) Many e-mail addresses can be applied for free of charge, such as yahoo, hotmail, sina, etc.

   (5) It is more convenient. You needn't go to the post office.

2. Writing an e-mail to a friend can be very freely. You can use smileys and abbreviations as you like. But writing an e-mail to a business partner may be quite formal. Using smileys and abbreviations may confuse or agitate him. So you should always know the situation when using e-mails.

3. Fax machines are easily found in companies. If you want to send a fax to someone, you should call him to receive the fax paper before sending the fax. If not, the fax paper may be dumped into the dustbin or goes under the desk accidentally.

4. The possible information can be inferred with an email address is :

   (1) The person who has this address may come from the UK.

   (2) Perhaps this person's company website is www.marketingman.net.

   　　Sometimes you get a businessman's e-mail address, but you don't know his other contact information. This inference may help you know his company's website and find his detailed contact information on the webpage.

## 难点解析

1. souvenirs in wood：souvenirs made of wood 木制的纪念品

   *e.g.* Then, with his knife, he began to carve all sorts of objects in wood; it was thus that Pinelli, the famous sculptor, had commenced.

   然后他又用小刀来雕刻各样的木头东西，大名鼎鼎的雕刻家庇尼里也就是这样开始的。

2. retail sale：零售

   *e.g.* The retail sales of consumer goods in urban areas reached 1,782.5 billion Yuan.

   城市消费品零售额达 17825 亿元。

3. tourist markets：旅游市场

   *e.g.* I learned that your company is going to extend business by developing new tourist markets.

   我注意到贵公司将扩大业务，开拓新的旅游市场。

4. as follows：如下，如下所述

*e.g.* Expenditure on the project breaks down as follows: wages £10 million, plant £4 million, raw materials £5 million.

该工程费用开支可分成如下几部分：工资一千万英镑，厂房设备四百万英镑，原料五百万英镑。

5. a replica of punt：平底船复制品

6. produce sth. to scale：按比例生产(制造)

*e.g.* The statue was made to scale, one inch to a foot.

这座塑像是按比例做的，大小是十二分之一英尺。

7. about 20cm in length：about 20cm long 大约 20 厘米长

*e.g.* The room is 15 feet in length and 10 feet in breadth.

这房间长 15 英尺，宽 10 英尺。

8. finished in dark gloss varnish：外涂深色上光漆。

*e.g.* The wood must be of good quality and finished in dark gloss varnish.

木材质量一定要好，外涂深色上光清漆。

9. specialize in exports：专营出口

*e.g.* I specialize in the sale of cotton piece goods. May I act as your agent?

我专营棉布买卖，我可作为你们的代理吗？

10. Enclosed please find：随函附上

*e.g.* Enclosed please find an invoice for 100 bales of cotton fabric.

随函附上棉布 100 包发货票一份。

11. as per your instructions：按照你方指示；as per 按照，根据

*e.g.* As per the contract, the construction of factory is now under way.

根据合同规定，工厂的建设正在进行中。

12. refer sb. to sb.：让某人咨询某人；让某人参看。

*e.g.* For further particulars I refer you to my secretary.

详细情况请问我的秘书。

13. have deals with sb.：和……做生意

*e.g.* We have had deals with them for more than 8 years.

我们和他们做生意 8 年多了。

14. experience in this line：在这个行业里的经验

*e.g.* We have a wide business connection in Australia as well as our many years of experience in this line.

除了多年的业务经验之外，我们在澳大利亚的业务关系也很广泛。

15. give our customers complete satisfaction：让我们的客户十分满意

*e.g.* We hope you will favor us with your order, which shall have our best attention to give you a complete satisfaction.

希望贵公司向我方订货，我们必尽最大努力使您满意。

16. Confirmation of Order：订购确认书

*e.g.* Enclosed is our Confirmation of Order in duplicate, of which please return us one copy
duly signed.

随函附上订购确认书，一式两份，请会签并退回我一份。

17. in reply：兹复(贵方来函)；回复

*e.g.* In reply, we confirm this order with the following particulars.

兹复贵方来函，我方确认订单详情如下。

In reply to your favor of the June 15, we quote you for the radio set as follows.

回复贵公司 6 月 15 日来函，兹将收音机报价如下。

**拓展提高**

## Letter One

**An Email for New Inquiry of Straw Hat**

From: tao0802@hotmail.com

To: davidcheng@163.com

Subject: New inquiry of straw hat

Attachment: quotation sheet

Dear Mr. Bao,

How are you? This is Cao Hua from Fashion France; we have bought the straw hats
from your company before.

Today I have a new inquiry, please check the attached file and fill it out and then
resend it to me.

Attention: the total quantity will be 423,000 per year, but it will be ordered in 8
times. Please quote us the price according to the different materials with detailed sample
time, production time and packaging information. Thanks!

If you have further question, please feel free to contact us!

Best regards,

Cao Hua

## Letter Two

**An Email for Completion of Packing**

From: jessie1985@hotmail.com

To: davidcheng@163.com

Subject: completion of packing (Order No. Ex012)
Attachment:

Dear David,

　　We are pleased to inform you that the Order No. Ex021 of 1,000 cartons of canned food has been packed as requested.

　　The packing charge was covered by the freight. The goods were shipped by Vessel Wilson on May 15.

Best Regards!
Jessie

## Notes

1. attach：to join, fasten, or connect 贴上，系，附上
   attached please find (书信用语)附上……请查收
   *e.g.* Fill it out and attach your check.
   　　请将它填妥后并附来支票。

2. resend：to send again 再发，再寄
   *e.g.* Sign your name on the sales contract and resend it to me.
   　　在销售合同上签上字，再发回给我。

3. fill out：填写完毕，变大，使长大；fill in 强调在何处填写以及填写的内容。
   *e.g.* Please fill out the application form and stamp with your company seal.
   　　请填写这份开票申请，并加盖公章。
   　　Fill in your address at the bottom of the application form.
   　　把你的地址填写在申请表下端。

4. it will be ordered in 8 times：分 8 次下单
   *e.g.* The total quantity will be 423,000 per year, but it will be ordered in 8 times.
   　　总数量是每年 423000 个，分 8 次下单。

5. quote us the price：向我方报价
   *e.g.* Will you quote us the price CIF 3% Marseilles?
   　　请给我们报包括 3%佣金、马赛交货的到岸价好吗？

6. sample time：样品交付期；production time 生产交付期
   *e.g.* Please quote us the price according to the different materials with detailed sample time,
   　　production time and packaging information.
   　　请根据不同的材料报价，说明详细的样品时间、生产周期和包装明细。

7. feel free to contact us：(委婉)随时联系我们。
   *e.g.* Business enquiry or comments about the web, please feel free to contact us.

任何商务洽谈或关于此网站的意见，欢迎联络我们。

8. canned food：罐头食品

    *e.g.* Our cartons for canned food are not only seaworthy but also strong enough to protect the goods from possible damage.

    我方罐头食品纸箱包装不仅可适合海运，而且很结实，能防止货物受损。

9. as requested：依照请求，按照要求

    *e.g.* As requested, we will inform you of the date of dispatch immediately upon completing shipment.

    按照要求，我们会在装运完成后立即将发货日期通知你方。

10. packing charges：包装费用

    *e.g.* We'll pack the goods in wooden cases instead of in cartons, but the extra packing charges will be for your account.

    我们将把货物的包装由纸箱改为木箱，但额外的包装费用应由你方负担。

## Letter Three

**A Fax for Marking Instructions**

Hangzhou Sunny Imp. & Exp. Co., Ltd.

Room 1109, 76 Yan'an Road,

Hangzhou, Zhejiang, China

Tel: 0086-571-82820577

Fax: 0086-57182820567

Company Website: http://www.sunny.cn

To: Smith & Company

Attn: Ransom, Sales Manager

Fax: 456-2678590

From: Martin Lu

Pages (incl. this page): 1

Subject: Marking Instructions

Dear Mr. Ransom,

    With reference to our Order No. 329 of 1,000 wine glasses, we would like to draw your attention to the marking instructions.

    The marking including our company initials, port of destination, order number, a "CAL" label and handling instructions should be listed as below:

    HS

Shanghai, China

"CAL"

Glassware, Handle with care!

Please follow the above marking instructions and advice us by fax of the shipping particulars.

Yours sincerely,

Martin Lu

Sales Manager

## Letter Four

**A Fax for Reminder for Overdue Account**

Smith & Company

84 Green Wood Street

Vancouver, Canada

Fax: 456-3678590

E-mail: smith@hotmail.com

To: Hangzhou Sunny Imp. & Exp. Co., Ltd.

Attn: Martin Lu, Sales Manager

Fax: 86-571-82820567

From: Ransom

Pages (incl.: this pages): 1

Subject: Reminder for overdue account

We would like to remind you that the following bills have not been settled:

March 7    Invoice No. 5467    USD 800

April 18    Invoice No. 5489    USD 600

Total                          USD1,400

We would appreciate it if you could make the payment by the end of May.

Please disregard this notice, if the payment has been made.

Yours sincerely,

Ransom

Sales Manager

## **Notes**

1. fax：a letter or message sent by fax; to send sb. a document, message, etc. by fax 传真

   *e.g.* They are shipped on October 15. We'll send you the shipment details by fax.

   货物已于 10 月 15 日送出。我会把出货明细表传真给你。

   We will certainly fax you an offer as soon as there is stock available.

   一有现货可供，我方将立即电告发盘。

2. with reference to：关于，根据

   *e.g.* We would like to send you a sample with reference to the last shipment.

   我们寄去有关上次交货的样品。

3. would like to draw your attention to：望你方注意

   *e.g.* May we draw your attention to our statement dated September 6 for the total amount of
   £7,500 covering your orders for August?

   敬请注意本公司 9 月 6 日对贵方 8 月的订单所提出的，总额 7500 镑的结算清单。

4. marking instructions：标记指示(说明)

   *e.g.* Please follow our marking instructions in packaging the goods.

   遵照我们的标记指示包装货物。

5. be listed as below：被列举如下

   *e.g.* The marking including our company initials, port of destination, order number, a "CAL"
   label and handling instructions should be listed as below:

   唛头包括公司名称、目的港、订单号、"CAL"图案以及搬运指示，细节如下：

6. Glassware, Handle with care! 玻璃器皿，小心轻放！

   *e.g.* On the outer packing, please mark wording, "Handle with care".

   在外包装上请标明"小心轻放"字样。

7. follow：to accept advice, instructions, etc. and do what you have been told or shown to do
   按照，遵循

   *e.g.* Please follow the instructions on the packet when you take the drug.

   吃药时请按照包装上的说明去服用。

8. advice us of the shipping particulars：告知我们运输细节

   advise sb. of sth. 告知某人关于某事的情况

   *e.g.* Please advise us of the name of the steamer.

   请告知我方船名。

9. reminder for overdue account：逾期未付账款提醒

   reminder 提醒，提示

   overdue account 逾期未付账款

   *e.g.* We regret that you have not reply to our previous two letter about the above overdue account.

   我们曾两次去函询问有关上述过期账目之事，你方迄今尚未作答，我们非常遗憾。

10. We would like to remind you that the following bills have not been settled：提请贵公司注意以

下账单未付

11. appreciate it if…：如果……将非常感激

    *e.g.* I would appreciate it if you can deliver your products ASAP.

    如果您能尽快发货，我会非常感激。

12. make the payment：付款

    *e.g.* How would you like to make the payment?

    您准备如何付款？

13. disregard this notice：忽略此通知

    disregard: to not consider sth.; to treat sth. as unimportant 忽视

    *e.g.* Please disregard this notice, if the payment has been made.

    如果钱已付，请勿在意此信。

    With the development of communication technology, telegrams and telexes which were widely used in government offices and state-owned import and export companies are no longer the primary means of communication and have already been replaced by fax the Internet. The following are two examples of a telex and a telegram.

## Letter Five

**A Specimen of a Telex**

33060 HZAIEC CN

278673 LEON UR

ATTN: FRANK LIU

TKS FR SHIPG ADV REGDS UNDR ORDR 305. PLS SEND US A CHEQUE TO COVER OR 5PCT COMM JUST AS U DID FR PREVIOUS ONES. RGDS

Interpretation:

    We thank you for your shipping advice regarding the shipment of goods under our Order No. 305. Please send us a cheque to cover our 5% commission just as you did in the past for our previous orders. Best regards.

## Notes

1. shipping advice：装运通知
2. regarding：关于；就……而论

## Letter Six

**A Specimen of a Telegram**

Date of dispatch: March 20, 2013

ABCCO LONGDON

OFFERING FOUNTAIN PEN WINGSUNG TATTUNG 80P 70P PER DOZEN (RE-SPECTIVELY) CFR MELBOURNE EQUAL SHIPMENT MAY/ JUNE REPLYHERE BEFORE 3RD APRIL

Interpretation:

We are now offering you the following fountain pens, 1,000 dozen each of Wingsung Brand and Tatung Brand at prices 80 and 70 pence per dozen respectively CFR Melbourne with equal shipment during May and June, subject to reply here before April 3.

## Notes

1. fountain pens：自来水笔

2. CFR Melbourne：墨尔本到岸价

3. subject to reply here before 3rd April：此报价 4 月 3 日之前有效

**技能操练**

**I. Choose the best answer from A, B, C and D.**

1. We are seeking a manufacturer to produce high quality souvenirs _____ wood.

    A. in        B. on        C. for        D. from

2. Expenditure on the project breaks down _____: wages £10 million, plant £4 million, raw materials £5 million.

    A. as following        B. as follow        C. as follows        D. like following

3. The item must be produced _____, with an actual size of about 20cm in length.

    A. to the scale        B. to scale        C. on scale        D. with scale

4. The wood must _____ good quality and finished in dark gloss varnish.

    A. be        B. be of        C. is of        D. be from

5. Each punt is to be wrapped _____ a small plastic bag.

    A. by        B. with        C. in        D. through

6. We are pleased to inform you that 1,000 cartons of _____ food has been packed as requested.

    A. canned        B. caned        C. having canned        D. being canned

7. _____ examining the goods we find that the goods were damaged due to the bad packing.

    A. In                B. On                C. Under           D. With

8. We would like _____ you that the shipping date is approaching.

    A. reminding          B. to remind          C. to call          D. calling

9. We look forward to _____ your further orders.

    A receive            B. hear from        C. receiving      D. hearing from

10. _____ our quotation as per your instructions, and I hope it will _____ to you.

    A. Enclosing is; be interest                B. Enclosed please find; be of interest

    C. Enclosed is; be interested                D. Enclosed is; be of interesting

## II. Translate the following phrases into English or vice versa.

1. 零售 _____

2. 如下所述 _____

3. 按比例 _____

4. 采购过程 _____

5. 报价单 _____

6. 专攻，专门从事于(某一科目)，专门研究 _____

7. 按照你方指示 _____

8. 请你方咨询中国工商银行 _____

9. 作为答复；兹复 _____

10. 售货合同 _____

11. sample time _____

12. production time _____

13. canned food _____

14. as requested _____

15. packing charges _____

16. with reference to _____

17. marking instructions _____

18. overdue account _____

19. make the payment _____

20. shipping advice _____

## III. Translate the following sentences from English into Chinese or vice versa.

1. 订单不能取消，因为货物已经生产。

_____

2. 随函附上空运提单以作参考。

_____

3. 去年我们给你方装运了价值 80 万美元的化工商品。

4. 报盘时，请以美元报最低价。

5. 希望你方按照合同条款修改信用证。

6. 我们非常遗憾地告知你方上周所订购的商品现在缺货。

7. As your price is on the rather high side, we have to decline your offer.

8. Please quote us the best price according to the different materials with detailed delivery information.

9. We are pleased to inform you that the order No. 745 of 1,000 boxes of green tea has been packed as requested.

10. I have a new inquiry today, please find the enclosed quotation sheet and fill it out and then resend it to me.

11. With reference to the above order, we would like to give the following packing instructions.

12. In your mail you asked us for a special discount of 5%. In fact, the quality of our products has enjoyed a high reputation in the world and our price has already been cut to its minimum.

**IV. Fill in the blanks with the proper words.**

1. We _____ _____ _____ remind you that the following bills have not been settled.
2. We _____ _____ _____ if you could make the payment by the end of May.
3. _____ _____ _____ our order No. 329 of 1,000 wine glasses, we would like to draw your attention to the marking instructions.
4. Please follow the above marking instructions and advice us _____ fax of the shipping particulars.
5. We are pleased to inform you that the order No. Ex021 of 1,000 cartons of canned food has been packed _____ requested.
6. The goods were shipped _____ Vessel Wilson _____ May 15.
7. If you have further question, please _____ _____ _____ contact us!
8. Enclosed _____ _____ our quotation as per your instructions.
9. I hope it will _____ _____ interest to you.
10. We are confident that _____ our experience _____ this line for more than 16 years,

we can give our customers complete satisfaction.

**V. Compose a dialogue in the following situation.**

Talking about Sales Packing and Outer Packing

Mr. Smith, the buyer and Mr. Chen, the seller are talking about the sales packing as well as transport packing or the outer packing. Mr. Smith says that the sales packing should be eye-catching to promote sales and that the outer packing should be strong enough to protect the garments from squeezing and collision due to possible jolting in transit. Mr. Chen tells Mr. Smith that they'll make sure that the packing is seaworthy, but they can't commit themselves to being responsible for every kind of mishap. In the end, they come to the agreement.

**VI. Make an English fax by using the following information.**

| | |
|---|---|
| 致：大同贸易公司 | 日期：2012 年 12 月 2 日 |
| 收件人：王军先生 | 传真编号：CE29 |
| 发件人：安妮·布朗 | 传真号：2098568 |
| 电话号码：3980888 | 电话号码：2098566 |
| 传真号：3980898 | 传真页数：1 |

主题：关于 CN18790 货物的运输

您 2012 年 11 月 30 日的传真已收到。

我们尚未收到 CN18790 货物的提货单原本。由于这批货物的估计到岸日期是 2012 年 12 月 18 日，所以我们必须在 12 月 15 日前收到提货单。

谨此致意。

安妮·布朗

## Read More

**Shipment and Delivery**

Shipment refers to the carriage of the goods from the seller to the buyer, and it is realized by transport services. Transport aids trade greatly. Transport is indispensable to import and export business. There are different modes of transport: sea transport, land transport, air transport, rail transport, etc. But generally speaking, sea transport is the most economical means of transportation, particularly when bulky commodities are involved. Now more than 2/3 of world trade in volume terms is conveyed by sea transport. Consequently, of the various means of transportation available, ocean freight is by far the most important one. In most movements of goods, usually three parties are involved: the consignor, the consignee and the carrier. In international trade, it is generally accepted that the contract is broken if the consignor (or the exporter) does not dispatch the goods in accordance with the time and mode of delivery as agreed upon between the consignee (or the importer) and the consignor (or the exporter). Therefore, in negotiating the clause dealing with the transportation of goods in a sales contract, the elements of time, types of shipping service, freight, etc., should be under careful consideration.

The shipment clause is an integral and important part of a contract signed between buyers and sellers. It involves the time of shipment, rate of shipment, ports of loading and destination, means of transport, shipping documents, etc.

Before shipment, the buyers generally send their shipping requirements to the sellers, informing them in writing of the packing and mark, mode of transportation, etc., known as the Shipping Instructions. On the other hand, the sellers usually send a Shipping Advice to the buyers as soon as the goods are loaded on board the ship, advising them of the shipment, especially under FOB or CFR terms. Shipping Advice, in general, may include: the contract, L/C number, name of commodity, number of packages, total quantity shipped, name of vessel and its sailing date, etc.

Shipment covers rather a wide range of work, besides those mentioned above, it also includes reserving shipping space, chartering vessel, making customs declaration, amending shipping terms, and so on.

# 实训项目 14

## Forms of Trade
## 贸易方式

**学习目标**

知识目标：了解补偿贸易，加工装配贸易的概念，贸易细节特点以及这几种贸易方式的区别。只有熟悉了这些贸易方式的概念，才能灵活自由地运用这些贸易方式以促进对外贸易和提高竞争力。

能力目标：能够撰写补偿贸易、加工装配贸易的信函，做到内容清楚，叙述完整，礼貌得体。

**工作任务**

### 工作任务 1

2012 年 10 月的中国出口商品交易会时，石家庄索卡进出口有限公司（以下称甲方）与 AP&T Advanced Automation（以下称乙方）达成了初步的一致，在补偿贸易的基础上进行交易。石家庄索卡进出口有限公司派出代表团赴瑞典进行考察，对机器设备表示满意。

> Shijiazhuang Soka Import & Export Co., Ltd.
> Telephone: 0086-311-89949639
> Fax: 0086-311-87628016
> Address: Room1603,
> Unit 3, Building 1,
> Han Lin Fu Di, Youlin Street,
> Qiaoxi District of Shijiazhuang, Hebei, CN

> **AP&T Advanced Automation**
> Pl 2012, Ulricehamnsvägen
> SE-520 24 Blidsberg
> Sweden
> Phone: 0046 325 66 18 00
> Fax: 0046 325 295 05
> E-mail: info@aptgroup.com
> Contact: Peder Jungmalm, Division Manager

请以石家庄索卡进出口有限公司经理 Anna Wang 的名义于 2012 年 12 月 12 日写信函，表达愿意与之建立补偿贸易关系。要求：

1. 表示愿意在补偿贸易的基础上从对方进口机器设备。
2. 表明在机器试运行后两年内分 4 批，以该机器和设备加工的钢丝绳偿还机器和设备的成本。
3. 表达与对方合作的诚意，并希望早日得到回复。

_____

_____

_____

_____

_____

_____

_____

## 工作任务 2

**Background：**

浙江华东电子有限公司专门加工生产各式电话机。该公司信誉好，产品质量可靠，做工精巧，设计美观大方，与很多国家的公司有过合作关系。英国海外贸易公司某成员，参加 2012 年 10 月的中国出口商品交易会时，对华东电子公司展出的电话机很感兴趣。2013 年 2 月，英国海外贸易公司需要在一年内生产 18000 部电话机，于是发函给华东公司并寄出 10 套电话装配部件和电话样品照片，要求其装配成成品并寄回检查其产品是否合格。

**Case 1**

华东公司收到信函和 10 套电话装配部件后立即发信函回复英公司并表明装配部件已经送到厂里，在 5 天内将装配成成品，7 天后将把成品航运到英公司，并表示质量一定让英公司满意，期待与英方公司的合作。

**Case 2**

英方公司收到成品后，经仔细检查后很满意电话质量，并开会讨论出了一些基本的协约，发信函给浙江华东公司。表示如华东公司对所提协约没有异议，产品经理将来中国进一步商讨此次加工贸易细节。

_____

_____

_____

_____

_____

_____

**操作示范**

**操作示范 1**

Shijiazhuang Soka Import & Export Co., Ltd.
Room1603, Unit 3, Building 1, Han Lin Fu Di, Youlin Street,
Qiaoxi District of Shijiazhuang, Hebei, CN
Telephone: 0086-311-89949639     Fax: 0086-311-87628016

November 12, 2012

AP&T Advanced Automation
Pl 2012, Ulricehamnsvägen，SE-520 24 Blidsberg，Sweden
Phone: 0046-325 66 18 00
Fax: 0046-325 295 05
E-mail: info@aptgroup.com
Attention: Peder Jungmalm, Division Manager

Dear Sirs,

Thank you very much for your hospitality to our delegation last month. We were pleased to take the opportunity to import the machines and equipment from you on the basis of compensation trade.

In compliance with our discussion, we shall repay the cost of the machines and equipment plus insurance and freight with the steel wire ropes processed with the said machines and equipment in 4 lots within two years after the trial operation of the machines.

Should the above be found acceptable to you, please let us know immediately. We await your early reply.

Yours truly,

Anna Wang

## 操作示范 2

Case 1:

**A letter to British Overseas Trading Company Ltd.**

Dear Sirs,

We are pleased to have received your inquiry for assembling telephones and have received the 10 sets of parts and components, blueprints, specification sheets and the photograph of the sample.

We have the honor of informing you that we have already transferred the above mentioned materials to our factory for assembling sample products. The sample products will be made and finished within 5 days.

We will send out the finished sample telephones within 7 days by airmail. We are sure that you will find them assembled perfectly in accordance with your requirements.

Thanks for your inquiry again and we're looking forward to your early reply.

Yours truly,

Zhejiang's Huadong Electronics Co., Ltd.

Case 2:

**A Reply**

Dear Sir or Madam，

We have received the sample products sent by you. After careful examination, we found that the telephones are very satisfactory. Therefore, we agreed to enter into cooperation with your firm on the basis of assembling trade agreement and summarized the essential points as follows:

1. You have to process and assemble 18,000 telephones within 1 year and deliver once a month 1,200 sets, and the shipping expense shall be at our account.

2. We shall supply with components, blueprints, specification sheets and assembling photograph.

3. The supplied materials and components shall be delivered to your warehouse at our expense.

4. We shall send over at our expense 10 technicians to your factory to render technical assistance during processing and assembling.

5. All the finished products shall bear the brand name designated by us.

If you agree to the above mentioned points, our product manger Mr. Black will make a trip to China to have a further discussion with you about the assembling business.

Looking forward to your early reply!

Yours sincerely,

British Overseas Trading Company Ltd.

## 知识链接

1. 贸易方式一共有多少种？分别是什么？

   Generally，there are seven kinds of form of trade as followed:

   A. distribution and agency,

   B. bidding,

   C. auction;

   D. commission sale,

   E. counter trade (barter trade, counter purchase and compensation trade),

   F. processing & assembling trade,

   G. futures trade.

2. 为什么要进行对销贸易和加工装配贸易？

   Compensation trade, processing and assembling trade are two common ways of trade, which are widely used in many countries. These two kinds of trade can make good use of foreign capital, technology and materials.

3. 根据上述情况，怎样写建交函？（写作技巧）

   A. inform your recipient what kind of trade he wants to cooperate with each other

   B. the details of cooperation

   C. express your wishes

## 一问一答

### Asks

1. What is form of trade?

2. What is the advantage in using compensation trade?

3. How many kinds does counter trade contain?

4. Why are processing trade and assembling trade two methods commonly used in transactions?

5. What is assembling trade?

### Answers

1. Form of trade, also called as mode of trade, is the specific way when transacting with other firms, namely how to sell or buy goods.

2. Compensation trade is an effective way to introduce and utilize foreign funds. On the part of importer, it can promote import when sufficient foreign exchange is not available and exploit foreign markets for his export goods by utilizing the sales capability of the foreign counterpart.

3. There are three kinds of counter trade: barter trade, counter purchase and compensation trade.

4. Since they are good ways of using foreign funds, technologies and materials to develop countries.

5. Assembling trade is a way that foreign trader supplies the domestic dealer with components, parts, or elements which are to be assembled by the latter.

## 难点解析

1. hospitality：殷勤好客；招待，款待

   *e.g.* Every visitor to Georgia is overwhelmed by the kindness, charm and hospitality of the people.

   来到佐治亚州的每位游客都被当地人的善良、可爱和热情好客所深深打动。

   I received the hospitality of the family.

   我受到这家人亲切的款待。

2. delegation：代表团

   *e.g.* The President named him to head the delegation.

   总统指定他率领代表团。

   Xiao Zhang has gone to accompany a delegation on a visit abroad.

   小张随同代表团出国访问去了。

3. take the opportunity：借此，利用这个机会，利用这个时机

   *e.g.* May I take the opportunity to express my thanks?

   我可不可以利用这个机会来表达我的感谢？

Excuse me , may I take the opportunity to introduce myself as an interpreter?

作为译员，我可以冒昧自我介绍一下自己吗？

4. compensation trade：补偿贸易

*e.g.* We are willing to use foreign patent technique and equipment in the form of compensation trade.

我们愿意以补偿贸易的方式采用外国专利技术和设备。

A total or a partial compensation trade depends upon your payment capability.

全额补偿还是部分补偿要看你们的支付能力。

Compensation trade benefits both parties who take part in it.

补偿贸易使双方都能获益。

5. in compliance with：与……一致

*e.g.* All the cases are strongly packed in compliance with your request.

按你方要求，所有箱子都包装得很牢固。

Audit the project quality system in compliance with ISO 9000.

根据 ISO 9000，审核项目及产品生产质量系统.

6. plus：（表示包容）外加； [口语]和

*e.g.* Work out the full weekly rent, plus your rates.

算出一周的房租外加税。

Send a cheque for £18.99 plus £2 for postage and packing.

请寄上 18.99 英镑的支票，外加 2 英镑的邮资和包装费。

7. trial operation：试运行

*e.g.* The vehicle has entered into trial operation stage.

该车已进入试运行阶段。

Trial operation of the sawer has proven its successful design.

实践表明，该热锯机的设计是成功的。

8. assemble：组装，装配

*e.g.* The workers who assemble cars work very skillfully.

装配汽车的工人们干得很熟练。

The shed comes in sections that you assemble yourself.

这个棚子有几个部分，要由自己组装起来。

9. transfer：转乘，转交

*e.g.* You can take the subway and then transfer to a bus.

你可先乘地铁然后转乘公共汽车。

It is a fast, easy way to communicate and transfer files.

那样通信、传达文件都比较快而且方便。

10. sample product：样品

finished sample telephone 样品电话成品

*e.g.* Before mass-production, please send me a sample of the finished product.

在批量生产前，请寄一个成品样品给我。

Is the product a raw material, a commodity or a finished product?

你的商品具体是个原料，是日用品还是一个成品呢？

Exactly ensure material as per order, in-processing production, inventory and finished product.

根据订单，制程，库存和成品的不同阶段保证物料的准确性。

Be applicable to hair, the processed goods or the finished product examination of loom cloth.

适用于毛呢、梳织布的半成品或成品之检验。

## 拓展提高

### Reply of Agreement of Compensation Trade

Dear Sirs,

We are pleased to learn from your mail of March 6 that you will consider compensation trade arrangements for the supply of our machines and equipment and up to now, we fully agree to your proposal.

As requested by you, we have made out a draft agreement with all the necessary terms and conditions for your consideration. Should you have any different views on the provisions, please do not hesitate to communicate with us.

Your early reply will be highly appreciated. We are looking forward to cooperating with you in the near future.

Yours faithfully,

Messrs. Carlson & Marwell

### Proposal for Payment of Compensation Trade

Dear Sirs,

We are glad to receive your draft agreement of the Compensation Trade that the price of these steel wire ropes is to pay for the machines and equipment you supply plus insurance and freight.

As to the payment, is it possible that our bank will open an irrevocable banker's acceptance L/C in your favor to cover the machines and equipment. The L/C will become valid after we receive your irrevocable sight L/C in our favor for equal amount of the resultant products within one week.

Should the above be found acceptable to you, please let us know immediately to bring the transaction to an early successful conclusion.

We await your early reply.

Yours truly,

×××

### A Processing Trade

Dear Sirs,

Thank you for your letter of June 22 inquiring about the possibility of manufacturing leather bags with the materials and according to your samples.

As one of the leading leather products manufacturers and exporters in China, we have been doing business of processing according to supplied samples and processing with supplied materials for years, in addition to our ordinary import and export transactions. Our leather products are superior in materials and excellent in workmanship. You can be assured that the processing and delivery of the leather bags will prove to your full satisfaction.

Enclosed please find our counter-sample, on which basis we quote our processing fee for each piece at USD…, including the cost of all accessories.

Delivery can be expected within two months after receipt of your materials.

We assure you of our close cooperation at any time and look forward to receiving your reply at an early date.

Yours sincerely,

×××

## Notes

1. make out：起草

2. draft：草稿，草案，草图

3. terms and conditions：条款，条件

4. provision：规定

5. at our account：at our expense 由我方支付

6. be found acceptable to：认为……可接受

   *e.g.* The leathers were found to be of acceptable quality for some types of leathers.
   结果表明某些品种的革质量可以达到国际认可标准。

   If found acceptable, your account shall be activated within 24 Hrs.
   如果发现可接受，您的账户将在 24 小时之内被激活。

7. in accordance with：按照

   *e.g.* One's opinion tends to differ in accordance with one's standpoint.
   不同的立场势必形成不同的见解。

   She was dismissed in accordance with the company's usual diplomacy procedures.

按照公司一般纪律程序,她被解雇了。

8. satisfactory：令人满意的；符合要求的

to your full satisfaction　令你完全满意

*e.g.* This arrangement is quite satisfactory, so far as I am concerned.

就我来说, 这样的安排很好。

After much discussion we came at a conclusion satisfactory to all.

经过充分讨论,我们得出了大家都很满意的结论。

9. deliver：投递；交付；递送

*e.g.* Will you take the goods with you or shall we deliver them to your house?

你自己把这些货物带走还是由我们送到你家里去?

You can contract with us to deliver your cargo.

你可以跟我们签订送货合同。

10. delivery：发送，交货

*e.g.* You have to pay a premium for express delivery.

寄快速投递你得付额外费用。

He was employed at the local grocery store as a delivery boy.

他受雇于当地杂货店当送货员。

11. on the basis of：在……的基础上

*e.g.* Have you ever do any business on the basis of assemble trade?

你们以前做过装配贸易吗?

We intend to do business with you on the basis of processing.

我们打算在加工的基础上和你方发展业务。

Our barter trade is conducted on the basis of equality.

我们是在平等的基础上进行易货贸易。

12. bring sth. to a conclusion：得出结论

*e.g.* I should never be able to come to a conclusion.

我永远也不会得出任何结论。

The discussion was brought to a conclusion.

讨论结束了。

13. be assured：保证

*e.g.* The state must be assured of the largest share of profits.

保证国家得大头。

Will you be assured of a career and adequate salary if you go there?

你到那里去能保证有事业和足够的收入吗?

14. Is there any possibility that you'll be back by the weekend? 周末以前你有可能回来吗?

*e.g.* There is a possibility of changing jobs.

换工作是有可能的事。

She cannot by any possibility do such a thing.

她绝不会做这种事。

## 技能操练

**I. Choose the best answer from A, B, C and D.**

1. In compensation trade, we pay for the cost of technological imports by delivery of end products _____ in processing or assembly deals, we charge a fee for processing raw materials or assembly of parts.

   A. while        B. when        C. whether        D. if

2. After expiration of the contracted period of two years, the supplied equipment and tools will become our property _____.

   A. with charge        B. free charge        C. uncharged        D. free of charge

3. All parts and components made in Shanghai must _____ the standards of quality, and be approved by Party A beforehand.

   A. add up to        B. measure up to        C. be measured up to     D. be made of

4. Party B undertakes to compensate Party A for the contract amount by exporting _____ cartons of canned pear.

   A. in two lots        B. in two lot        C. with two lots        D. with two lot

5. In case the delivered value of feather exceeds that of machinery equipment, Party B shall ship such additional spare parts as indicated by Party A to _____ the difference.

   A. get off        B. set off        C. get up        D. set up

6. Party B shall establish in favor of Party A an irrevocable Banker's Acceptance L/C in payment _____ the equipment _____ an amount not less than HK$ 22 million.

   A. of … for        B. to … for        C. for … at        D. for… for

7. The factory was awarded the contract for the _____ with supplied drawings.

   A. processing Gear Boxes            B. processings of Gear Box

   C. process of Gear Box              D. processing of Gear Boxes

8. We don't need the exact total right now; an _____ figure will suffice.

   A. approximate        B. rough        C. gross        D. estimated

9. There is a _____ that your quality products will sell well in our city.

   A. possibility        B. credit        C. consideration        D. potential

10. If you find a compensation trade acceptable, please don't _____ to tell us.

    A. hesitate        B. regret        C. notify        D. submit

**II. Translate the following words phrases into English or vice versa.**

1. 补偿贸易 _____

2. 好客，殷勤 _____

3. 代表团 _____

4. 与……一致 _____

5. 偿付，偿还的款项_____

6. 一批货_____

7. 加工费_____

8. 组装，装配_____

9. 商议，磋商，谈判_____

10. 草稿，草案，草图_____

11. trial operation_____

12. validity_____

13. resultant product_____

14. bring sth. to a conclusion_____

15. irrevocable sight L/C_____

16. assembling with supplied parts and components_____

17. terms and conditions_____

18. provision_____

19. processing with supplied materials_____

20. accessory_____

## III. Translate the following sentences from English into Chinese or vice versa.

1. The natives are noted for their hospitality.

_____

2. We shall inform you of the date of the delegation's arrival.

_____

3. The growth of demand reduced finished product inventory.

_____

4.This bicycle is quite satisfactory—just the thing I want.

_____

5. You can be assured that she will recover in a couple of weeks.

_____

6. They will pay about $ 673 million plus interest.

_____

7. 王先生, 现在请您谈谈这批货的包装方式。

_____

8. 这个设备已经在试运转了。

_____

9. 我知道现在不早了, 但我要转些钱。

_____

10. 我认为补偿贸易安排更适合我们公司。

_____

11. 这次罢工严重地延误了邮件的投递。

_____

**IV. Fill in the blanks with the proper words.**

1. We should make decisions in _____ with specific conditions.

2. We _____ _____ _____ to introduce our company as exporters dealing exclusively in leather goods.

3. What if the sale is made on the _____ of sight draft?

4. Performs all duties in _____ with company safety standards.

5. These examples bring us to a _____.

6. I _____ you that she can be trusted to do the job.

7. Take your umbrella because there's a _____ that it will rain.

**V. Compose a dialogue in the following situation.**

Mr. Hadavas, an official of Messrs. Carlson & Maxwell, was named to head a delegation to visit Shijiazhuang Import & Export Co. Ltd. and discuss the possibility of compensation trade.

**VI. Write a letter with the ideas given below, expressing your wish to do assembling trade with them on the basis of supplied materials, components and equipments.**

(1) Recommend to assemble 36,000 refrigerators within a period of three years.

(2) Finished products: a neutral brand. 60% to Hong Kong and 40% to Sydney.

   Shipment: once half a year.

   Shipping expenses: for your account.

(3) Payment: sight L/C, no later than 30 days before shipping.

## Read More

### Compensation Trade

Compensation trade is a form of counter trade in which incoming investment is repaid from the revenues generated by that investment.

There are two kinds of compensation trade, i.e. direct compensation trade (buyback) and indirect compensation trade (counter purchase).

Processing and assembling trade refers to the business activity of importing all or part of the raw and auxiliary materials, parts and components, accessories, and packaging materials from abroad in bond, and re-exporting the finished products after processing or assembly by domestic enterprises.

It includes processing with supplied materials and with imported materials.

# 参考答案

## 实训项目 1

**I. Choose the best answer from A, B, C and D.**

1–5: BCADC    6–10: AABAA

**II. Compose a dialogue in the following situation.**

In the first round, their conversation was as follows:

**J:** Shall we start?

**Y:** Yes. I'd be glad to answer any questions you may have.

**J:** Your product leaves me a deep impression. But I'm a little worried about the prices.

**Y:** Don't worry. Before we quote the price, please tell us the exact quantity you want.

**J:** I'm not sure still. I know your research costs are high, but I prefer 20% discount.

**Y:** No, no, no. You must be kidding. That's a big cut, and it will make us no profit.

**J:** If we promise future business that will reduce your costs for products, right?

**Y:** Yes, but it's hard to see how you can place such large orders. (Pause) We need a guarantee of future business, not just a promise.

**J:** We said we wanted 500 pieces over a 3–month period. What if we place orders for 6 months, with a guarantee?

**Y:** If you can guarantee that on paper, I think we can discuss this further. But even with volume sales, our costs won't go down much.

**J:** So, what are your proposals?

**Y:** We could give you a cut, but not 20%. We can grant 10% at most. That's the best we can do.

**J:** That's a big change from 20! 10 is beyond my deadline. (pause) Any other ideas?

**Y:** I don't think I can make a decision right now. Why don't we talk again tomorrow?

**J:** Sure. I must talk to my office anyway. I hope we can find some common ground on this.

### NEXT DAY

**J:** Yoyo, sorry to tell you that we cannot accept your quotation; let's came up with something else.

**Y:** I hope so, Jay. My aim is to negotiate hard on this order—but I'm trying very hard to reach some middle ground.

**J:** I understand. We suggest a structured deal. For the first 3 months, we get a discount of 15%, and the next 3 months we get 12%.

**Y:** Jay, I can't bring those numbers back to my office—they'll reject it directly.

**J:** Then you'll have to think of something better, Yoyo.

**Y:** How about 12% the first 3 months, and the second 3 months at 10%, with a guarantee of 1500 units?

**J:** That's a large number to sell, with such low profit.

**Y:** It's about the best we can do, Jay. (pause) We need to figure something out today. If I go back empty-handed, I may be coming back to you soon to ask for a job. (smiles)

**J:** (smiles) OK, 12% the first 6 months, 10% for the second?

**Y:** So, that's the deal.

**J:** Yes, nice cooperation!（shake hands）

**III. Write an envelope with following Information.**

China Import and Export Corporation (Chongqing Branch)                    stamp

Xilin Road, Yonghang District,

Chongqing

China, 100023



Mr. Turner Smith, the sales manager,

Hamster Electronic Corporation

8 Shenton way

Sydney

Australia

# 实训项目 2

**I.Choose the best answer from A, B, C and D.**

1–5: BBACA    6–10: AADAA

**II. Translate the following phrases into English or vice versa.**

1. enter into/establish business relations
2. specialize in
3. for your reference
4. fall within our business activities
5. enclose
6. Chambers of Commerce
7. enjoy a great reputation
8. status enquiry
9. price list
10. wholesaler

11. 一收到
12. 共同的利益
13. 商务参赞处
14. 商业信用征信所
15. 渴望，期望
16. 具体询盘
17. 主要的，重要的
18. 冒昧地
19. 关于
20. 发送、寄送

## III. Translate the following sentences from English into Chinese or vice versa.

1. 我们从一个朋友处得知贵公司的消息,很高兴告知贵方我们专营汽车配件和零部件的出口业务,并愿意与贵公司建立业务关系。

2. 感谢你方 2013 年 1 月 9 日表示愿意同我们建立业务关系的来信。

3. 我们在这一行业有 20 余年的经验,因此我们产品及服务都会令客户满意。

4. 英国联合汽车公司销售部要求我们向你们查询一家客户的资信状况。

5. 非常感谢你们的帮助,我们真诚地期待着你们的答复。

6. 从信中我们高兴地获知,你们特别有意向向我方市场运送电子机械产品。

7. We have the pleasure to introduce ourselves to you with the hope that we may have an opportunity to cooperate with you in your business extension.

8. We expect you to try our services and realize that they will meet your full satisfaction.

9. We enclose a copy of our recent catalogue for your information.

10. We shall be obliged if you would let us know if the company is reliable in repaying debts.

11. We are well-reputed exporters of all kinds of Chinese goods especially electronic and HI–FI products.

12. Although the market is not very brisk at present, we are able to do a fairly good business with you if your prices are competitive.

## IV. Fill in the blanks with the proper words.

1. compliance/accordance
2. to
3. with
4. to
5. stipulates/states
6. in; to
7. lower than
8. please find
9. Through/By
10. the liberty to

## V. Compose a dialogue in the following situation.

**Mr. Henry:** Hello, Ms. Wang. Nice to see you.

**Ms. Wang:** Hello, Mr. Henry. Glad to meet you. Welcome to Guangzhou Trade Fair.

**Mr. Henry:** You told me that Guangzhou Trade Fair is very big and influential in the world. Thousands of businessmen from more than 150 countries and regions are to trade with China. Today I find it is worthy to come.

**Ms. Wang:** Yes, meanwhile, you're able to get more information about our company and other companies as well.

**Mr. Henry:** I really appreciate it. By the way, what about your company?

**Ms. Wang:** Our company is in Wenzhou, the city of leather shoes, specializing in exporting leather shoes.

**Mr. Henry:** Oh, great. I just want to find chances to import some Chinese leather shoes but I want good quality and competitive price.

**Ms. Wang:** That's right. Maybe our products are your choice. You can have a look first.

**Mr. Henry:** OK. Er, do you sell shipping weight or landing weight?

**Ms. Wang:** Shipping weight. Prior to every shipment the cargo is inspected and weighed by China Import and Export Commodities Inspection Bureau, which will issue certificates of quality and weight. The certificates are to be taken as final.

**Mr. Henry:** I see. And what are your usual terms of payment?

**Ms. Wang:** Irrevocable L/C payable by draft at sight accompanied with a full set of shipping documents.

**Mr. Henry:** Could you make a firm offer for ten days?

**Ms. Wang:** We often offer three or four days. Anyway, in view of our further cooperation, we will do utmost to meet your requirement. Here is our brochure for you.

**Mr. Henry:** Thank you very much. We would like to have a talk for details tomorrow morning, will you be available?

**Ms. Wang:** Certainly. See you tomorrow morning.

**Mr. Henry:** See you tomorrow morning.

**VI. Write a letter with the ideas given below, expressing your wish to establish business relations with them.**

Dear Sirs,

You are recommended by the Bank of China in Paris who has informed us that you are one of the important importers for shoes in France. We avail ourselves of this opportunity to approach you for the establishment of business relations with you.

We are a private enterprise, which was founded 20 years ago, handling the export of shoes including men shoes, women shoes and children shoes, etc. In order to acquaint you with our business, we enclose a copy of our export list covering the main items suppliable at present.

If you are interested in our business, please tell us your usual trade terms and we will forward samples to you.

We hope your early reply.

Yours sincerely,

Mary

# 实训项目 3

**I. Choose the best answer from A, B, C and D.**

1–5: DBCBB     6–10: ABAAB

**II. Translate the following phrases into English or vice versa.**

1. 佣金

2. 大量的订单

3. 包含

4. 装运时间

5. 最小订单数量　　　　　　　　　6. 物美价廉

7. 由我方付款　　　　　　　　　　8. 首次订购

9. 进口值　　　　　　　　　　　　10. 各自地

11. latest catalogue　　　　　　　　12. in receipt of

13. frankly speaking　　　　　　　　14. manufacturer

15. in stock　　　　　　　　　　　16. enquiry

17. competitive price　　　　　　　18. demand exceeding supply

19. supply exceeding demand　　　　20. place an order

## III. Translate the following sentences from English into Chinese or vice versa.

1. After receipt of your specific enquiry, we will forward you our quotation list at once.

2. We are studying your catalogue, and we will inform you the products we want to buy.

3. We shall appreciate it, if you could send us samples and relative brochures.

4. We are sending you our No.143 enquiry list, please make an quotation based on FOB.

5. At present, the supply exceeds demand in our market.

6. We allow 8% discount for an order exceeding 100 units.

7. 很遗憾，你方所询的货物现在无货。

8. 现随函寄上一份我公司目前可以供应的主要商品目录，如果你方需要该表所列项内的任何商品，我公司一接到你方详细货单，将尽力为你方提供所需商品。

9. 请贵公司发来 3 吨二级核桃仁报价，九月份交货，并请注明有关各项贸易的条件。

10. 我们很想和你方建立贸易关系，但我方很难接受你们的还盘，也不能再让步。

11. 而且，我方已经将价格压到生产费用的边缘了。

12. 可以说我们的产品到处受到热烈欢迎。

## IV. Fill in the blanks with the proper words.

1. for　　　　　　　　　　　　　　2. by

3. to　　　　　　　　　　　　　　4. with

5. under　　　　　　　　　　　　　6. in

7. upon/after　　　　　　　　　　　8. to

9. with　　　　　　　　　　　　　10. to

## V. Compose a dialogue in the following situation.

**A:** I'm glad to have the opportunity of visiting your corporation. I hope we can do business together.

**B:** It's a great pleasure to meet you, Mr. Clife. I believe you have seen our exhibits in our show room. What is particularly you're interested in?

**A:** I'm interested in your hardware. I've seen exhibits and studied the catalogs. I think some of the items will find a ready market in Canada. It's the list of requirements. I'd like to have your lowest quotations CIF Vancouver.

**B:** Thank you for your enquiry. Would you tell us the quantity you require so that we can work out the offer?

**A:** I'll do that. Meanwhile, could you give me an indication of the price?

**B:** Here is our FOB price. All the prices in the list are subject to our confirmation.

**A:** What about commission? From European suppliers I usually get a 3%–5% commission for my imports. It's the general practice.

**B:** As a rule, we do not allow any commission. But if the order is a sizable one, we will consider it.

**A:** You see, we do business on a commission basis. The commission on your prices will make it easier for me to promote sales. Even 2% or 3% would help.

**B:** We'll discuss this when you place your order with us.

**VI. Write a letter with the ideas below.**

Dear Ms. Dan,

I am writing to make an enquiry on:

(1) 100% cotton cloth, color No.12, standard width 200 yards;

(2) silk of 30% nylon, color No.9 standard width 400 yards.

We would also like to make sure if you can make delivery of the above in two weeks after the June 12 and if you could, what is the quote (CIF)?

I look forward to your early quotation, as we are making an order from one of our close contacts.

# 实训项目 4

**I. Choose the best answer from A, B, C and D.**

1–5: DCDAA                    6–10: BCDBC

**II. Translate the following phrases into English or vice versa.**

1. firm offer                    2. be subject to

3. final confirmation            4. captioned goods

5. counter-offer                 6. quotation

7. long-standing business relation    8. conclude the transaction

9. terms and conditions          10. article number

11. 虚盘                         12. 专营

13. 不可撤销的信用证              14. 根据你方要求

15. 现行的价格                    16. 报盘

17. 首次订单                      18. 良好平均品质

19. 偏高                         20. 平均价格

**III. Translate the following sentences from English into Chinese or vice versa.**

1. 如果你方报价具有竞争力且交货期合适，我们将很高兴向你方订货。

2. 希望你方向我方报具有竞争力的儿童衬衫的成本、保险加运费的利物浦价格。

3. 如蒙报花生最低价，我们将非常感谢。

4. 你方还盘价格与现行市场价不符。

5. 在大量订购之前，我们想要你方产品的样本以便熟悉你们货物的质地和工艺。

6. 我们不妨在这里补充说明一下，由于需求量大，该盘有效期到本月末截止，过期后我们无法在把货物保留着不销售。

7. There is no possibility of getting business done unless you reduce your price by 3%.

8. We take pleasure in sending you an offer for 50 sets of Milling Machine Type 70 as follows.

9. We offer firm 50 m/t Bitter Apricot Kernels at USD 120 FOB prompt shipment, subject to our final fax confirmation.

10. We wish to inform you that we can supply the goods under the caption.

11. If you can see our way clear to improving the quality of our products, we may place substantial orders.

12. It is understood that a Letter of Credit in our favor will be established immediately.


**IV. Fill in the blanks with the proper words.**

| | |
|---|---|
| 1. in | 2. to; to |
| 3. till | 4. for |
| 5. of; in; in | 6. from |
| 7. to | 8. to |

**V. Compose a dialogue in the following situation.**

**Miss Wang:** Mr. Joe, do you have offers for all the articles listed here?

**Mr. Joe:** Oh, yes, this is the price list, but it serves as a guide line only. Is there anything you are particularly interested in?

**Miss Wang:** Yes, I'm interested in your embroidered table cross. It found a ready market in our country last year. So once again, the main item of our order is embroidered table cross. This time, we will have 50,000 pieces.

**Mr. Joe:** If the order is so large, we'll offer you our most favorable terms. We'll give you a 5% discount.

**Miss Wang:** Thank you. That does seem to be a nice offer. Now, what would be the earliest possible date of shipment?

**Mr. Joe:** By this coming July. Do you have any specific requirements for packing? Here are the samples of packing available now. You may have a look.

**Miss Wang:** Oh, wonderful. These three are all right, but I prefer small boxes. They are the most beautiful. You know nice packing helps find a market. Then what about the terms of payment?

**Mr. Joe:** Letter of Credit at sight. Here is our official offer with special price CIF London.

**Miss Wang:** How long will you keep your offer open?

**Mr. Joe:** Three days.

**Miss Wang:** Finc, thank you.

### VI. Write a letter with the idea below.

Dear Sir,

Thank you for your enquiry of May 5 requesting for reams of A4 white paper of different qualities suitable for poster work. We are enclosing 3 samples marked A, B and C, and technical details concerning quality are printed on each. The price for 500 or 1,000 reams of these qualities are quoted below:

| Quantity | Size | Quality | List Price (per ream) |
| --- | --- | --- | --- |
| …… | …… | …… | …… |

Delivery may be guaranteed within 2 weeks of the date of receipt of your order.

This is our very keen quotation and we feel sure that after consideration you will want to take up this offer. Our terms of payment are initially cash with order.

We are looking forward to your early reply.

Yours truly,

× × ×

# 实训项目 5

### I. Choose the best answer from A, B, C and D.

1–5: BDCDC                          6–10: BDBAD

### II. Translate the following phrases into English or vice versa.

1. promotion

2. have a good market

3. make a choice

4. current price

5. reach a standard

6. fine craftsmanship

7. the reviver

8. reasonable price

9. favorable terms

10. lay in stock

11. 属于……的范围

12. 回顾

13. 实惠的价格

14. 随访信

15. 中小型企业

16. 扩大业务范围

17. 试订

18. 很受欢迎

19. 折扣

20. 商标

### III. Translate the following sentences from English into Chinese or vice versa.

1. 请在你的地区尽力推销这种新产品。

2. 根据你方要求，我们把样品另寄你处。

3. 由于所需型号脱销，我们将用下列型号代替。

4. 你方会有兴趣从所附的价格单上看到，对于所有可供型号，我们将从现行价格基础上给予你方 15%的折扣。

5. 此次写信告知您，本公司已被指定为著名的熊猫彩电的代理商。我方可现货供应许多新型的优质彩电，同时还提供零件和良好的售后服务。

6. 这是个难得的良机，你方可以按我们不可能重报的价格买到这些高质量的产品。我们希望你方充分利用这个机会。

7. We can offer you the latest toys that are attractive, durable and reasonably priced. They are of various patterns and for children of different ages. We are sure that the toys will be popular among children and good for their intelligence.

8. We can supply several varieties of green tea.

9. We recommend your immediate acceptance because our stocks are almost exhausted.

10. We give you this special discount for the order with the view of developing the business relations between us.

11. The quality of Art. No. 101 is better than that of Art. No. 102.

12. As this product is now in great demand and the supply is rather limited, we would recommend you to accept this offer as soon as possible.

**IV. Fill in the blanks with the proper words.**

1. manufactures          2. performs; market

3. equipped; allows        4. retail; lowest

5. features

**V. Compose a dialogue in the following situation.**

**J:** Now, Mr. Liu, let's have a word about delivery. Can you make prompt shipment?

**L:** "Prompt shipment", such terms are ambiguous. People can interpret this phrase differently.

**J:** We must have the seafood for the winter sale. That's all I want.

**L:** For the winter sale? Why, that would mean the goods must arrive at London in early November. We're now in late September. Even if we had the goods ready, I don't think we could ship them right away.

**J:** I know there's a great demand on shipping lately.

**L:** That is so. I was informed by our shipping department yesterday that liner space for Europe up to the end of next month had been fully booked. I'm afraid we can do very little about it.

**J:** We understand tramps are still available.

**L:** Yes, but tramps are scarce. Generally, no refrigeration facilities are provided on them, and I'm not sure whether there would be enough tonnage to make a full cargo, even if a tramp could be obtained.

**J:** Is there any chance if transhipment is allowed?

**L:** But transhipment adds to the expenses, risks of damage and sometimes may delay arrival, because there's also a shortage of transhipment space for Europe. Anyhow, we'll try. We have good connections with China Resources Shipping & Storage Co., Ltd. in Hong Kong. This company has a great reputation for its competence in the shipping world. Since it has long-term agency agreements with many world famous shipping companies, it can easily meet the clients' varied demands.

**J:** We prefer direct shipment, of course, but if you can't get hold of a direct vessel, we may agree to have the goods transhipped at Hong Kong. You know, good quality, competitive price, all would mean nothing if goods could not be put on the market on time.

**L:** Yes, fully understood. We'll find out the situation about the connecting steamer right away.

**J:** As far as I know, Jardine Shipping Agent (HK) Ltd. has a liner sailing from Hong Kong for Europe around mid-October. If you could manage to catch that vessel, everything would be all right.

**L:** It's very hard for us to accept a designated carrier. There are so many factors that might make the goods miss the intended sailing. Besides, are you sure the vessel will call at London? And is she already carrying a full load?

**J:** I guess if we start immediately, there's still hope. If worst comes to worst, please ship the goods to London or Liverpool. How about Liverpool as an optional port of destination?

**L:** Good. Then what would you say if we put it like this: "Shipment, first available steamer in October. port of destination, London or Liverpool. Transhipment at Hong Kong allowed."

**J:** Fine. It seems I've no alternative. Thank you, Mr. Liu. I'm sorry if these arrangements cause you a lot of inconvenience.

**L:** Oh, no, we're only very glad to help you in any way we can.

## VI. Write a letter with the idea below.

Dear Sirs,

As requested, we are sending you herewith our proforma invoice No. 009 in triplicate for 200 KWH Meters, Model HH 23.

A sample will be sent to you by separate parcel soon for your reference.

We understand that the above proforma invoice will help you apply for an import licence. Please let us know by telex as soon as you have obtained the said licence.

You will no doubt find that the price mentioned in the proforma invoice very favorable to you if you compare your price with that of other manufacturers.

Your early reply is awaited.

Yours truly,

John

Manager

# 实训项目 6

**I. Choose the best answer from A, B, C and D.**

1–5: CACBD    6–10: ABCAC

**II. Translate the following phrases into English or vice versa.**

| | |
|---|---|
| 1. captioned item | 2. contract order |
| 3. in duplicate | 4. for our file |
| 5. place a trial order | 6. the enclosed sheet |
| 7. a small order | 8. in stock |
| 9. out of stock | 10. to your satisfaction |
| 11. 据贵方来信 | 12. 供应现货 |
| 13. 现按所示价格 | 14. 确认予以接受 |
| 15. 如附寄的销售合同所示 | 16. 签退一份供我方存档 |
| 17. 有现货 | 18. 谢绝你订单 |
| 19. 很难接受新的订单 | 20. 确保订单的执行 |

**III. Translate the following sentences from English into Chinese or vice versa.**

1. 我方已接受贵方货号 244 的 20000 码货物。

2. 请寄给我方产品颜色分类并据合同开相关信用证。

3. 我们很高兴发现贵方质料品质优良。

4. 现寄去 2000 打胶鞋小额订单。

5. 如此订单可接受，请传真告之。

6. 已收到贵方目录与价格表，现按所示价格订购下列物品。

7. We enclose a trial order. If the quality is up to our expectation, we shall send further orders in the near future.

8. The material supplied must be absolutely waterproof, and we place our order subject to this guarantee.

9. Your order is receiving our immediate attention, and you can depend on us to effect delivery well within your time limit.

10. We are preparing to accept return of the rejected goods within 15 days if their quality is found unsatisfactory.

11. Enclosed please find Sales Confirmation in duplicate.

12. Your order is ready for delivery.

**IV. Fill in the blanks with the proper words.**

| | | | | |
|---|---|---|---|---|
| 1. pleasure | 2. requirement | 3. upon receipt of | 4. list | 5. stock |
| 6. satisfactory | 7. open | 8. supply; dispatch | 9. lead to | 10. additional |

### V. Compose a dialogue in the following situation.

**A:** Hello. May I speak to Mr. Liu?

**B:** Speaking. Who's calling please?

**A:** This is James Hall. I am calling about placing a trial order, after I received your samples yesterday.

**B:** How many are you able to order?

**A:** What is the smallest order for your T-shirt?

**B:** 1,000 pieces.

**A:** OK, I see. We are able in a position to order 1,500 pieces. If they are sold well in my area, we will consider placing a repeat order.

**B:** Wonderful, that is what we expect.

**A:** How about the discount and commission?

**B:** 3% on the price offered and 3% commission as we both agree upon last time.

**A:** OK. If we place an order now, when will you ship it?

**B:** We should be able to get that off to you right away.

**A:** Good. We are in urgent need to reply our customers. I will send an email to confirm my order.

**B:** OK. I am waiting for your email.

### VI. Write a letter according to the following situation.

Dear Sir,

Thank you for your speedy samples, along with the quotation for your household slippers of November 4.

We have made selections from the samples you sent to us. We found the quality of the slippers meets our requirement and we take pleasure of placing 15,000 household slippers.

As it is the first time for your goods to be introduced here, hope you will send them to us when you are at your earliest convenience.

We shall be obliged if you will kindly let us have the shipping advice immediately after you effect shipment.

Yours faithfully,

×××

## 实训项目 7

### I. Choose the best answer from A, B, C and D.

1–5: BCBCA                    6–10: CBABA

### II. Translate the following phrases into English or vice versa.

1. terms of packing                    2. seaworthy

3. wooden case

4. with an inner lining of stout waterproof material

5. transshipment

6. designated packing

7. marks

8. shipping advice

9. freight space

10. rough handling

11. 装箱单

12. 装运港

13. 适合海洋运输包装

14. 内包装

15. 交货

16. 直达轮

17. 分两批

18. 当事人

19. 外包装

20. 年需求量

## III. Translate the following sentences from English into Chinese or vice versa.

1. The goods are packed in seaworthy wooden cases.

2. All the packing will be specially reinforced and this, we hope, will prevent damage.

3. Please stencil our initials and order number on the outer packing.

4. The reason that the goods are popular with our customers is that it is made from a kind of waterproof material.

5. Please inform us of the details of the goods as soon as they are delivered.

6. They haven't informed us whether they can arrange transshipment of the goods in Hong Kong.

7. 请发电子邮件告诉我们唛头和目的地。

8. 我方保证我们将按时完成你们的订货，既不推迟也不提前。

9. 那里的存货并不充裕，相反越来越少。

10. 这批货物必须在许可证期满前运到。

11. 兹通知 21 号合同项下的货物已于今日由和平轮运出。

12. 我们已经修改了尺寸，请相应通知你方工厂。

## IV. Fill in the blanks with the proper words.

1. packed   2. from   3. with   4. of   5. of   6. amend   7. shipment   8. regret   9. from   10. on

## V. Compose a dialogue on the following situation.

**A:** What about the export packing?

**B:** Well, they are packed in cartons, 50 pieces to one carton, gross weight around 40 kilos a carton.

**A:** Cartons? Could you use wooden cases instead?

**B:** Why use wooden cases?

**A:** I'm afraid the cardboard boxes are not strong enough for such a long voyage.

**B:** No need to worry about that. Cartons are quite seaworthy. They are extensively used in our shipments to continental ports. There is never any complaint from our clients.

**A:** If you could guarantee compensation in case the insurance company refuses to honor a claim for faulty packing, we would be quite willing to accept cartons.

**B:** I'm sorry, but we can't take on any responsibility that is beyond our powers.

**A:** I can understand your position. Perhaps I'm asking too much. Well, I will take cartons.

**B:** Thanks for your cooperation.

**VI. Write a letter with the ideas given below.**

Dear Sirs,

Thank you for your fax dated April 2.

First of all, please accept our sincerely apology for losing your customer because of the delayed shipment. Unfortunately, in spite of round-the-clock attempt for shipping the goods before our Spring Festival Holiday, we failed. On the other hand, long lasting of the Spring Festival Holiday made the situation worse. Now at this stage when the goods are containerized in Keelung and ready to be loaded on the vessel, we are hearing such a sorrowful news from you.

We kindly ask you not to decline the orders at this stage and try to persuade your customers to accept the goods. Be sure that your try in this respect will strengthen our future cooperation undoubtedly. Please reply by fax.

Yours truly,

×××

# 实训项目 8

**I. Choose the best answer from A,B,C and D.**

1–5: A ADAD          6–10: ABACA

**II. Translate the following phrases into English or vice versa.**

1. payment in advance          2. cash on delivery

3. against this credit          4. a complete set of documents

5. have adequate stocks          6. draw a draft at sight in duplicate

7. delivery date can be met          8. receive our immediate attention

9. certificate of origin          10. full invoice value plus 10%

11. 向华丰公司取款          12. 商业承兑汇票

13. 货到目的地后凭单付款          14. 合同总值

15. 不可撤销的信用证          16. 电汇

17. 资信情况          18. 凭单证付现

19. 分期付款          20. 领事发票

**III. Translate the following sentences from English into Chinese or vice versa.**

1. 买方建议用承兑交单作为付款方式，但卖方不愿例外。

2. 我们不同意开具 30 天期的承兑交单汇票。

3. 因此，最好是采用付款交单方式或承兑交单方式。

4. 我建议这次用付款交单或承兑交单方式来付款。

5. 如果您能接受付款交单或承兑交单付款，那可帮了我们大忙。

6. 您能否来个例外，接受承兑交单或付款交单付款方式？

7. We insist on a Letter of Credit.

8. L/C at sight is normal for our exports to France.

9. You must be aware that an irrevocable L/C gives the exporter the additional protection of banker's guarantee.

10. For payment we require 100% value, irrevocable L/C in our favor with partial shipment allowed clause available by draft at sight.

11. What do you say to 50% by L/C and the balance by D/P?

12. Please notify us of L/C number by telex immediately.

**IV. Fill in the blanks with the proper words.**

| 1. to | 2. opened | 3. in a position | 4. under | 5. extended |
| 6. amend | 7. equivalent | 8. interest | 9. documents | 10. lead to |

**V. Compose a dialogue in the following situation.**

**A:** We've settled the questions of price, quality and quantity. Now what about the terms of payment? What is your regular practice?

**B:** We usually accept payment by L/C.

**A:** We would like to make payment for baskets by installments.

**B:** I'd need to check with my company about that. But what kind of installments do you have in mind?

**A:** What we'd like to do is to make a down payment first, and then after delivery, we pay off the rest in four installments.

**B:** It would be very difficult to arrange a deal like this.

**A:** "Payment by installments" is one of the terms of payment that have been widely accepted and commonly used by our sellers abroad.

**B:** But we seldom use this kind of payment terms in our business. As I stressed at the very beginning we usually require payment by L/C, especially for new customers.

**A:** Can you make any compromise this time? Say, 50% by down payment and the balance by L/C?

**B:** I can't give you my word now. I have to consult my director to see if we can do it in this way.

**A:** Thanks. I will wait for your news.

**VI. Write a letter with the ideas given below**

Dear Sirs,

Thank you for your order of 5,000 pieces of shirts, but we regret being unable to accept your terms of payment, 50% by L/C at 30 days' sight, the balance 50% by D/P at sight.

The specimen contract we sent to you last time for your reference indicates clearly that our usual terms of payment for trial orders are the buyer shall pay 100% of the sales proceeds in advance by T/T through Bank of China to reach the sellers within 10 days upon counter-signature of the S/C.

As soon as we hear from you in the affirmative, we will airmail to you the contract for your counter-signature.

We look forward to your favorable reply.

Yours faithfully,

××× ×

## 实训项目 9

**I. Choose the best answer from A, B, C and D.**

1–5: ACDBA            6–10: DACDD

**II. Translate the following phrases into English or vice versa.**

1. sight L/C                        2. issue an L/C

3. in your favor                    4. commission

5. negotiable bank                  6. beneficiary

7. partial shipment                 8. blank endorsed

9. insurance policy                 10. bill of lading

11. 欧洲主要港口                    12. 转运

13. 差异                            14. 修改

15. 规定                            16. 总金额计……

17. 按照                            18. 期满

19. 互利                            20. 预先

**III. Translate the following sentences from English into Chinese or vice versa.**

1. 我们已收到你方第 555 号信用证，但发现其中有下列不符之处。

2. 现高兴地通知，你方由利物浦渣打银行开出的、用以支付有关我方第 111 号售货合同的第 666 号信用证刚刚收到。但经审核后，我们遗憾地发现某些地方与合同规定的条款不符。

3. 收到你方第 999 号信用证，谢谢。经核对条款，我们遗憾地发现你方信用证要求 2003 年 10 月装船，但我方合同规定是 11 月份装运。

4. 佣金应该是 3%而不是 5%。

5. 货物应于六七月间装运，而不是 6 月 30 日或 30 日前装运。

6. 货物按发票金额的 110%投保，而不是 150%。

7. Please amend your L/C No. 789 as follows.

8. Increase the unit price from $0.78 to $0.87 and total amount to $1,234,500.

9. Please amend the credit to allow transshipment.

10. Please amend L/C No. 898 to read "This credit will expire on December 31, 2012 in China."

11. Please extend the shipment date and the validity of your L/C No. 518 to the end of October and November 15, 2012 respectively and make arrangement for the amendment advice to reach us by September 30, 2012.

12. Please rush the amendment to the L/C.

## IV. Fill in the blanks with the proper words.

1. to      2. opened, in favor of, covering      3. under      4. extend      5. instead of

6. into    7. in             8. In            9. in             10. under

## V. Compose a dialogue in the following situation.

**A:** Hello. Thank you for your L/C established in time.

**B:** Not at all.

**A:** But I'm quite sorry to mention that there are some terms to be amended in order to keep accordance with our contract.

**A:** OK, no problem.

**B:** Please amend the foregoing L/C to read piece length in 30 yards instead of 40 yards.

**A:** Oh, sorry, that is our mistake.

**B:** Also, you should amend the L/C to read "Partial shipments and transshipment allowed". We have changed the original terms in the previous letter.

**A:** Yes, I know and we are very sorry for the faults.

**B:** It doesn't matter. Our contract stipulates shipments in Dec. 1, 2011 but there are not enough shipping space for your goods. We have no alternatives but to decline date of shipment. Please extend the shipment date to the January 15, 2010.

**A:** OK, but that is the deadline. We have promised to supply the cloth in February to our customers. You know reputation is important.

**B:** I see. That's all right.

**A:** Hope to receive your goods as soon as possible. See you.

**B:** See you.

## VI. Write a letter with the ideas given below.

Dear Sirs,

We have received your L/C No. 234 covering the shipment of 1,000 pieces of shirts. After we checked with the L/C carefully, we found there are some discrepancies with the stipulations in the sales contract. We request you to make the following amendments:

The quantity should be 1,500 pieces rather than 1,000 pieces.

Transshipment is allowed not prohibited.

Commission is 3%, not 5%

Insurance is not included because this is on CFR basis.

Please confirm the amendments as early as possible, so that we may arrange shipment accordingly.

Yours faithfully,<br>× × ×

# 实训项目 10

**I. Choose the best answer from A, B, C and D.**

1–5: DACBD          6–10: BDABC

**II. Translate the following phrases into English or vice versa.**

1. 水渍险      2. 保险费      3. 投保人      4. 投保金额
5. 保险单    6. 仓至仓条款   7. 盗窃提货不着险  8. 中国人民保险公司
9. 发票金额  10. 投保人

**III. Translate the following sentences from English into Chinese or vice versa.**

1. 我们所收取的费率适中。当然，保险费因投保范围不同而有所不同。

2. 请报香港至青岛保额为 500 万美元的电视机投保平安险的最低费率。

3. 我们已经为贵方 1202 号订单项下的货物按发票金额的 120%投保至目的港。

4. 按照我们的惯例，只保基本险，按发票金额 110%投保。如果要加保其他险别，例如破碎险、渗漏险、盗窃提货不着险、钩损和污染险等，额外保费由买方承担。

5. 我们已经将这些货物按发票金额的 110%投保了一切险。

6. 平安险不包括单独海损性质的部分损失。

7. 针对这种性质的货物只保水渍险是不够的。请加保偷盗提货不着险。

8. 我们请贵方为我们的货物向中国人民保险公司投保保险金额为 2 万美元的水渍险。

9. For the goods sold on the CIF basis, insurance is to be covered by us for 110% of the invoice value against All Risks.

10. This batch of plastic toys is to be insured against All Risks with the PICC based on warehouse to warehouse clause.

11. The insurance company is responsible for the claim as far as it is within the scope of coverage.

12. We shall cover W. P. A. for 110% of the invoice value.

13. We leave the insurance arrangement to you but we wish to have the goods covered against All Risks.

14. An insurance claim should be submitted to the insurance company or its agents as promptly as possible so as to provide the insurance company or its agents with ample time to pursue

recovery from the relative party at fault.

15. Please note that the insurance covers F. P. A. and War Risks only. Should additional insurance coverage be required, the extra premium incurred would be for the buyer's account.

**IV. Fill in the blanks with the proper words.**

1. policy      2. insurer      3. insured      4. premium      5. insurance

6. owned/operated      7. agents      8. covered      9. effect      10. account

**V. Write a letter for Everbright Trading Co. to People's Insurance Company of China enquiring about the insurance rate.**

Dear Sirs,

We shall shortly have a shipment of 100 cases of silk blouses, valued USD 4,000, to be shipped by S.S. Wilson from Ningbo to Singapore, due to leave on October 10. Please quote us your rate for W. P. A.

As the shipping date is round the corner, we hope to have your reply as soon as possible.

Yours truly,

×××

# 实训项目 11

**I. Choose the best answer from A, B, C and D.**

1–5: BBDDC        6–10: AABCD

**II. Translate the following phrases into English or vice versa.**

1. 销售代理人      2. 运输代理人      3. 采购代理人      4. 保险代理人

5. 独家代理人      6. 佣金代理人      7. 总代理人      8. 广告代理人

9. 总经销      10. 独家发盘      11. 专卖权      12. 包销

**III. Translate the following sentences from English into Chinese or vice versa.**

1. 我们已决定按下列条款授权贵方为在美国的销售代理。

2. 由于贵方在我地区还没有直接的代表，我方请求担任贵方在我地区的独家代理。

3. 我们建议先试行一年。如果都满意，可以到期时续签协议。

4. 我们认为考虑独家代理的建议时机还不够成熟。

5. 目前的业务量不足使我方委托你方为独家代理。

6. 我们将在收妥货款后，按照实际出货发票金额汇付你方 5%的佣金。

7. 关于在你方提出的地区内担任我方中国芦笋代理的请求，我方已经决定委任你方为我们的代理。

8. 代理问题仍在考虑中，希望贵方仍继续努力推销我方产品。

9. We shall pay you a commission of 5% on the net value for all sales orders received through you, to which would be added a del credere commission of 2.5%.

10. With wide and varied experience in the trade, we are convinced that we are in a position to take good care of your import business as a buying agent in the most effective manner.

11. We accept the terms and conditions as set out in the draft agency agreement and look forward to a happy and successful working relationship with you.

12. We regret to inform you that our agency representation has taken over by someone else.

13. We are willing to be your agent for canned food because we have a large domestic market and a perfect marketing system.

14. Having considered your proposal and investigated your financial standing, we have decided to appoint you as our sole agent in China, subject to the following terms and conditions.

15. As to the advertisement campaign, you should do your utmost and we will absorb 50% of all the costs and expenses.

**IV. Write a letter.**

Dear Sirs,

We are grateful to your enquiry regarding sole agent for the sale of our Man-made Leather Bags in South Africa.

After serious consideration, we decided not to commit ourselves at this stage, when the record of transaction shows only a moderate volume of business.

Please do not misinterpret our above remarks. They do not imply dissatisfaction. We are quite satisfied with the amount of business you have done with us. However, we are of the opinion that a bigger turnover must be reached to justify establishing an agency. We think it advisable to postpone this matter until your future sales warrant such a step.

We hope that you will appreciate our position and continue giving us your cooperation.

Yours faithfully,

×××

# 实训项目 12

**I. Choose the best answer from A, B, C and D.**

1–5: DABDA                          6–10: CAAAA

**II. Translate the following phrases into English or vice versa.**

1. 到达时的情况……              2. 抱怨

3. 要求调换                          4. 检查，检验

5. 采取措施                          6. 提出索赔

7. 符合标准                          8. 解释

9. 公证行　　　　　　　　　　　10. 有瑕疵的货物

11. Mate's Receipt　　　　　　　12. short-delivered

13. at any rate　　　　　　　　　14. recourse to

15. attribute to　　　　　　　　　16. lose no time

17. at your disposal　　　　　　　18. prompt execution

19. in consequence of　　　　　　20. entertain a claim

## III. Translate the following sentences from English into Chinese or vice versa.

1. 很遗憾通知你方，发来的货不令人满意。

2. 很遗憾通知你方货物与样品不符。

3. 如果这批货在本月底前不能到达我方，我们将拒收，因为它对我们的季节销售已无用了。

4. 在检查中我们发现里面所有的货都弄脏了，其中许多是由于海水渗入受损的。

5. 尽管这些货的质量没达到我们通常的行业要求，但如果你降价，如……，我们准备接受。

6. 当打开这批货时，我们发现货物的质地比我们的样品要差得多，而且色度略为不同。

7. 我们希望贵公司对这一点品质上之瑕疵能加以说明，同时希望知道贵公司对此事之处理方法。

8. 在检查收到的货物时，我们发现有几件货品未列到你方发票上，现附上未列入货品的清单。

9. 兹发现到货仅有 6952 箱，而非贵方运出的 7000 箱，我们为此深感遗憾。

10. Upon examination, we find that all the cases weigh short by from 5 to 12 kg.

11. Would you kindly let me know if you will take them back, or allow me to sell them at a discount of 20 percent.

12. We have shipping documents to prove that the goods were received by the carrier in perfect condition. Therefore, they must have been damaged en route.

13. We have been supplying the same material for sometime and have had no complaints about it so far.

14. We were sorry to receive your complaint that the material you received was not of the quality expected.

15. Such deviation between the products and the samples is normal and permissible, therefore, the claim for compensation cannot be allowed.

16. We are most anxious to compensate you for the shortage in weight mentioned in you letter of… by offering you an allowance of … percent.

17. It would not the fair if the loss be totally imposed on us as the liability rests with both parties. We are ready to meet you half way, i. e., to pay 50% of the loss only.

18. We trust that the arrangements we have made will satisfy you and look forward to receiving your further orders.

## IV. Fill in the blanks with the proper words.

1. on; ex; for　　　　2. over　　　3. After/On/Upon; with; sample　　　4. between

5. to; shipment/consignment; in　　6. without　　7. At; were　　8. with

9. After; at; of; ex; under; in compliance with　　　　10. with; for; for

**V. Compose a dialogue in the following situation.**

**F:** (Agitated and furious) Your last shipment arrived at our port in June. Much to out regret, after inspection we found the quality inferior and unfit for production. We have no choice but to lodge a claim against you for quality.

**C:** Be patient, please. First tell us the whole story, then we may proceed to settle the problem. Have you brought along your sample? Will you let me have a look?

**F:** Of course! Here it is.

**C:** How strange!

**F:** What do you think of it?

**C:** Have a look. Your cutting is covered with a lot of spots while there is no spot at all on our shipping sample. Compare these two samples, what conclusion will you offer?

**F:** These two samples do look different. But our cutting is taken from your arrived goods.

**C:** Our products were strictly inspected by authorized department before loading. And the bill of lading was clean. This shows that the goods were in good condition at the time of loading.

**F:** The arrived goods are just like this cutting, which is also a true fact.

**C:** Apparently the goods were damaged in transit. How is this then? Please get your survey report and show us. If your have evidence and your evidence is convincing, we shall meet the claim according to the international practice. On the other hand, if the damage occurred during transportation, you are going to file your claim with the shipping company. OK?

**F:** All right. So be it at present.

**VI. Write a claim letter according to the following particulars.**

Dear Sirs，

　　The first shipment per S.S. *PEACE* arrived at our port two days ago.

　　Upon examination，we find the quality of the products is too inferior to meet the requirement at our local market. Please let us know how you are going to dispose this shipment. Shall we return them to you or shall we hold them for you？

　　　　We await your prompt response.

　　　　　　　　　　　　　　　　　　　　　　　　　　　　　　　　　　　Sincerely,

　　　　　　　　　　　　　　　　　　　　　　　　　　　　　　　　　　　×××

# 实训项目 13

**I. Choose the best answer from A, B, C and D.**

1–5: ACBBC　　　　　　　　　　6–10: ABBCB

**II. Translate the following phrases into English or vice versa.**

1. retail sale　　　　　　　　2. as follows　　　　　　　　3. to scale

4. procurement process　　　　5. quotation sheet　　　　6. specialize in

7. as per your instructions　　　8. refer you to Industrial and Commercial Bank of China

9. in reply　　　　　　　　　　10. sales contract　　　　11. 样品交付期

12. 生产交付期　　　　　　　　13. 罐头食品　　　　　　14. 依照请求，按照要求

15. 包装费　　　　　　　　　　16. 关于，根据　　　　　17. 标记指示(说明)

18. 逾期未付账款　　　　　　　19. 付款　　　　　　　　20. 装运通知；装船通知

## III. Translate the following sentences from English into Chinese or vice versa.

1. The order can't be canceled, as the goods have already been manufactured.

2. The airway bill copy is attached for your immediate reference.

3. Last year we shipped to you 800,000's worth of chemicals.

4. In case of offer, please quote us your lowest price in US dollar.

5. You are requested to revise the L/C as per the terms and conditions of our contract.

6. We feel regret to inform you that the articles you ordered last week are out of stock at present.

7. 由于你方价格太高，我们只得谢绝你方报盘。

8. 根据不同的材料，以及详细的交货细节，报我们最优惠的价格。

9. 很高兴地通知你方，745 号订单项下的 1000 箱绿茶已经按你方要求包装妥当。

10. 现在我有一个新的询盘，请把附件中的报价单填好，然后回发给我。

11. 关于上述订单，我们做如下包装指示。

12. 从来函中得知你方要求给予 5% 的优惠折扣。然而，本公司产品品质享有盛誉，报的价格
实际上已经贴近成本价。

## IV. Fill in the blanks with the proper words.

1. would like to　　　2. would appreciate it　　3. With reference to　　4. by

5. as　　　　　　　　6. by; on　　　　　　　　7. feel free to　　　　　8. please find

9. be of　　　　　　10. with; in

## V. Compose a dialogue in the following situation.

**Smith:** Mr. Chen, I wonder if you could tell me a bit about the packing of your ladies pajamas.

**Chen:** Certainly. You know, we have definite ways of packing garments. For ladies pajamas, we use polythene wrappers, ready for window display. Would you like to have a look at the samples?

**Smith:** Ah yes. Eye-catching packaging will surely help promote sales. With intense competition from all sources, we must make the merchandise not only superior in quality but also attractive in appearance.

**Chen:** That's right. One important function of packing is to stimulate the buyer's desire to buy. We'll try our best to make your end-users fall in love with the products at first sight. We'll make sure that the pajamas will appeal to the eye as well as to the purse.

**Smith:** That's good. What about the outer packing?

**Chen:** They will be packed 10 dozen to one carton, gross weight around 25 kilos a carton.

**Smith:** Carton? Wouldn't it be safe to use wooden cases? I'm concerned about the possible jolting, squeezing and collision that may take place when these cartons are moved about. And the dampness or rain may get into them, making the goods spotty.

**Chen:** Well, cartons are comparatively light and easy to handle. They are not stowed away with heavy cargo, and are always handled with care. All our cartons are lined with plastic sheets, so they are waterproof.

**Smith:** Well, if you can guarantee compensation from the insurance company, and no risk of a claim being dishonored for faulty packing, we would be willing to accept cartons.

**Chen:** I'm sorry, but we can't take on any responsibility that is beyond our control. We'll make sure that the packing is seaworthy, but we can't commit ourselves to being responsible for every kind of mishap. If you want us to use wooden cases, we can arrange that, but the charge will be much higher.

**Smith:** I see. I'll accept cartons.

### VI. Make an English fax by using the following information:

FAX   MESSAGE

| | | | |
|---|---|---|---|
| TO: | Datong Trading Co. | DATE: | Dec. 2, 2012 |
| ATTN: | Mr. Wang Jun | REF No: | CE29 |
| FROM: | Anne Brown | FAX: | 2098568 |
| TEX: | 3980888 | TEL: | 2098566 |
| FAX: | 3980898 | NO. OF PAGE: | 1 |
| SUBJECT: | Shipment CN18790 | | |

Your fax dated 30/ 11/ 2012 was received.

Regarding the shipment CN18790, we have not received the original of lading from you. The ETA of the shipment is 18/ 12/ 2012, so we must receive the B/L on 15th the latest.

Best regards!

Anne Brown

## 实训项目 14

### I. Choose the best answer from A,B,C and D

1–5: ADCAB                              6–10: CDAAA

### II. Translate the following phrases into English or vice versa.

1. compensation trade                    2. hospitality

3. delegation                            4. in compliance with

5. repayment

6. lot

7. processing fee

8. assemble

9. negotiate

10. draft

11. 试运转

12. 有效，效力，正确

13. 直接产品

14. 得出结论

15. 不可撤销即期信用证

16. 来件装配

17. 条款，条件

18. 规定

19. 来料加工

20. 辅料；（机器的）附件

**III. Translate the following sentences from English into Chinese or vice versa.**

1. 当地人以殷勤好客而闻名。

2. 我们将把代表团到达的日期通知你。

3. 需求的增长减少了成品库存。

4. 这辆自行车买得很称心。

5. 你放心，她将在两三周内康复。

6. 他们将支付约 6.73 亿美元再加上利息。

7. Mr. Wang will you tell me about the way of packing for this lot?

8. The equipment has already gone into trial operation.

9. I know it's late, but I need to transfer some money.

10. I think the compensation trade arrangement suits us better.

11. The strike caused a great delay in the delivery of the mail.

**IV. Fill in the blanks with the proper words.**

1. accordance    2. take the opportunity         3. basis        4. compliance

5. conclusion    6. assure        7. possibility

**V. Compose a dialogue in the following situation.**

**Mr. Mark:** Welcome to our factory！Let me introduce our team today. This is Ian Roger, the manager of Purchasing Department; this is Michelle, who is responsible for Quality Control; and this is Henry, the Project manager.

**Mr. Hadavas:** It's a great pleasure to meet you. Through the Chamber of Commerce of China in the United States, we intend to discuss the possibility of compensation trade with you.

**Mr. Mark:** As we have talked in the emails before, here is the material for your reference. Now let me introduce our factory to you first. We have been in the line of steel wire rope for more than 20 years. There are a great many production machinery & testing machinery as listed.

**Mr. Hadavas:** I see. Your factory also enjoys great reputation with long history. But the machines and equipments have not been updated in recent 7 years. Besides, the monthly production capacity is a bit low with 3,000 tons per month.

**Mr. Mark:** Yes, we need to update and introduce more machines and equipments, but we are lack of money.

**Mr. Hadavas:** Can we have the possibility of compensation trade? We are a comprehensive dealer of steel wire rope, machines and equipments. With our machines, you can widen your range of products and improve production capacity.

**Mr. Mark:** How shall we repay the cost of the machines and equipments?

**Mr. Hadavas:** You should pay with the steel wire ropes processed with the said machines and equipment. Here is the material for the compensation trade, based on our careful calculation.

**Mr. Mark:** Let me see. We shall repay in 4 lots within two years after the trial operation of the machines. It covers the cost of the machines and equipment plus insurance and freight.

**Mr. Hadavas:** Yes, all right.

**Mr. Mark:** We'll have our accountancy department check it, and give you a reply as soon as possible. Best wishes for our cooperation!

**VI. Write a letter with the ideas given below, expressing your wish to do assembling trade with them on the basis of supplied materials, components and equipments.**

Dear Sirs,

In compliance with the previous several pleasant discussions with your Vice President early this month, now we wish to do assembling trade of refrigerators in the following 3 points:

(1) With the components, materials, and necessary equipments and tools supplied by your company, we shall assemble 36,000 refrigerators within a period of three years.

(2) All the finished products will bear a neutral brand. 60% of the finished products will be shipped to Hong Kong and 40% to Sydney. Shipment of the products is to be effected once half a year. All the shipping expenses will be for your account.

(3) Payment for the assembling fee and shipping expenses is to be made by sight L/C to be opened by you no later than 30 days before the shipping schedule.

Please give the above points your careful consideration. Your early reply will be highly appreciated.

Yours faithfully,

× × ×